WRITING SPACE

The Computer, Hypertext, and the History of Writing

Jay David Bolter
University of North Carolina

LEA LAWRENCE ERLBAUM ASSOCIATES, PUBLISHERS
1991 Hillsdale, New Jersey   Hove and London

Lawrence Erlbaum Associates, Inc., Publishers
365 Broadway
Hillsdale, New Jersey 07642

Library of Congress Cataloging-in-Publication Data

Bolter, J. David, 1951-
    Writing space: the computer, hypertext, and the history of
writing / by Jay David Bolter.
        p.   cm.
    Includes bibliographical references and index.
    ISBN 0-8058-0427-7. -- ISBN 0-8058-0428-5 (pbk.)
    1. Word processing. 2. Hypertext systems. 3. Electronic
publishing. 4. Authorship—Data processing. 5. Text processing
(Computer science)   I. Title.
Z52.4.B65   1991
652.5--dc20   90-46380
                                                                         CIP

Printed in the United States of America
10   9   8

WRITING SPACE

The Computer, Hypertext, and the History of Writing

Contents

8 Interactive Fiction   121

9 Critical Theory and the New Writing Space   147

Part III: The Mind as a Writing Space

10 Artificial Intelligence   171

Preface

Because the subject of this printed book is the coming of the electronic book, I have found it particularly difficult to organize my text in an appropriate manner—appropriate, that is, to the printed page. In my mind the argument kept trying to cast itself intertextually or "hypertextually." Electronic text falls naturally into discrete units—paragraphs or sections that stand in multiple relation to one another. An electronic text is a network rather than the straight line suggested by the pages of a printed book, and the network should be available for reading in a variety of orders. Texts written explicitly for this new medium will probably favor short, concentrated expression, because each unit may be approached from a different perspective with each reading. Electronic writing will probably be aphoristic rather than periodic. A printed book, on the other hand, usually demands a periodic rhetoric, a rhetoric of subordinations and transitions.

The printed book also requires a printed persona, a consistent voice to lead the reader on a journey through the text. It has been hard for me to establish and maintain such a voice in this essay. For us in this period of transition, the idea of electronic writing is highly ambiguous. I found myself wanting to be true to this ambiguity by playing the advocate of the new technology in one paragraph and the devil's advocate in the next. In the end I had to remain the advocate, to argue rather cheerfully that the computer is a revolution in writing. I would in fact like to argue just as strongly for the continuity of electronic writing—that this new medium grows naturally and easily out of the late age of print. Somehow, the computer is both revolutionary and evolutionary. Such ambivalence is felt by many, perhaps all, authors, but ambivalence must be suppressed as a condition of writing nonfiction for publication in print. An author can take a position and add qualifications, but he or she cannot both take and reject a position in any convincing way. We shall see that an author can do this in the writing space provided by the computer. Indeed, a many-voiced text that is large enough to contain and admit its own contradictions may be the only convincing form of writing in the electronic medium.

This printed book can be about, but cannot be, an electronic book. As I will argue, there are many printed books in this late age of print that in some way aim to become electronic texts—everything from the Fifteenth Edition of the *Encyclopaedia Britannica* to *Glas* by Jacques Derrida. In this printed book, however, I have tried to follow the conventions of print. But I have also added an electronic shadow: a diskette that contains a hypertextual version of *Writing Space*. (The diskette can be obtained by sending in the order form enclosed in this book.) In the hypertext the rules of print are ignored. The argument falls into short paragraphs, sometimes single sentences. In place of a single reading order, the reader is given a choice of paths to follow. And I have tried to animate the text with several voices, some of which are skeptical about electronic writing.

*   *   *

In an electronic text it would be unnecessary to thank those who have read and critiqued the "manuscript"—not because the author is independent of such help, but because an electronic text acknowledges its dependence upon others with every link that it establishes between itself and the rest of the textual world. An electronic text cannot pretend to be an "original" work in the conventional sense. However, a printed book can and must. A printed book pretends to be closed and complete, and the author who applies for a copyright is making a legal claim that his or her work is original. The writer of a printed book should therefore acknowledge the debt owed to others, and in my case the debt is very great.

I must first acknowledge Michael Joyce, the author of "Afternoon," whose conversation and writing have been a constant source of ideas: I can no longer say that any of my ideas about electronic writing are free of his creative influence. John B. Smith and his colleagues Stephen F. Weiss, Marcy Lansman, and Gordon Ferguson (all in the Computer Science Department at the University of North Carolina) have helped me tremendously in understanding the computer as a new technology of writing.

I also wish to thank Jane Yellowlees Douglas, who read the entire manuscript and whose hypertextual critique helped me to focus the argument. Other readers who provided valuable criticism include Stuart Moulthrop, Peter Timmerman, Phil Mullins, Laurence Stephens, and Julia Hough. Pamela McCorduck offered perceptive comments on my chapter on artificial intelligence. In published work, in private drafts, and in conversations and letters, George Landow has helped me to understand the importance of hypertext both for pedagogy and for critical theory. Richard Lanham's elegant and original thinking on electronic writing has greatly helped me clarify my own ideas. Nancy Kaplan, John McDade, and Diane Balestri have also contributed greatly to my nascent understanding of hypertext. Murray Anderegg provided valuable assistance in computational mathematics.

I wish to thank Hollis Heimbouch of Lawrence Erlbaum Associates for her valuable criticism of my manuscript and her considerable help and advice in editing this volume. Thanks also to the editorial and production staff (particularly John Eagleson) at Lawrence Erlbaum Associates.

Finally, I thank my wife, Christine de Catanzaro, for her understanding and boundless support in this project.

Acknowledgments

Illustrations taken from other works are credited where they appear in my text. I wish also to acknowledge the following sources for the use of my own previously published work.

Portions of Chapter 2 were adapted from an earlier article and are reprinted with permission from *Language and Communication*, vol. 9, no. 2/3, "Beyond Word Processing: The Computer as a New Writing Space," pp. 129-142, ©1989 Pergamon Press PLC.

Portions of various chapters were adapted from "Text and Technology," *Library Resources and Technical Services* 31(1) (January/March, 1987) pp.12–23, ©1987 American Library Association and are reprinted with permission.

Portions of Chapter 8 were adapted from "The Idea of Literature in the Electronic Medium," *Topic* vol. 39 (Fall, 1985), pp. 23-34 and are reprinted with permission.

On the subject of acknowledgments, I would like to remind the reader how difficult the problem of copyright has become. Several illustrations that I wished to use had to be omitted, because it was not possible to secure permission in a timely fashion. It seems that everything is now being copyrighted, trademarked, or appropriated in some form. Everyone is rushing to divide up the world of signs for his or her own economic benefit. The mechanisms for legal protection of intellectual property are becoming more and more sophisticated at precisely the time when the notion of copyright itself is being vitiated by the computer and other electronic devices. This is clear evidence that we are living in the late age of print.

Chapter

1

Introduction

THE LATE AGE OF PRINT

Opening the window of his cell, he pointed to the immense church of Notre Dame, which, with its twin towers, stone walls, and monstrous cupola forming a black silhouette against the starry sky, resembled an enormous two-headed sphinx seated in the middle of the city.

The archdeacon pondered the giant edifice for a few moments in silence, then with a sigh he stretched his right hand toward the printed book that lay open on his table and his left hand toward Notre Dame and turned a sad eye from the book to the church.

"Alas!" he said, "This will destroy that." (Hugo, *Notre-Dame de Paris, 1482*, 1967, p. 197)

In Victor Hugo's novel *Notre-Dame de Paris, 1482*, the priest remarked "Ceci tuera cela": this book will destroy that building. He meant not only that printing and literacy would undermine the authority of the church but also that "human thought... would change its mode of expression, that the principal idea of each generation would no longer write itself with the same material and in the same way, that the book of stone, so solid and durable, would give place to the book made of paper, yet more solid and durable" (p. 199). The medieval cathedral crowded with statues and stained glass was both a symbol of Christian authority and a repository of medieval knowledge (moral knowledge about the world and the human condition). The cathedral was a library to be read by the religious, who walked through its aisles looking up at the scenes of the Bible, the images of saints, allegorical figures of virtue and vice, visions of heaven and hell. (See *The Art of Memory* by Frances

Yates, 1966, p. 124.) Of course, the printed book did not eradicate the encyclopedia in stone; it did not even eradicate the medieval art of writing by hand. People continued to contemplate their religious tradition in cathedrals, and they continued to communicate with pen and paper for many purposes. But printing did displace handwriting: the printed book became the most highly valued form of writing. And printing certainly helped to displace the medieval organization and expression of knowledge. As Elizabeth Eisenstein has shown, the printing press has been perhaps the most important tool of the modern scientist. (See *The Printing Press as an Agent of Change* by Elizabeth Eisenstein, 1979, especially vol. 2, pp. 520ff.)

Hugo himself lived in the heyday of printing, when the technology had just developed to allow mass publication of novels, newspapers, and journals. Hugo's own popularity in France (like Dickens' in England) was evidence that printed books were reaching and defining a new mass audience. Today we are living in the late age of print. The evidence of senescence, if not senility, is all around us. And as we look up from our computer keyboard to the books on our shelves, we must ask ourselves whether "this will destroy that." Computer technology (in the form of word processing, databases, electronic bulletin boards and mail) is beginning to displace the printed book. Until recently it was possible to believe that the computer could coexist with the printed book. Computers were for scientific analysis and business data processing. Pragmatic writing (business letters, technical reports, and stock prices) could migrate to the computer, but texts of lasting value—literature, history, scholarship—would remain in printed form. Now, however, this distinction between lasting texts and pragmatic communication is breaking down. Computers are being used for all kinds of writing, not just office memos and stock quotations. We shall see that the computer has even fostered a new genre of literature, one that can only be read at the computer screen. Major book publishers in the United States already translate their texts into computer-readable form for photocomposition; books pass through the computer on the way to the press. Many, perhaps most, of these texts will someday cease to be printed and will instead be distributed in electronic form.

The printed book, therefore, seems destined to move to the margin of our literate culture. The issue is not whether print technology will completely disappear; books may long continue to be printed for certain kinds of texts and for luxury consumption. But the idea and the ideal of the book will change: print will no longer define the organization and presentation of knowledge, as it has for the past five centuries. This shift from print to the computer does not mean the end of literacy. What will be lost is not literacy itself, but the literacy of print, for electronic technology offers us a new kind of book and new ways to write and read. The shift to the computer will make writing more flexible, but it will also threaten the definitions of good writing and careful reading that have been fostered by the technique of printing. The printing press encouraged us to think of a written text as an unchanging artifact, a monument to its author and its age. Hugo claimed that a printed book is more solid and durable than a stone cathedral; no one would make that claim, even metaphorically, for a computer diskette. Printing also tended to magnify the distance between the author and the reader, as the author became a monumental figure, the reader only a visitor in the author's cathedral. Electronic writing emphasizes the impermanence and changeability of text, and it tends to reduce the distance between author and reader by turning the reader into an author. The computer is restructuring our current economy of writing. It is changing the cultural status of writing as well as the method of producing books. It is changing the relationship of the author to the text and of both author and text to the reader.

REWRITING THE BOOK

As early as the 1450s and 1460s, Gutenberg and his colleagues were able to achieve the mass production of books without sacrificing quality. Gutenberg's great book, the 42-line Bible, does not seem to us today to have been a radical experiment in a new technology. It is not poorly executed or uncertain in form. The earliest incunabula are already examples of a perfected technique; there remains little evidence from the period of experimentation that must have preceded the production of these books. Indeed, Gutenberg's Bible can hardly be distinguished from the work of a good scribe, except perhaps that the spacing and hyphenation are more regular than a scribe could achieve. The early printers tried to make their books identical to fine manuscripts: they used the same thick letter forms, the same ligatures and abbreviations, the same layout on the page. It took a few generations for printers to realize that their new technology made possible a different writing space, that the page could be more readable with thinner letters, fewer abbreviations, and less ink.

Today we find ourselves in a similar interim with the electronic book. We have begun by using word processors and electronic photocomposition to improve the production of printed books and typed documents. Yet it is already becoming clear that the computer provides a new writing surface that needs conventions different from those of the printed page. In fact, the page itself is not a meaningful unit of electronic writing. The electronic book must instead have a shape appropriate to the computer's capacity to structure and present text. Writers are in the process of discovering that shape, and the process may take decades, as it did with Gutenberg's invention. The task is nothing less than the remaking of the book.

Electronic technology remakes the book in two senses. It gives us a new kind of book by changing the surface on which we write and the rhythms with which we read. It also adds to our historical understanding of the book by providing us with a new form that we can compare to printed books, manuscripts, and earlier forms of writing. Electronic writing turns out to be both radical and traditional. It is mechanical and precise like printing, organic and evolutionary like handwriting, visually eclectic like hieroglyphics and picture writing. On the other hand, electronic writing is fluid and dynamic to a greater degree than any previous technique. The coming of the new electronic book helps us to understand the choices, the specializations, that the printed book entails. We see that, like the specializations on outer branches of an evolutionary tree, the printed book is an extreme form of writing, not the norm.

THE USES OF ELECTRONIC WRITING

Those who tell us that the computer will never replace the printed book point to the physical advantages: the printed book is portable, inexpensive, and easy to read, whereas the computer is hard to carry and expensive and needs a source of electricity. The computer screen is not as comfortable a reading surface as the page; reading for long periods promotes eyestrain. Finally—and this point is always included—you cannot read your computer screen in bed. But electronic technology continues to evolve: machines have diminished dramatically in size and in price during the past 40 years, and computer screens are becoming much more readable. It is not hard to imagine a portable computer with the bulk and weight of a large notebook and whose screen is as legible as a printed page. We can also envision an electronic writing system built into the top of a desk or lectern (like those used in the Middle Ages and the Renaissance), where the writer can work directly by applying a light pen instead of typing at a keyboard.

In any case, ease of use is only one measure of a writing technology. The great advantage of the first printed books was *not* that you could read them in bed. Gutenberg might well have been appalled at the thought of someone taking his beautiful folio-sized Bible to bed. For generations, most important printed books remained imposing volumes that had to be read on bookstands, so that people often read (and wrote) standing up. Mass production by printing did eventually make books cheaper and more plentiful, and this change was important. However, the fixity and permanence that printing gave to the written word were just as important in changing the nature of literacy. The book in whatever form is an intellectual tool rather than a means of relaxation. If the tool is powerful, writers and readers will put up with inconveniences to use it. In any technique of writing, structure matters more than appearance or convenience, and the electronic book, whether it is embodied in today's boxy microcomputer or in a slim electronic notebook of the future, gives text a new structure. In place of the static pages of the printed book, the electronic book maintains text as a fluid network of verbal elements.

Writers are only beginning to exploit the possibilities of this new structure; electronic writing in general is still in its infancy. The electronic incunabula include computer-controlled photocomposition, the word processor, the textual database, the electronic bulletin board and mail. As already mentioned, electronic texts are by no means rare: most of what we read today has passed through the computer on its way to our hands. In the United States it is common to produce newspapers, magazines, and printed books by means of electronic photocomposition. The texts are typed into the computer, revised and arranged by editors and typographers, and then output as camera-ready copy, photographic sheets or plates that the printer can use in his presses. However, computer-controlled photocomposition does not teach us how to write electronically. Publishers are simply using the computer to enhance the older technology, to make printing faster and less expensive.

The same is true of word processing. Word processors do demonstrate the flexibility of electronic writing in allowing writers to copy, compare, and discard text with the touch of a few buttons. Words in the computer are ultimately embodied in the collective behavior of billions of electrons, which fly around in the machine at unimaginable speeds. Change is the rule in the computer, stability the exception, and it is the rule of change that makes the word processor so useful. (See Mullins, 1988.) On the other hand, the word processor has been enthusiastically accepted by so many writers precisely because it does not finally challenge their conventional notion of writing. The word processor is an aid for making perfect printed or typed copy: the goal is still ink on paper. Like programs for photocomposition, the word processor is not so much a tool for writing, as it is a tool for typography. With a sophisticated word processor and a laser printer, users can create their own camera-ready copy. The program allows small organizations and even individuals to bypass the publishing industry. This change is important, but it is not a revolution in writing. (On the interplay between fluidity and fixity in word processing, see Balestri, 1988.)

The word processor treats text like a scroll, a roll of pages sewn together at the ends, and its visual structures are still typographic. A word processor stores its text as a simple sequence of letters, words, and lines. It remembers margins and pagination; it may remember which letters are to be printed in boldface, in Times Roman, or in 14-point type. But a conventional word processor does not treat the text as a network of verbal ideas. It does not contain a map of the ways in which the text may be read. It does not record or act on the semantic structure of the text. A true electronic text does all this, for a true electronic text is not a fixed sequence of letters, but is instead from the writer's point of view a network of verbal elements and from the reader's point of view a texture of possible readings.

An electronic text permits the reader to share in the dynamic process of writing. The text is realized by the reader in the act of reading. Electronic reading is already a feature of many current computerized texts. There are, for example, databases containing Supreme Court decisions for lawyers, newspaper articles for journalists, and even Greek or Shakespearean tragedies for scholars. Each such database constitutes a potential text of vast proportion and complexity: it offers millions of combinations of articles or passages that some reader might at some time request. No one reader examines every entry in such a database; instead the reader searches for appropriate phrases and retrieves only those passages that satisfy the search. The reader calls forth his or her own text out of the network, and each such text belongs to one reader and one particular act of reading.

The same principle of reader participation is embodied in computer-assisted instruction, commonly used in business and schools. Computer-assisted instruction is sometimes effective, often not, but in all cases it requires the dynamic reading of a multiply organized text. The computer presents the student with a question or problem. The student responds, and, based on that response, the computer may present another question, give the student a message, or take the student back to review material that he or she does not seem to understand. The teacher who wrote the program must anticipate and provide for a wide variety of responses from the student. The teacher is the writer whose text the machine juggles and displays to the student. The student also becomes a writer as he or she coaxes answers from the machine. The whole lesson is a composite of the two texts, one by the teacher and one by the student. Meanwhile, electronic bulletin boards take the principle of multiple authorship even further, allowing hundreds of participants from distant locations to exchange texts and questions. Each participant moves quickly and repeatedly between the roles of reader and writer.

All of these programs suggest what the computer can do as a technology of reading and writing. And yet they are all attempts to transfer previous techniques of writing into an electronic idiom. The word processor makes the computer into an electronic typewriter. A textual database makes it a file cabinet filled with copies of printed records. Computer-assisted instruction with its steady rhythm of question and answer is modeled on the exercises included in printed textbooks. And electronic bulletin boards are just what the name implies: a place for posting typed or written messages. But if we combine the dynamic writing of the word processor with the dynamic reading of the bulletin board or textual database and add the interactivity of computer-assisted instruction, then we do have a textual medium of a new order. This new medium is the fourth great technique of writing that will take its place beside the ancient papyrus roll, the medieval codex, and the printed book.

THE NEW VOICE OF THE BOOK

Writing in the classical and Western traditions is supposed to have a voice and therefore to speak to its reader. A printed book generally speaks with a single voice and assumes a consistent character, a persona, before its audience. A printed book in today's economy of writing must do more: it must speak to an economically viable or culturally important group of readers. Printing has helped to define and empower new groups of readers, particularly in the 19th and 20th centuries: for example, the middle-class audience for the 19th-century British novel. But this achievement is also a limitation. An author must either write for one of the existing groups or seek to forge a new one, and the task of forging a new readership requires great talent and good luck. And even a new readership, brought together by shared interests in the author's message, must be addressed with consistency. No publisher would accept a book that combined two vastly different subject matters: say, European history and the marine biology of the Pacific, or Eskimo folklore and the principles of actuarial science. It would be hard to publish a book that was part fiction and part non-fiction—not a historical novel, a genre that is popular and has a well-defined audience, but, let us say, a combination of essays and short stories that treat the same historical events. We might say that these hypothetical books lack unity and should not be published. Yet our definition of textual unity comes from the published work we have read or more generally from the current divisions of academic, literary, and scientific disciplines, which themselves both depend on and reinforce the economics of publishing. The material in a book must be homogeneous by the standard of some book-buying audience.

This strict requirement of unity and homogeneity is relatively recent. In the Middle Ages, unrelated texts were often bound together, and texts were often added in the available space in a volume years or decades later. Even in the early centuries of printing, it was not unusual to put unrelated works between two covers. On the other hand, it is natural to think of any book, written or printed, as a verbal unit. For the book is a physical unit; its pages are sewn or glued together and then bound into a portable whole. Should not all the words inside proceed from one unifying idea and stand in the same rhetorical relationship to the reader?

Because an electronic text is not a physical artifact, there is no reason to give it the same conceptual unity as the printed book, no reason not to include disparate materials in one electronic network. The writer or editor need not envision and address only one homogeneous readership; an electronic book may speak with different voices to different readers (and each reader is a different reader each time he or she approaches a text). Thus, an electronic encyclopedia may address both the educated novice and the expert: its articles may be written on several levels of expertise to suit the needs and background of various readers. Our traditional canon of unity no longer applies to the electronic book, whose shadowy existence in electronic storage does not convey the same sense of physical unity. The text may reside on a diskette or in the computer's internal memory, where it cannot be seen or directly touched by the reader. If the user is calling up a remote database, then the text may be hundreds or thousands of miles away and arrive only in convenient pieces through the telephone wires.

An electronic book can tailor itself to each reader's needs. As the reader moves quickly or deliberately through the textual network, he or she seldom feels the inertia that pulls a reader through the pages of a printed book. A reader who consults the *New York Times* Information Service does not want to read every article in the database; the student in computer-assisted instruction does not need or want to read every response the computer has to offer for every possible wrong answer. The reader exercises choice at every moment in the act of reading. Electronic reading is therefore a special instance of what economists now call "market segmentation." In the classic industrial age, economies of scale required that products be homogeneous: each factory produced one or a few kinds of toothbrushes, soft drinks, or deodorants in vast quantities. In today's more automated and flexible factories, goods are tailored to segments of the buying public. Before the invention of photocomposition, the printing press was a classic industrial machine, producing large quantities of identical texts. Marshall McLuhan called printing the first example of the assembly line and mass production (McLuhan, 1972, p. 124). Photocomposition and then the computer as photocomposer have already made printing more flexible, allowing publishers to target books to well-defined markets. However, a true electronic book goes further still, changing for each reader and with each reading.

The vanishing of the fixed text alters the nature of an audience's shared experience in reading. All the readers of *Bleak House* could talk about the novel on the assumption that they had all read the same words. No two readers of an electronic book can make that assumption; they can only assume that they have traveled in the same textual network. Fixed printed texts can be made into a literary canon and therefore promote cultural unity. In the 19th and early 20th centuries, when the canon of literature was often taken as the definition of a liberal education, the goal was to give everyone the experience of reading the same texts—Shakespeare, Milton, Dickens, and so on. This ideal of cultural unity through a shared literary inheritance, which has received so many assaults in the 20th century, must now further suffer by the introduction of a new form of highly individualized writing and reading.

Critics accuse the computer of promoting homogeneity in our society, of producing uniformity through automation, but electronic reading and writing have just the opposite effect. The printing press was the great homogenizer of writing, whereas electronic technology makes texts particular and individual. An electronic book is a fragmentary and potential text, a series of self-contained units rather than an organic, developing whole. But fragmentation does not imply mere disintegration. Elements in the electronic writing space are not simply chaotic; they are instead in a perpetual state of reorganization. They form patterns, constellations, which are in constant danger of breaking down and combining into new patterns. This tension leads to a new definition of unity in writing, one that may replace or supplement our traditional notions of the unity of voice and of analytic argument. The unity or coherence of an electronic text derives from the perpetually shifting relationship among all its verbal elements.

COMPUTING AS WRITING

So far we have been considering the computer as a vehicle for human (what computer specialists call "natural") language, and that will be our focus throughout this book. But we cannot ignore the fact that the computer is used to manipulate numbers as well as words. The computer reminds us that any definition of writing must now include mathematics and symbolic logic along with verbal writing and graphics. And in all its various uses, the computer is best understood as a new technology for writing. Even computer programming is a kind of writing. Programming languages (like PASCAL or C) constitute a restricted and yet powerful mode of communication, a mode based on imperative sentences and the unambiguous use of symbols. Admittedly, their rigid syntax makes these computer languages unusual; natural language is far less precise. And unlike natural language, computer language is made to be written down: it belongs on the page or the computer screen. It is not easy to speak PASCAL or C, so that even a good programmer must see the lines of code in order to understand them. What the programmer sees is a network of symbols whose interaction defines the program's operation. Computer programs are by definition electronic texts, and a computer system is a sophisticated collection of programmed texts that act on and interact with each other—applications, system utilities, compilers, assemblers, and so on. All programs are texts that read texts and write other texts.

Computer programming is simply the newest version of the symbol manipulation that mathematicians and logicians have practiced for centuries. Programming is embodied logic: the establishment of logical relationships among symbols that are embodied in and empowered by the memory chips and processors of the digital computer. Mathematics has been a special kind of writing at least since the evolution of modern notation in the 17th century. The set of mathematical equations that defines a physical theory is a symbolic text of the highest order. And science itself has been a formal language since the time of Descartes and Leibniz, or indeed Galileo with his claim that the book of nature was written in the language of mathematics. In the 19th and 20th centuries, the desire to make language formal and rigorous has led to modern symbolic logic, to semiotics, to logical positivism, and ultimately to computer programming.

Formal language is, therefore, the natural language of computers. It is English, French, or Russian that poses problems when taken into the machine. Formal languages are operational: they direct the computer's actions. Human languages are merely stored in the machine, as texts to be divided, recombined, and presented to readers. Yet the computer can activate even these human texts in new and surprising ways. The computer as a writing technology invites us to recognize the similarities as well as the obvious differences between formal and natural language. It becomes easier to understand natural language too as a network of interconnecting signs.

In everything it does, the computer is called on to read and write either formal or natural language. Today the machine is indispensable in physics, chemistry, and biology, where it is a tool for reading and writing Galileo's language of nature. When the computer reads and writes numbers for scientists, it does so by executing a text of programmed instructions. It may print out its results in numbers and words, or it may display its results graphically, giving the user a map or a graph to read. It may be called on to simulate some aspect of nature or human technology and to present that simulation as a picture on the screen or as a graphic or numerical text. Even a graphics program does not draw: it writes. A computer graphic is a set of symbolically positioned bits: a texture of dots that our eyes convert to continuous lines on the screen. Even when the computer is controlling machinery in an automated factory, the controls are in fact a language of discrete commands that the computer constructs and sends to the machinery. The computer is performing a kind of writing on the world. All computing is reading and writing. The computer is therefore a technology for all writers—scientists and engineers as well as scholars, novelists, and poets. A text in the computer is always an interplay of signs, which may be mathematical and logical symbols, words in English, or graphics and video images treated symbolically.

WRITING SPACES

Writing is the creative play of signs, and the computer offers us a new field for that play. It offers a new surface for recording and presenting text together with new techniques for organizing our writing. In other words, it offers us a new writing space. In the following chapters, we shall see how the computer's writing space resembles and differs from the space of its predecessors, particularly the papyrus roll, the codex, and the printed book.

By "writing space" I mean first of all the physical and visual field defined by a particular technology of writing. All forms of writing are spatial, for we can only see and understand written signs as extended in a space of at least two dimensions. Each technology gives us a different space. For early ancient writing, the space was the inner surface of a continuous roll, which the writer divided into columns. For medieval handwriting and modern printing, the space is the white surface of the page, particularly in a bound volume. For electronic writing, the space is the computer's videoscreen where text is displayed as well as the electronic memory in which text is stored. The computer's writing space is animated, visually complex, and to a surprising extent malleable in the hands of both writer and reader.

How the writer and the reader understand writing is conditioned by the physical and visual character of the books they use. Each physical writing space fosters a particular understanding both of the act of writing and of the product, the written text. In this late age of print, writers and readers still conceive of all texts, of text itself, as located in the space of a printed book. The conceptual space of a printed book is one in which writing is stable, monumental, and controlled exclusively by the author. It is the space defined by perfect printed volumes that exist in thousands of identical copies. The conceptual space of electronic writing, on the other hand, is characterized by fluidity and an interactive relationship between writer and reader. These different conceptual spaces foster different styles and genres of writing and different theories of literature.

In the act of writing, the writer externalizes his or her thoughts. The writer enters into a reflective and reflexive relationship with the written page, a relationship in which thoughts are bodied forth. It becomes difficult to say where thinking ends and writing begins, where the mind ends and the writing space begins. With any technique of writing—on stone or clay, papyrus or paper, and particularly on the computer screen—the writer comes to regard the mind itself as a writing space. The writing space becomes a metaphor, in fact literate culture's root metaphor, for the human mind.

In the following chapters, we will explore the computer as a literal, conceptual, and metaphoric writing space. Chapter 2 is an introduction to the current art of electronic writing, to the way textual elements and graphic images are deployed on the computer screen and organized in electronic memory. In Chapters 3-5 we will compare the physical and visual space provided by the computer with that of earlier techniques of writing. In Chapters 6-9 we will consider the computer as a conceptual space: the nature of the electronic book and the styles of fiction and non-fiction appropriate to it. Finally, because changes in our conception of the writing space lead to changes in our conception of ourselves as writers and readers, we will consider in Chapters 10-13 the electronic writing space as a new metaphor for the human mind and for our culture's collective mentality.

The Visual Writing Space

Chapter

2

The Computer as a New Writing Space

Consider this simple example of electronic writing. (See Fig. 2.1.) The text is a continuous prose paragraph, displayed on the computer screen for the reader to read in the traditional way. Some of the words are in boldface; the style indicates that there is a note on that word or phrase, something more to be said. To retrieve the note, the reader points with the cursor at the text in boldface and presses a button. A second window then opens on the screen and presents a new paragraph for the reader to consider. The reader examines the note and may then return to the original paragraph.

In one sense this is simply the electronic equivalent of the footnote used in printed books for hundreds of years. Instead of looking to the bottom of the page or the end of the book, the reader aims the cursor and the computer retrieves and displays the reference. The machine is merely handling the mechanics of reading footnotes. But there is this important difference: the second window can also contain boldface phrases that in turn lead the reader to other paragraphs. The process can continue indefinitely as the reader moves from one window to another through a space of paragraphs. The second paragraph is not necessarily subordinate to the first. A phrase in boldface may lead the reader to a longer, more elaborate paragraph. One paragraph may be linked to many and serve in turn as the destination for links from many others. In a printed book, it would be intolerably pedantic to write footnotes to footnotes. But in the computer, writing in layers is quite natural, and reading the layers is effortless. All the individual paragraphs may be of equal importance in the whole text, which then becomes a network of interconnected writings. The network is designed by the author to be explored by the reader in precisely this peripatetic fashion.

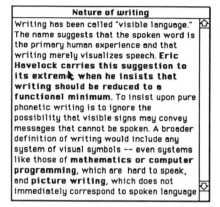
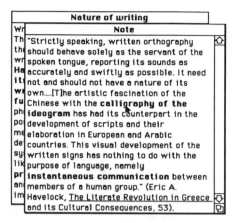

FIG. 2.1. (a) To examine a note, the reader points to and activates a phrase in boldface. (b) A new window appears and presents the associated text, which contains boldface phrases of its own.

Such a network is called a *hypertext*, and, as we shall see, it is the ability to create and present hypertextual structures that makes the computer a revolution in writing. The computer as hypertext invites us to write with symbols that have both an intrinsic and extrinsic significance. That is, the symbols have a meaning that may be explained in words, but they also have meaning as elements in a larger structure of verbal gestures. Both words and structures are visible, writeable, and readable in the electronic space.

WRITING PLACES

With or without the computer, whenever we write, we write topically. We conceive of our text as a set of verbal gestures, large and small. To write is to do things with topics—to add, delete, and arrange them. The computer changes the nature of writing simply by giving visual expression to our acts of conceiving and manipulating topics. A writer working with a word processor spends much of the time entering words letter by letter, just as he or she does at a typewriter. Revising is a different matter. With most word processors, writers can delete or replace an entire word; they can highlight phrases, sentences, or paragraphs. They can erase a sentence with a single keystroke; they can select a paragraph, cut it from its current location, and insert it elsewhere, even into another document. In using these facilities, the writer is thinking and writing in terms of verbal units or topics, whose meaning transcends their constituent words. The Greek word *topos* meant literally a place, and ancient rhetoric used the word to refer to commonplaces, conventional units or methods of thought. In the Renaissance, topics became headings that could be used to organize any field of knowledge, and these headings were often set out in elaborate diagrams. (See Ong, 1958, pp. 104-130.) Our English word *topic* is appropriate for the computer because its etymology suggests the spatial character of electronic writing: topics exist in a writing space that is not only a visual surface but also a data structure in the computer. The programmers who designed word processors recognized the importance of topical writing, when they gave us operations for adding or deleting sentences and paragraphs as units. They did not, however, take the further step of allowing a writer to associate a name or a visual symbol with such topical units. This important step lends the unit a conceptual identity. The unit symbol becomes an abiding element in the writer's thinking and expression, because its constituent words or phrases can be put out of sight.

On a printed or typed page, we indent and separate paragraphs to indicate the topical structure. Within each paragraph, however, we have only punctuation, occurring in the stream of words, to mark finer structure. A better representation of topical writing is the conventional outline, in which major topics are designated by Roman numerals, subtopics by capital letters, sub-subtopics by Arabic numerals, and so on. Each point of an outline serves to organize and situate the topics subordinate to it, and the outline as a whole is a static representation, a snapshot, of the textual organization. The conventions of outlining turn the writing surface into a tiered space in which the numbering and indentation of lines represent the hierarchy of the author's ideas. A paragraphed text is the flattening or linearization of an outline.

The word processor, which imitates the layout of the typed page, also flattens the text. It offers the writer little help in conceiving the evolving structure of the text. Although the word processor allows the writer to define a verbal unit in order to move or delete it, the definition lasts only until the operation is complete. But if the word processor offers the writer only temporary access to his or her structure, another class of programs called *outline processors* makes structure a permanent feature of the text. An outline processor sets the traditional written outline in motion. A writer can add points to an electronic outline in any order, while the computer continually renumbers to reflect additions or deletions. The writer can promote minor points to major ones, and the computer will again renumber. The writer can collapse the outline in order to see only those points above a certain level, an action that gives an overview of the evolving text. In short the writer can think globally about the text: one can treat topics as unitary symbols and write with those symbols, just as in a word processor one writes with words. (See Fig. 2.2.)

Writing in topics is not a replacement for writing with words; the writer must eventually attend to the details of his or her prose. The outline processor

Electronic Writing Space

I. Introduction

II. Writing places

III. Electronic trees

IV. Hypertext

V. Hypermedia

VI. The First Hypertext

VII. Writers and Readers

.
.
.

(a)

Electronic Writing Space

I. Introduction
  A. Example
    1. Figure 1
  B. Footnote
  C. Hypertext
II. Writing places
  A. Topos
  B. Print format
  C. Word processor
    1. Conventional
    2. Desktop publishing
  D. Outline processor
    1. Figure 2
  E. Topical writing
    1. With the computer
    2. In print

.
.
.

(b)

II. Writing places

A. Topos

> With or without the computer, whenever we write, we write
> topically. We conceive of our text as a set of verbal gestures, large
> and small. To write is to do things with topics -- to add, delete, and
> arrange them. The computer changes the nature of writing simply by
> giving visual expression to our acts of conceiving and manipulating
> topics. A writer working with a word processor spends much of his
> time entering words letter by letter, just as he does at a typewriter.
> Revising is a different matter. With most word processors, the

B. Print format

> On a printed or typed page, we indent and separate paragraphs to
> indicate the topical structure. Within each paragraph, however, we
> have only punctuation, occurring in the stream of words, to mark
> finer structure. A better representation of topical writing is the
> conventional outline, in which major topics are designated by Roman
> numerals, subtopics by capital letters, sub-subtopics by Arabic
> numerals, and so on. Each point of an outline serves to organize and
> situate the topics subordinate to it, and the outline as a whole is a

C. Word processor

> The word processor, which imitates the layout of the typed page, also
> flattens the text. It offers the writter little help in conceiving the
> evolving structure of his text. Although the word processor allows

.
.
.

(c)

FIG. 2.2. An outline processor can reveal or hide detail as the writer
requires. It may show only the major points (a), the full outline (b), or the
prose paragraph attached to each point of the outline (c).

contains within it a conventional word processor, so that the writer can attach text to each of the points in the outline. But in using an outline processor, writers are not aware of a rigid distinction between outlining and prose writing: they move easily back and forth between structure and prose. What is new is that the points of the outline become functional elements in the text, because when the points move, the words move with them. In this way the computer makes visible and almost palpable what writers have always known: that the identifying and arranging of topics is itself an act of writing. Outline processing is writing at a different grain, a replication on a higher level of the conventional act of writing by choosing and arranging words. The symbols of this higher writing are simply longer and more complicated "words," verbal gestures that may be whole sentences or paragraphs.

In an outline processor, then, the prose remains, but it is encased in a formally operative structure. With a pen or typewriter, writing meant literally to form letters on a page, figuratively to create verbal structures. In an electronic writing system, the figurative process becomes a literal act. By defining topical symbols, the writer can, like the programmer or the mathematician, abstract himself or herself temporarily from the details of the prose, and the value of this abstraction lies in seeing more clearly the structural skeleton of the text. It is not possible or desirable that the prose writer should become a mathematician or that human language should be reduced to a system of logical symbols. The result of giving language wholeheartedly over to formalism would simply be the impoverishment of language. On the other hand, the electronic medium can permit us to play creatively with formal structures in our writing without abandoning the richness of natural language.

ELECTRONIC TREES

It is no accident that the computer can serve as an outline processor. The machine is designed to create and track such formal structures, which are important for all its various uses. The computer's memory and central processing unit are intricate hierarchies of electronic components. Layers of software in turn transform the machine's physical space of electronic circuits into a space of symbolic information, and it is in this space that a new kind of writing can be located. Like the space of the modern physicist, the space of the computer is shaped by the objects that occupy it. The computer programmer forms his or her space by filling it with symbolic elements and then by connecting these elements as the program requires. Any symbol in the space can refer to another symbol by using its numerical address. Pointers hold together the structure of computer programs, and programming itself may be defined as the art of building symbolic structures in the space that the computer provides—a definition that makes programming a species of writing.

One such programming structure, which represents hierarchy, is called a *tree*. Trees (and their relatives such as *lists*, *stacks*, and *networks*) are ubiquitous in programs that must record and track large bodies of information or information subject to frequent change. Tree diagrams, in which elements are connected by branches as in a genealogical tree, have a long history in writing as well. They date back at least to the early Middle Ages and are not uncommon in medieval and Renaissance books, where they served for the spatial arrangement of topics (Ong, 1958, pp. 74-83, 199-202, 314-318). The traditional outline is a strict hierarchy that can just as easily be represented by a tree diagram. Part of the outline that we saw earlier (Fig. 2.2) is represented by the following tree (Fig. 2.3).

Both the tree and the outline give us a better reading of structure than does ordinary paragraphing, because they mold the visual space of the text in a way that reflects its structure. A printed page of paragraphs is by comparison a flat and uninteresting space, as is the window of a word processor. A writer can use a word processor to type an outline, and, if the word processor permits graphics, the writer can insert a tree diagram into the text. But the outline or diagram will then be stored as a picture, a sequence of bits to be shown on the screen; the picture will not be treated as a data stucture and will not inform the space in which the writer is working. The writer will not be able to change the structure by manipulating the outline, as he or she can in an outline processor, and that ability is necessary for true electronic writing. In using an outline processor, the writer can intervene at any level of the evolving structure. And if the writer gives the reader a diskette rather than a printed version, then the reader too gains immediate access to that structure. All this

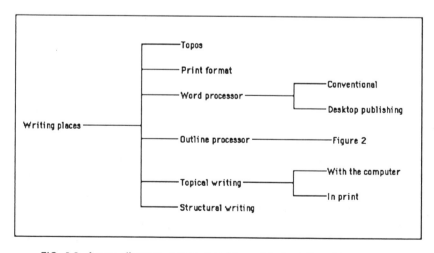

FIG. 2.3. A tree diagram represents hierarchical relationships among elements.

is possible, because the writing space itself has become a tree, a hierarchy of topical elements.

The electronic writing space is extremely malleable. It can be fashioned into one tree or into a forest of hierarchical trees. A hierarchy defines a strict order of subordination: each point in an outline is arranged under exactly one heading; each topical unit in a tree diagram (except the root) has exactly one incoming arrow. In any printed or written text, one such hierarchical order always precludes others. The static medium of print demands that the writer settle on one order of topics, although the writer may find that the topics could be arranged equally well in, say, three orders corresponding to three electronic outlines. Unlike the space of the printed book, the computer's writing space can represent any relationships that can be defined as the interplay of pointers and elements. Multiple relationships pose no special problem. A writer could therefore maintain three outlines, each of which deployed the same topics in a different order. These outlines may all reside in the computer's memory at the same time, each activated at the writer's request. The writer may choose to examine topics from any of the three vantage points and then switch to another; he or she may alter one outline while leaving the others intact; he or she may alter any of the outlines themselves without revising the text in any one of the topics. The structure of an electronic text is in this sense abstracted from its verbal expression.

This multiplicity and abstraction already render the electronic writing space more flexible than its predecessors. And if all writing were only hierarchical, then the outline processor itself would be revolutionary in its freeing of writing from the frozen structure of the printed page. But there is one further step to be taken in liberating the text.

HYPERTEXT

The goal of conventional writing is to create a perfect hierarchy, but it is not always easy to maintain the discipline of such a structure. All writers have had the experience of being overwhelmed with ideas as they write. The act of writing itself releases a flood of thoughts—one idea suggesting another and another, as the writer struggles to get them down in some form before they slip from his or her conscious grasp. "I only wish I could write with both hands," noted Saint Teresa, "so as not to forget one thing while I am saying another" (see Peers, 1972, vol. 2, p. 88). Romantics like Carlyle founded their psychology of literature upon this experience. The experience is not limited to saints and poets: many, perhaps most, writers begin their work with a jumble of verbal ideas and only a vague sense of how these ideas will fit together. The writer may start by laying out topics in an arrangement less formal than an outline: he or she may organize by association rather than strict subordination. Teachers of writing often encourage their students to begin by sketching out topics and connecting them through lines of association, and they call this activity "prewriting." What students create in prewriting is a network of elements—exactly what computer programmers mean by the data structure they call a network. The computer can maintain such a network of topics, and it can reflect the writer's progress as he or she trims the network by removing connections and establishing subordination until there is a strict hierarchy. In the world of print, at least in nonfiction, associative writing is considered only a preliminary.

Association is not really prior to writing, as the term "prewriting" suggests. Association is always present in any text: one word echoes another; one sentence or paragraph recalls others earlier in the text and looks forward to still others. A writer cannot help but write associatively: even if he or she begins with and remains faithful to an outline, the result is always a network of verbal elements. The hierarchy (in the form of paragraphs, sections, and chapters) is an attempt to impose order on verbal ideas that are always prone to subvert that order. The associative relationships define alternative organizations that lie beneath the order of pages and chapters that a printed text presents to the world. These alternatives constitute subversive texts-behind-the-text.

Previous technologies of writing, which could not easily accommodate such alternatives, tended to ignore them. The ancient papyrus roll was strongly linear in its presentation of text. The codex, especially in the later Middle Ages, and then the printed book have made better efforts to accommodate association as well as hierarchy. In a modern book the table of contents (listing chapters and sometimes sections) defines the hierarchy, while the indices record associative lines of thought that permeate the text. An index permits the reader to locate passages that share the same word, phrase, or subject and so associates passages that may be widely separated in the pagination of the book. In one sense the index defines other books that could be constructed from the materials at hand, other themes that the author could have formed into an analytical narrative, and so invites the reader to read the book in alternative ways. An index transforms a book from a tree into a network, offering multiplicity in place of a single order of paragraphs and pages. There need not be any privileged element in a network, as there always is in a tree, no single topic that dominates all others. Instead of strict subordination, we have paths that weave their way through the textual space. Thus, the outline and tree that we saw earlier (Figs. 2.2 and 2.3) can become the network shown in Fig. 2.4. If all texts are ultimately networks of verbal elements, the computer is the first medium that can record and present these networks to writers and readers. Just as the outline processor treats text as a hierarchy, other computer programs can fashion the text into a general network or hypertext.

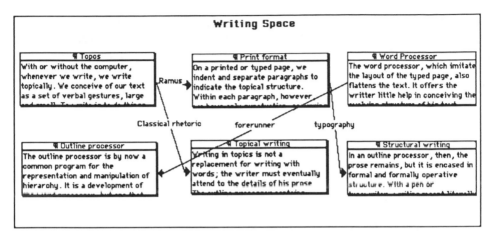

FIG. 2.4. A hypertext is a network of textual elements and connections.

Hypertext has only recently become a discipline in computer science. (See Smith & Weiss, 1988.) The term "hypertext" was coined two decades ago by Ted Nelson. Working with mainframe computers in the 1960s, Nelson had come to realize the machine's capacity to create and manage textual networks for all kinds of writing. "Literature," he wrote, "is an ongoing system of interconnecting documents." By literature he meant not only belles-lettres but also scientific and technical writing: any group of writings on a well-defined subject. "A literature is a system of interconnected writings. We do not offer this as our definition, but as a discovered fact" (Nelson, 1984, p. 2/7; see also Nelson, 1974 and Conklin, 1987, pp. 22-23). Actually this "fact" had been discovered independent of and long before the computer, but the machine has provided Nelson and others in the last two decades with the technology needed to realize and indeed to reify writing as a network. Even before Nelson, the scientist and engineer Vannevar Bush had envisioned using electro-mechanical technology as a hypertextual reading and writing system. In 1945 Bush proposed (but never built) what he called a "memex," a device that would serve as an interactive encyclopedia or library. The reader of the memex would be able to display two texts on a screen and then create links between passages in the texts. These links would be stored by the memex and would be available for later display and revision; collectively they would define a network of interconnections. Because electronic storage was not yet capacious or reliable, Bush chose microfilm as the storage medium for his memex. Fortunately the development of electromagnetic and optical disks has rendered microfilm obsolete for this purpose. But computer technology was already far enough advanced for Bush to see the possibility of hypertext and to express himself enthusiastically. His article proclaims nothing less than "a new relationship between thinking man and the sum of knowledge" (see Bush, 1945, p.101).

Whether realized on microfilm or in computer memory, a hypertext consists of topics and their connections, where again the topics may be paragraphs, sentences, individual words, or indeed digitized graphics. A hypertext is like a printed book that the author has attacked with a pair of scissors and cut into convenient verbal sizes. The difference is that the electronic hypertext does not simply dissolve into a disordered bundle of slips, as the printed book must. For the author also defines a scheme of electronic connections to indicate relationships among the slips. In fashioning a hypertext, a writer might begin with a passage of continuous prose and then add notes or glosses on important words in the passage. As we suggested earlier (Fig. 2.1), the glosses themselves could contain glosses, leading the reader to further texts. A hypertextual network can extend indefinitely, as a printed text cannot.

A computer hypertext might serve, for example, to collect scholars' notes on complex texts such as Joyce's *Ulysses* and *Finnegans Wake*. The computer can record and update the collective work of many scholars who continue today adding to, refining, and revising the glosses; it can connect notes to other notes as appropriate. Such exegesis, currently recorded in books and journals, would be both easier to use and more appropriate as a hypertext, because *Ulysses* and particularly *Finnegans Wake* are themselves hypertexts that have been flattened out to fit on the printed page. But an author does not have to be as experimental as Joyce to profit from hypertext. A historian might choose to write an essay in which each paragraph or section is a topic in a hypertextual network. The connections would indicate possible orders in which topics could be assembled and read, and each order of reading might produce a different literary and analytic result. A mathematician might choose to write a hypertextbook that could tailor itself to different students with differing degrees of mathematical proficiency. Hypertext can serve for all sorts of more popular materials as well: directories, catalogues, how-to manuals—wherever the reader wishes to move through the text in a variety of orders. In fact thousands of such hypertexts are already available, written for display by Hypercard, a program for the Apple Macintosh computer.

In general, the connections of a hypertext are organized into paths that make operational sense to author and reader. Each topic may participate in several paths, and its significance will depend upon which paths the reader has traveled in order to arrive at that topic. In print, only a few paths can be suggested or followed. In an electronic version the texture of the text becomes thicker, and its paths can serve many functions. Paths can, as in a tree structure, indicate subordination. They can also remind the writer of relationships among topics that had to be sacrificed for the sake of an eventual hierarchy. They can express cyclic relationships among topics that can never be hierarchical. They can categorize topics for later revision: the writer might wish to join two paths together or intersect two paths and preserve only those elements common to both. In the electronic medium, hierarchical and associative thinking may coexist in the structure of a text, since the computer can take care of the mechanics of maintaining and presenting both networks and trees. In the medium of print, the writer may use an index to show alternatives, but these alternatives must always contend with the fixed order of the pages of the book. The canonical order is defined by the book's pagination, and all other suggested orders remain subordinate. A hypertext has no canonical order. Every path defines an equally convincing and appropriate reading, and in that simple fact the reader's relationship to the text changes radically. A text as a network has no univocal sense; it is a multiplicity without the imposition of a principle of domination.

In place of hierarchy, we have a writing that is not only topical: we might also call it "topographic." The word "topography" originally meant a written description of a place, such as an ancient geographer might give. Only later did the word come to refer to mapping or charting—that is, to a visual and mathematical rather than verbal description. Electronic writing is both a visual and verbal description. It is not the writing of a place, but rather a writing *with* places, spatially realized topics. Topographic writing challenges the idea that writing should be merely the servant of spoken language. The writer and reader can create and examine signs and structures on the computer screen that have no easy equivalent in speech. The point is obvious when the text is a collections of images stored on a videodisk, but it is equally true for a purely verbal text that has been fashioned as a tree or a network of topics and connections.

Topographic writing as a mode is not even limited to the computer medium. It is possible to write topographically for print or even in manuscript. Whenever we divide our text into unitary topics and organize those units into a connected structure and whenever we conceive of this textual structure spatially as well as verbally, we are writing topographically. As we shall see in a later chapter, many literary artists in the 20th century have adopted this mode of writing. Although the computer is not necessary for topographic writing, it is only in the computer that the mode becomes a natural, and therefore also a conventional, way to write.

HYPERMEDIA

The first generation of personal computers could only display about one or two hundred different signs—the letters of the alphabet, numerals, punctuation, and some special characters. The writer had to choose from those shapes and therefore symbols that were wired into the displays or into their interface cards. Now the advent of inexpensive, bit-mapped graphics has removed that limitation. With bit-mapping, each pixel, each tiny square or rectangle on the screen, is under programmed control: permissible shapes are no longer frozen into the hardware. The letters of the alphabet themselves are defined by software, so that the system can provide not only the Roman alphabet in pica, but other styles, type fonts, and sizes as well. Images can be represented on the screen as easily as letters of the alphabet. These machine images have the same advantage of dynamic control as do the letter forms, and they suffer from the same problem of graininess, since the images too consist of a finite number of pixels.

Some word processors already permit the writer to insert diagrams and pictures directly into the text. But in word processing the graphic image is not really part of the text; it is merely allowed to coexist with the verbal text. As we have seen in the figures presented earlier, the computer has the capacity to integrate word and image more subtly, to make text itself graphic by representing its structure graphically to the writer and the reader. The computer can even dissolve the distinction between the standardized letter forms and symbols of the writer's own making. True electronic writing is not limited to verbal text: the writeable elements may be words, images, sounds, or even actions that the computer is directed to perform. The writer could use his or her network to organize pictures on videodisk or music and voices on an audio playback device. Instead of moving from paragraph to paragraph in a verbal text, the reader might be shown videotaped scenes of a play in a variety of orders. The reader might move through an aural landscape created by various recorded sounds or walk through a city by viewing photographs of various buildings. (Such was the Aspen project. See Brand, 1987, pp. 141-142.) Any combination of these elements is possible. The same computer screen might display verbal text below or beside a video image; it might combine sound and verbal writing. These combinations have come to be called *hypermedia* and are already quite sophisticated.

The introduction of video images might seem to turn electronic writing into mere television. Television itself often displays words on the screen, but it robs the displayed words of their cognitive value. Text on television is mere ornamentation; words appear most often to reinforce the spoken message or to decorate the packages of products being advertised. In fact, hypermedia is the revenge of text upon television (Joyce, 1988, p. 14). In television, text is absorbed into the video image, but in hypermedia the televised image becomes part of the text. This incorporation is literally true in MIT's Project Athena, in which the reader can run a videotape in a window on his computer screen. The video image therefore sits among the other textual elements for the reader to examine. (For a description of Project Athena, see Balkovich,

Lerman, & Parmelee, 1985.) The Intermedia system developed at Brown University is another instance, in which texts and images are read and written in the same computer environment. (See Yankelovich, Haan, Meyrowitz, & Drucker, 1988.) Once video images and sound are taken into the computer in this fashion, they too become topical elements. Writers can fashion these elements into a structure. They can write with images, because they can direct one topical image to refer to another and join visual and verbal topics in the same network (see Fig. 2.5). A journalist might select examples from a library of digitized still pictures and form them into a pictorial essay. An art historian might take images of Renaissance painting and attach explanatory comments. In fact, one can link the comments not only to the whole painting, but also to given areas of the image. The eyes of one portrait may refer to a comment, which may in turn link to eyes of other portrait examples. Other parts of the painting would lead to other comments and other examples. The reader would begin with the first picture and then choose to read the network of examples and explanations in a variety of orders, based on an interest in hands, eyes, or other elements of Renaissance technique. In each case the elements of the pictures have themselves become signs that refer to verbal topics and to other pictures. The image is functioning symbolically within the writer's text.

Such multimedia texts are by no means the death of writing. A hypermedia display is still a text, a weaving together of elements treated symbolically. Hypermedia simply extends the principles of electronic writing into the domain of sound and image. The computer's control of structure promises to create a synaesthesia in which anything that can be seen or heard may contribute to the texture of the text. These synaesthetic texts will have the same qualities as electronic verbal texts. They too will be flexible, dynamic, and interactive; they too will blur the distinction between writer and reader.

THE FIRST HYPERTEXT

Although experiments have been conducted since the 1960s, workable hypertext systems such as Intermedia are relatively recent. It was not until the advent of personal computers and workstations that hypertext could be made available to a large audience of writers and readers. On the other hand, the principle of hypertext has been implicit in computer programming for much longer. Hypertext is the interactive interconnection of a set of symbolic elements, and many kinds of computer programs (databases, simulation programs, even programs for artificial intelligence) are special cases of that principle. Hypertext shows how programming and conventional prose writing can combine in the space provided by the computer. It puts at the

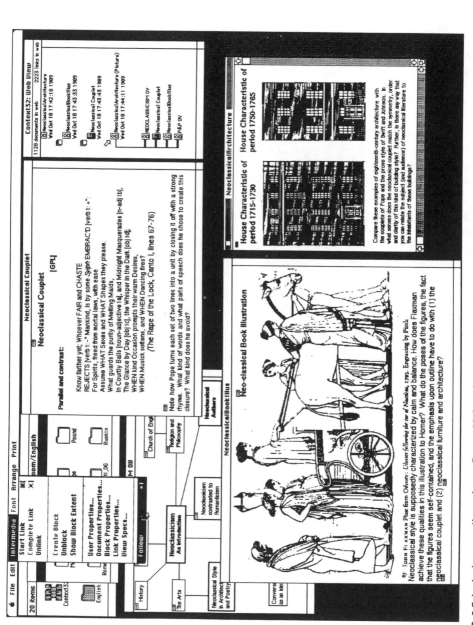

FIG. 2.5. In the Intermedia project at Brown University, text and graphics can be combined into a single hypertextual web. Here, in a complex set of windows on the Macintosh computer screen, a passage from Pope is related to examples of Neoclassical architecture and book illustration. The link icon is a small box that contains a right pointing arrow. Wherever that icon occurs, the reader can choose to follow the link to another element in the hypertext. Reprinted with the kind permission of Professor George P. Landow.

disposal of writers data structures (trees and networks) that have been used for decades by programmers. Conversely, it makes us realize that the programmer's data structures are formalized versions of the textual strategies that writers have exploited for centuries.

Important anticipations of hypertext can be found in the computerized communications networks, such as ARPANET or BITNET, put in place in the 1960s and 1970s. Such a network constitutes the physical embodiment of hypertext. Each element or *node* in the network is a computer installation, while the connections among these elements are cables and microwave and satellite links. Each computer node serves dozens or hundreds of individual subscribers, and these subscribers both produce and read messages created by others within their computing facility, around the nation, or around the world. Some messages travel a single path through the communications links until they reach their marked destination, while general messages spread out to all the elements in the net. At any one moment the network holds a vast text of interrelated writings—the intersection of thousands of messages on hundreds of topics. It is a hypertext that no one reader can hope to encompass, one that changes moment by moment as messages are added and deleted.

Subscribers use these networks both for personal mail and to conduct ongoing discussions in so-called "newsgroups." When one subscriber in a newsgroup "publishes" a message, it travels to all the dozens or hundreds of others who belong to that group. The message may elicit responses, which in turn travel back and forth and spawn further responses. The prose of these messages is almost as casual as conversation, precisely because publication in this medium is both easy and almost unrestricted. The transition from reader to writer is completely natural. The reader of one message can with a few keystrokes send off a reply. Readers may even incorporate part of the original message in the reply, blurring the distinction between their own text and the text to which they are responding. There is also little respect for the conventions of the prior medium of print. Subscribers often type newspaper articles or excerpts from books into their replies without concern for copyright. The notion of copyright seems faintly absurd, since their messages are copied and relayed automatically hundreds of times in a matter of hours.

Writing for such a network is by nature topographical: relatively small units of prose are sent and received. The medium itself encourages brevity, since two correspondents can send and receive several messages in one day. And the addresses of the messages provide a primitive system of links. To reply to a given message is to link your text to the earlier one, and both message and reply may then circulate for days around the network provoking other reponses. No user is bound to read or reply to anything; instead, any message can refer to any other or ignore all previous messages and strike out in a new direction. A communications network is therefore a hypertext in which no one writer or reader has substantial control, and because no one has control, no one has substantial responsibility. The situation is different for hypertext systems for microcomputers, where there is one author and one reader. There the twin issues of control and responsibility are paramount.

WRITERS AND READERS OF HYPERTEXT

When we receive a written or typed letter, we hold in our own hands the paper that the sender also has handled. We see and touch the inkmarks that he or she has made. With electronic mail we receive bits of information that correspond to the tapping of keys on the writer's keyboard. We read this information as patches of light on our computer screen, and we touch nothing that the writer has touched. Like all other kinds of writing, electronic writing is an act of postponement or deferral. As writers, we defer our words by setting them down on a writing surface for later reading by ourselves or by others. The reader's task is to reactivate the words on the page and to devise for them a new context, which may be close to or far removed from the author's original context. There is always a gulf between author and reader, a gap that the technique of writing first creates and then mediates. In one sense the computer opens a particularly wide gap because of the abstract nature of electronic technology. On the other hand, the author has a unique opportunity to control the procedure of reading, because he or she can program restrictions into the text itself.

Computer-assisted instruction, for example, is nothing other than a hypertext in which the author has restricted the ways in which the student/ reader can proceed. In typical computer-assisted instruction the program poses a question and awaits an answer from the student. If the student gives the correct answer, the program may present another question. If the student's answer is wrong, the program may explain the student's error. If the student makes the same error repeatedly, the program may present a review of the point that the student has failed to grasp. In most cases, these questions and explanations are texts that the teacher/programmer has composed and stored in advance. However, good programming can make these simple programs seem uncannily clever in replying to the student. In fact such a program takes on a persona created for it by the teacher/programmer, as it transfers the teacher's words into the new context of the student's learning session. In general, the reader of an electronic text is made aware of the author's simultaneous presence in and absence from the text, because the reader is constantly confronting structural choices established by the author. If the program allows the reader to make changes in the text or to add new connections (as some hypertext systems do), then the game becomes still more complex. As readers we become our own authors, determining the structure of the text for the next reader, or perhaps for ourselves in our next reading.

Electronic text is the first text in which the elements of meaning, of structure, and of visual display are fundamentally unstable. Unlike the printing press or the medieval codex, the computer does not require that any aspect of writing be determined in advance for the whole life of a text. This restlessness is inherent in a technology that records information by collecting for fractions of a second evanescent electrons at tiny junctions of silicon and metal. All information, all data, in the computer world is a kind of controlled movement, and so the natural inclination of computer writing is to change, to grow, and finally to disappear. Nor is it surprising that these constant motions place electronic writing in a kaleidoscope of relationships with the earlier technologies of typewriting, printing, and handwriting.

Chapter

3

Writing as Technology

Writing is a technology for collective memory, for preserving and passing on human experience. The art of writing may not be as immediately practical as techniques of agriculture or textile manufacture, but it obviously enhances the human capacity for social organization—by providing a culture with fixed laws, with a history, and with a literary tradition. Eventually writing also becomes the preserver and extender of other technologies, as an advanced culture develops a technical literature. Writing is and has always been a sophisticated technology: skill is required to learn to read and write, and penetrating intelligence is needed to invent or improve some aspect of the technology of literacy.

It is not difficult to recognize the printing press, the typewriter, or the Linotype machine as technologies. These modern means of book production are complex and to a degree self-activating or self-directing. The mechanization of writing began with the printing press in the fifteenth century. The press was the first text "processor," the first technology of writing to duplicate words en masse. In replacing the scribe who formed his or her letters one at a time, the press registered several pages of text onto a large sheet of paper with each impersonal pull. As Marshall McLuhan recognized, "the invention of typography . . . provid[ed] the first uniformly repeatable commodity, the first assembly-line, and the first mass-production" (see *The Gutenberg Galaxy* by McLuhan, 1972, p. 124). Printing had the additional virtue that it could produce books nearly identical to the best manuscripts: the press rivaled handwriting in quality while far surpassing it in quantity. Elizabeth Eisenstein notes that "[t]he absence of any apparent change in product was combined with a complete change in methods of production, giving rise to the paradoxical combination of seeming continuity with radical change" (Eisenstein, 1983, p. 20). This paradox made the mechanization of the word easier to accept, and many scholars in the 15th century immediately saw the advantages of this new technology. Gradually, over several generations, printing did change the visual character of the written page, making the writing space technically cleaner and clearer. The book had taken on a thoroughly different and modern look by the late 18th century. In the 19th and 20th, steam and electric presses, and automatic typesetting brought further mechanization, removing the need for human muscle and further distancing the human controller from the printing process.

The computer in turn changes the technology of writing by adding new flexibility to the rapidity and efficiency of printing: the computer allows a writer or reader to change a text as easily as he or she can duplicate it. The capacity to adjust the text to each user's needs is unmechanical, uncharacteristic of the classic industrial machine, and this capacity derives from the unmechanical materials of electronic technology. The computer's central processor itself contains no grinding gears or indeed any moving parts above the level of electrons, and even the mechanical components of a computer system, such as disk drives and laser printers, are characterized by rapid movement and fine control. The digital computer has helped to give us a new definition of the machine, as a complex interrelation of logical parts—an abstraction that, unlike the steam engine and the dynamo, produces information rather than power. If the printing press is the classic writing machine, the computer provides us with a technology of writing beyond mechanization.

The medieval manuscript and ancient papyrus roll in turn represent technologies of writing before mechanization. These earlier technologies also required devices—pen and paper or parchment in the Middle Ages or reed pen and papyrus in the ancient world. And working from such raw materials as rags, animal skins, or plants to produce a finished book required a considerable technical knowledge. Still, the manuscripts were produced at the relatively leisured pace of the writing hand, not the insistent rhythm of the machine. We can see on each page or in each column the variations in size and shape of letters that indicate direct human production. The development of printing has affected our view of all previous writing. A medieval manuscript, rubricated and bound in leather, would perhaps have struck a Greek in Plato's time as a complicated and ingenious device. Now we admire it as art, simple in conception and intricate in execution. What we also admire is the apparent negation of technology, the fact that the codex is not a printed book, not the product of a machine.

WRITING AS A STATE OF MIND

Does the word "techne" not denote a possession or state of mind? (Plato, *Cratylus*, 414B-C)

There is good etymological reason to broaden our definition of technology to include skills as well as machines. The Greek root of "technology" is *techne*, and for the Greeks a *techne* could be an art or a craft, "a set of rules, system or method of making or doing, whether of the useful arts, or of the fine arts" (Liddell and Scott, 1973, p. 1785). In the ancient world physical technology was simpler, and the ancients put a correspondingly greater emphasis on the skill of the craftsman—the potter, the stone-mason, or the carpenter. In his dialogue the *Phaedrus*, Plato calls the alphabet itself a *techne*. He would also have called the ancient book composed of ink on papyrus a *techne*; Homeric epic poetry was also a *techne*, as was Greek tragedy. All the ancient arts and crafts have this in common: that the craftsman must develop a skill, a technical state of mind in using tools and materials. Ancient and modern writing is a technology in just this sense. It is a method for arranging verbal thoughts in a visual space. The writer always needs a surface upon which to make his or her marks and a tool with which to make them, and these materials help to define the nature of the writing. Writing with quill and parchment is a different skill from writing with a printing press, which in turn differs from writing with a computer. However, all writing demands method, the intention of the writer to arrange ideas systematically in a space for later examination by a reader.

In *Orality and Literacy* Walter Ong has argued that writing is "interiorized" and that the process of interiorization makes it difficult for us to recognize writing as a technology (Ong, 1982, pp. 81-82). Yet this process is not peculiar to writing. Every technological skill is internalized by its users, until at last it becomes "second nature," an ability that the expert exercises without conscious or labored effort. And as the skill becomes natural, the technological device itself seems to become a part of the user. If we drive a car daily, we become accustomed to the feel of the machine and learn to regard its power and handling as extensions of our arms and legs. Construction workers may have a similar feeling about their massive cranes or bulldozers, carpenters about their hammers, surgeons about their scopes and scalpels, and musicians about their instruments. However, in all these cases, experts spend time away from their cars, cranes, or instruments: they can detach themselves from their technological prostheses. For writers, for all literate people, this detachment is not so easy. As writers we do not write all the time, but our technical relationship to the writing space is always with us. Literacy is the realization that language can have a visual as well as an aural dimension, that one's words can be recorded and shown to others who are not present, perhaps not even alive, at the time of the recording. Literate people know that words can be placed in a visual space and have continued existence in that space. They always know this. When they are speaking, they know that their words can be written down. Students of culture as uncongenial as Walter Ong and Jacques Derrida have insisted that writing exercises this constant influence upon our mental life.

Literate men and women indeed reveal their literacy when they are speaking as well as writing. Cultures with a long tradition of literacy develop a standard literary language. Illiterates are denied access to that language, while men and women educated in the tradition tend to speak in a combination of colloquial and literary terms. They have larger vocabularies, and they speak, as they write, in a variety of styles and levels. They often structure their speech as they do their writing, talking in sentences and even paragraphs. They write in their mind as well as on paper or at a keyboard; indeed, they are writing whenever they think or verbalize in that methodical way characterized by writing.

Spoken language can therefore itself be a *techne*. It can require method—most obviously in the many different kinds of oral poetry and storytelling that have existed throughout history and are still important today in much of the third world. The oral poet applies method to language in order to create verse forms and story structures, although in this case the structures are appreciated by listening rather than by reading. The oral poet is a writer, who writes in the minds of his or her audience. Perhaps in this sense there is no language without *techne*, without intentional structure or art. Even today in North America, when the art of conversation is apparently dead, we never speak in a wholly unrhetorical and unstructured way. Wholly naive or artless language is only hypothetical; it exists only as an imagined counterpoint to all structured speaking and writing.

Writing, like language itself, is therefore both natural and artificial. Even if the human capacity for language is innate, wired into our genes, we nevertheless use our innate capacity in an artificial, rhetorical way. Writing is certainly not innate. Yet writing can be taken in and become a habit of mind. What is natural seems more intimately and obviously human. For that reason we do not wish to dwell on the fact that writing is a technology; we want the skill of writing to be natural. We like our tools and machines well enough, but we also like the idea of being able to do without them. Putting away our technology gives us a feeling of autonomy and allows us to reassert the difference between the natural and the merely artificial. Since the time of Rousseau, much of the hostility directed against modern technology has been rooted in the belief that, as our technology becomes more complex, we are becoming creatures of our own creations. Today, the computer is a perfect target for such an assault on technology, because of the computer's apparent autonomy.

But in the case of writing as elsewhere, it is not possible to put away technology. Writing with pen and paper is no more natural, no less technological than writing at a computer screen. It is true that the computer is a more complicated and more fragile device than a pen. But we cannot isolate ourselves from technology by reverting to older methods of writing. The production of today's pens and paper also requires a sophisticated manufacture. Without electricity, industrial organization, and networks of transportation and distribution, we could not provide ourselves with adequate supplies of these simple writing materials. In any case, it is not the complexity of the devices that matters so much as the technical state of mind, which is common to all methods of writing. The ancient Sumerian inscribing clay tablets with wedge-shaped marks was adopting the same technical attitude toward his materials as the contemporary writer seated at a computer terminal: both are shaping a writing space by filling it with visual signs.

ECONOMIES OF WRITING

Each culture and each age has its own economy of writing. There is a dynamic relationship between the materials and the techniques of writing, and a less obvious but no less important relationship between materials and techniques on the one hand and the genres and uses of writing on the other. Economies of writing—materials, techniques, and uses—evolve and expand and sometimes deteriorate and collapse.

The earliest economies flourished in Mesopotamia and in Egypt, where picture writing was gradually replaced by phonetic systems, in which written symbols were associated directly and consistently with sounds in the language. (The Egyptians may have borrowed the idea of phonetic writing from the Sumerians. The Chinese and the Mayans in the New World may have been the only other peoples to invent phonetic writing independently. See Sampson, 1985, pp. 46-47.) Both the Sumerians and the Egyptians developed complicated word-syllable scripts, whose symbols sometimes stood for whole words, sometimes more abstractly for combinations of consonants and vowels. The Sumerians and their successors wrote principally on stone and clay, the Egyptians on stone and papyrus, a paper-like surface made from a reedy plant that grew along the Nile. While the Egyptians developed a monumental style for their hieroglyphics in stone, the Sumerians adopted a wedge-shaped stylus that worked well in clay and led to their distinctive cuneiform. Writing on stone and even on wet clay was a slow process. The chief advantage, in which the two have yet to be surpassed, was longevity. Egyptian hieroglyphics inscribed on the walls and stone slabs have often survived for thousands of years, and we possess millions of clay tablets from the Sumerians and their successors in Mesopotamia. Papyrus, on the other hand, has only survived in dry climates and by accident. Nonetheless, its flexibility and portability made papyrus preferable for day-to-day uses. Egyptian writing on papryus became progressively more cursive and less like the traditional and beautifully stylized hieroglyphic images inscribed on stone.

The ancient Greeks and Romans borrowed both the materials and the elements of their writing economy. The Greek alphabet was taken from the Phoenicians, while papyrus from Egypt served as the chief writing material for the Greeks and the Romans. The ancient book was a roll, consisting of sheets of papyrus glued together at the ends. Greek and Latin texts were written in narrow columns perpendicular to the length of the roll, an arrangement that made ancient books more strictly linear than modern ones. The reader could not easily flip to the middle of the book in search of a passage; instead the reader had to start at the beginning and scroll his or her way through. Each roll, 20 to 25 feet in length, held much less text than a modern book, so that longer works, such as the Homeric poems, had to be stored on many rolls. The roll later became a structural unit in writing, and Greek and Roman authors often conceived and wrote their works in units appropriate to the roll. The paged book or codex, which came into use in the second and third centuries A.D., opened a range of new possibilities for writing, by defining a writing space both more varied and more accessible than that of the roll. (See Reynolds & Wilson, 1978, pp. 30-32.) In either form, roll or codex, ancient books offered their readers few visual aids for the understanding of the structure of a text. The books had little punctuation and did not make consistent use of page numbers, indices, or tables of contents. Ancient scribes did not even leave extra space to mark boundaries between words. Instead each line of text was a continuous row of twenty or more letters, and separating one word from the next was part of the reader's task of decipherment.

The paged book became a more sophisticated technology in the Western European economy of writing. In the Middle Ages parchment provided a more durable and more attractive writing surface than papyrus, which in any case became hard to obtain from Egypt. Paper was introduced from the Far East as a cheaper replacement for parchment in the later Middle Ages. Although not as tough as parchment, paper made from rags could be produced in greater quantities and could therefore supply growing demand for reading materials. (On the replacement of parchment by paper, see Febvre & Martin, 1971, pp. 39-60. See also Gaur, 1984, pp. 44-47.) Upon these new materials, medieval scribes set out to create a new writing space; they used word division, punctuation, rubrication (decorated initial letters), and in some cases headings, and letter styles to organize the writing visually on the page. They also began to insert critical notes and glosses into the margins of the text, sometimes in several layers. In the medieval codex, the page became a web of text and interpretation, tradition and innovation.

Finally, the invention of printing in the 15th century initiated the modern economy of writing. Printing has defined for us the contemporary, highly organized and standardized writing space. The techniques of spatial organization used in modern printing include most of those devised in the Middle Ages and others besides. If legibility is measured by reading efficiency, the printed book is more legible than any previous technology. Good readers can manage 600 words a minute as they devour a printed novel (Levin & Addis, 1979, p. 33). Such speeds are unthinkable for an ancient papyrus or medieval codex. Typographic standardization also permits us to consult a modern encyclopedia with far greater ease than an ancient could consult Pliny the Elder or a medieval scholar Vincent of Beauvais. But with this gain in legibility, our books have lost the organic beauty they possessed in the age of manuscripts. The printing press gives us stiff, mechanically correct letters in place of the sometimes beautiful, sometimes wretched medieval hands. This price is one we have willingly paid. For 500 years the printing of alphabetic texts has remained our dominant technology for writing and reading, where our culture locates its most important and lasting writing.

Each new technology must find its place in the current economy of writing, and in so doing it may supplement or replace older technologies. The codex effectively replaced the roll in late antiquity. Papyrus was replaced in the Middle Ages by parchment and paper. In the late 19th and early 20th centuries, the typewriter replaced handwriting for business communcations. (That change created secretarial jobs for millions of young women, because before the typewriter, clerks were generally male. See Zuboff, *In the Age of the Smart Machine*, 1988, pp. 115-116.) Now the word processor is replacing the typewriter.

No one technology of writing has ever proven adequate for all needs. The economy of writing is always diversified, as secondary technologies occupy places around the dominant one. These secondary technologies may even have been dominant ones that were pushed aside. Secondary technologies survive by meeting some need better than the dominant technology. The wax tablet remained in use from ancient times through the Middle Ages, because it was convenient for rough drafts and other ephemera. (See Rouse & Rouse, 1989.) Stone has served as a medium for thousands of years when the writer wants a permanent, public display. Although printing completely replaced handwriting in book production, it did not make handwriting obsolete. Printing led to increased literacy, and, as more people learned to read, more have learned to write. In today's complex economy, pen and paper serve for notes or personal communications; word processing and typewriting are used for texts not important enough or not ready for typesetting. We also have (or have had) the stenograph, the mimeograph, microfilm and microfiche readers, the overhead projector, and the xerox copier—all serving in some capacity that the press and printed books cannot.

The economy of print has succeeded in absorbing all of these technologies, even the word processor. Hypertextual electronic writing, however, now threatens to rearrange our economy by promoting an ideal of writing very different from the ideal of print. In the process, electronic writing gives new life to marginal techniques of the past. Electronic writing shares with the wax tablet the quality of rapid change. It shares with the typewriter its keyboard (at least at present), its method of discrete selection of alphabetic elements, and its machine-like uniformity. The computer can serve as a copier, a note pad, a calendar, or a teletype machine. In fact, it is hard to think of a marginal technology in the history of writing that the computer cannot imitate, just as it is hard to think of a dominant technology (the papyrus roll, the codex, the printed book) whose elements the computer does not borrow and reinterpret. Electronic writing will therefore be felt across the whole economy and history of writing: this new technology is a thorough rewriting of the writing space.

HARD AND SOFT STRUCTURES

Alphabetic literacy differs from literacy in syllabic writing or in Chinese word-writing. The skills needed to write and read a papyrus roll are different from those required to produce and read a printed book, and now electronic writing demands yet another set of skills. (By classical Chinese or Japanese standards, most of us in the West are barely literate, because our handwriting is poor and we have no interest in calligraphy.) In each case the needed skills go beyond the mechanical ones of holding the pen or turning the pages. The writer must learn how to structure and locate text in the visual space provided, just as the reader must learn how to make sense of texts in that space. Such verbal-visual structures are conventions that change in time, as anyone knows who has tried to find his or her way through a medieval or ancient manuscript. Ancient papyrus and medieval codices present the modern reader with different and alien writing spaces. When ancient, medieval, or even Renaissance texts are prepared for modern readers, it is not only the words that are translated: the text itself is translated into the space of the modern printed book. In translating dialogues by Plato, the editor marks each change of speaker, punctuates sentences, divides long replies into paragraphs, and gives the whole book a table of contents and perhaps an index. Greek readers in the 4th century B.C. would have had none of these visual cues as they scrolled their way through the papyrus. Plato, Chaucer, and even Shakespeare long after the invention of printing are not merely respelled for modern editions; they are restructured and therefore rewritten.

A writing space is characterized by the interplay of writing materials and writing techniques used. The materials define structural units and relationships that are tangible and hard to change. Thus, the principal hard structures in the age of print are the page and the paged book—folded, sewn or glued, and bound. The order of the pages in a book is fixed at the time of binding, text is arranged to run from one page to the next, and, with the important exception of reference works, the reader is expected to move through a book in that order. Printers have learned how to arrange text in order to make the opening (two pages visible when the book lies flat) attractive and legible. Beyond the opening, the book itself is our principal unit of meaningful text. Except in the case of multiple volume works, we expect each book to be whole, to present some complete narrative, interpretation, or body of information. There were analogous structures in all earlier technologies: the stone or clay tablet, the waxed writing board, the papyrus roll, the ancient scrinium or bookcase, and so on. Hard structures, then, are tangible qualities of the materials of writing.

Soft structures are those visually determined units and relationships that are written on or in the hard structures. Soft structures are drawn, painted, or incised on the surface of the writing material and transform that surface into an articulated writing space. Soft structures are by definition more flexible and can evolve more easily. Once you have invented the paged book, you can hardly avoid regarding the page as a structural unit. However, you still have great freedom in exploiting the surface that the page provides. Sometimes, it is true, a culture can change hard structures while retaining soft ones. The fundamental unit of soft structure in the ancient world was the alphabet, and writers have continued to use the alphabet on stone, wax writing boards, papyrus rolls, and written and printed books from 700 B.C. to the present. But more often, soft structures change without a change in materials. The medieval codex permitted remarkable changes in the visual presentation of text: through the creation of new scripts and through the gradual development of punctuation, marginalia, and marks of emphasis and organization. Today, the technology of print has a large repertoire of soft structures (punctuation, paragraphing, chapter divisions) that have evolved over hundreds of years. Newspapers and magazines have soft structures of their own. And all forms of printed matter can rely on styles of type, point size, type fonts, and even colors of the ink to organize and give visual meaning to the page.

ELECTRONIC STRUCTURES

Electronic technology presents writers with a new set of hard structures, defined by the hardware of the machine. Text is stored or "written" and retrieved or "read" by means of a variety of electronic, electro-mechanical, and now optical devices. For immediate use, text resides in transistor memory, where it is in direct connection with the central processing unit. For longer periods of storage, the text may be transferred to magnetic disk or tape. The newest and most capacious storage technology is the optical disk, written and read by a laser beam. All these methods allow rapid access: transistor memory provides the fastest access, optical disk the slowest, but even on an optical disk the time to locate and return a portion of text is measured in fractions of a second. All (except the current optical disks) can record a new text almost as quickly as they can deliver an old one.

Text is stored in these devices as strings of bits, which are in turn realized as voltage differences in transistors, patches of magnetized material on disk or tape, or tiny dots burned into the surface of the optical disk. For purposes of display, a printer can shift the text back to the older medium of the typed page. The videoscreen, however, offers a new surface with its own peculiar characteristics. The screen too can alter its contents rapidly and so fashion a writing space that changes at the writer's command. The screen can also combine words and images in the same textual space, for it presents all information as a set of discrete units or *pixels*.

Taken together, these hard structures constitute perhaps the greatest single technological change in the history of writing, principally because of their speed and autonomy of operation. The Roman rhetorician Quintilian found it good that "when we write, . . . our hand cannot keep up with our thoughts, and so we have time to weigh our words" (10.3.18-19). Quintilian would not have approved of a typist who can enter 80 or 100 words a minute at a keyboard, and he would have been appalled at the speed with which the computer can transfer words. Once a text has been stored in any layer of the computer's tiered memory, the machine can fetch, process, and present text in milliseconds. The computer can also copy text with unparalleled ease and speed—an important facility, considering that throughout the history of literacy the difficulty of making copies has been the chief impediment to the spread of the written word. The most unusual feature is that these new electronic hard structures are not directly accessible either to the writer or to the reader. The bits of the text are simply not on a human scale. Electronic technology removes or abstracts the writer and reader from the text. If you hold a magnetic or optical disk up to the light, you will not see text at all. At best you will see the circular tracks into which the data is organized, and these tracks mean nothing to the human eye. The human writer or reader needs a different device in order to examine electronic text, either a videoscreen or a printer. The text is filtered through layers of hardware and software as it passes from writer to reader, even if the writer is reading his or her own text.

Writing in any medium is an act of appropriation. Writing pulls words or ideas out of their original time and stores them away for later use. Even the writer who simply puts ink on paper defers his or her words. Printing, the mechanization of writing, defers in another sense: the author no longer writes on the page, but must instead work through layers of technology and a number of middlemen (the publisher, the copy editor, the printer). Yet, the printed product is still readable by human beings without further technological assistance. The more recently developed microfilm and microfiche are not directly readable: they require machines to project and enlarge the image to a scale suitable for the human eye. But microfilm technology does not make the crucial step of translating or coding text in a digital form. In the electronic medium several layers of sophisticated technology must intervene between the writer or reader and the coded text. There are so many levels of deferral that the reader or writer is hard put to identify the text at all: is it on the screen, in the transistor memory, or on the disk? The ephemeral character of electronic text makes possible new methods for organizing and visualizing the text. We identified the key to these new soft structures in the preceding chapter: it is the electronic link, by which we can establish and maintain connections between any two (numerical, verbal, or graphic) units of information. The electronic link allows us to build and explore trees and networks of such elements, to turn texts into hypertexts.

Chapter

4

The Elements of Writing

In Books lies the soul of the whole Past Time: the articulate audible voice of the Past . . . (Carlyle in "The Hero as Man of Letters," *Heroes and Hero Worshop*, 1890, p. 197)

There is a deeply rooted cultural assumption that the purpose of writing is to give voice, to speak our thoughts. Thought is supposed to be prior to writing: it is mysterious, hidden, and incorporeal, whereas writing is extroverted, visible, and embodied. Contemporary literary theory has called this assumption into question, and we will explore in a later chapter the collusion and collision of electronic writing with contemporary theory. In this chapter, we simply note that writing need not give voice to anything. Phonetic writing is not the only kind of writing; there are other principles by which a writing space can be constructed. The only quality that all writing shares is that it is discrete: writing is always the arrangement of discrete signs on or in a surface. The elements of writing may represent words, syllables, or individual sounds in a spoken language, or they may be visual signs with no fixed reference to speech. Writing can even dispense with visible signs and a visible surface altogether: it is possible to write in the mind, to inscribe human memory as if it were a piece of paper. Such mental writing too requires the arrangement of discrete elements.

The digital computer provides a richly textured writing space. Computer writing can be as abstract as alphabetic writing. It can be as fast and effortless (as apparently untechnological) as mental writing. Computer writing is primarily visual, rather than oral, and can be as silent as the picture writing of preliterate peoples. This eclectic character is the reason that computer writing is so important for the history of writing. The computer rewrites the history of writing by sending us back to reconsider nearly every aspect of the earlier technologies. In particular, the electronic medium gives a renewed prominence to the long discredited art of writing with pictures.

PICTURE WRITING

In alphabetic writing each sign represents a sound. We cannot specify what a particular letter of the alphabet means, except to say that it stands for a particular sound in our spoken language. Alphabetic writing is in this sense secondary writing, as it refers the reader to another system. Picture writing is primary in the sense that it is not tied to spoken language in this fashion. This freedom from spoken language is true of all picture writing—the contemporary electronic version as well as the preliterate forms. The signs in picture writing, stylized images, constitute their own silent language. The writer and reader may use words to describe and interpret the pictorial message, but the message is not wedded to any particular set of words. Two readers could explain the same message in different words, and speakers of different languages could share the same system of picture writing. Perhaps picture writing seems closer to the reader precisely because it does not depend upon the intermediary of spoken language and seems to reproduce places and events directly.

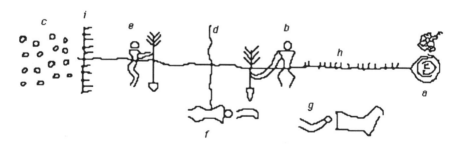

FIG. 4.1. "In 1858 a war party of Mille Lacs Ojibwa Indians, a, under the leadership of Shahâsh'king, b, went to attack Shákopi's camp, c, of Sioux at St. Peter's river, d. Shákopi is represented at e. The Ojibwa lost one man, f, at the St. Peter's river, while the Ojibwa killed five Sioux, but succeeded in securing only one arm of an Indian, g. The line h is the trail followed between Mille Lacs, a, and Shákopi's camp, c. The spots at c designate the location of the lodges, while the vertical line with short ones extending from it, i, signifies the prairie with trees growing near the camp" (taken from Mallery, 1972, vol 2, pp. 559-560; see also Jensen, 1969, p. 41).

By the standards of phonetic writing, picture writing lacks precision. The picture elements extend over a range of verbal meanings; each element means too much rather than too little. If the writer is drawing a battle, the writer's own comrades might not be distinguished from the enemy, and victory may be hardly distinguishable from defeat. When we look at the above representation of a battle between tribes of American Indians, we have exactly this experience. (See Fig. 4.1.) We cannot tell whose side the writer is on. The explanatory text below the figure removes the ambiguity, but certainly reading the verbal text keyed to portions of the picture is an utterly different experience from reading the picture itself. The description puts the picture elements in a logical and chronological order. A viewer can examine the picture itself in many ways, starting at the left or the right. The picture is nearly symmetric, and there is nothing to indicate that the right or Ojibwa side is favored over the left or Sioux side. How could the reader, even a 19th-century Ojibwa reader, guess that Shahâsh'king, the figure at b, is the author of this picture text? Nothing in picture writing corresponds to a first-person narrative, for the obvious reason that picture writing has no voice at all. And there is also no indication of the passage of time: the Ojibwa march seems contemporary with the battle at the river. Shahâsh'king's text captures meaning, as pictures must, at a level prior to the word. When we examine this picture, we are not reading about a skirmish that occurred on a particular day in the year 1858; instead, we are seeing the schema of that battle. In order to get a text to our (still print-bound) way of thinking, in order to instantiate the schema, we must return to the writer. The picture elements themselves are generic: signs for men, tepees, and weapons. As we gaze at the picture, it comes to represent not so much a particular battle as a fragment of the conceptual world of the Indian writer who produced it, an image from the intellectual rather than the physical landscape of the Ojibwa. Picture writing often, perhaps always, has this suggestive power.

WRITING OF THE SECOND ORDER

Picture writing is usually regarded as the historical precursor of phonetic writing. (See Jensen, 1969, pp. 50-53. See also Gelb, 1963. A different view is presented by Roy Harris in *The Origin of Writing*, 1986.) The bridge from picture writing to phonetic was the realization that picture elements could be identified with sounds in the language—a realization made by the Sumerians in the 4th millennium B.C., by the Egyptians perhaps independently, by the Chinese, and possibly by the Mayans centuries later (Sampson, 1985, pp. 46-47). The first step would have been to establish a correspondence between pictures for objects and the names of those objects, so that the pictogram became a logogram, a coded element telling the reader to pronounce a word in his or her language. Initially, the logogram was a double sign, referring both to an idea and to a word in the reader's language. But the principle was established: from that moment picture writing was in the service of spoken language. The picture element stood in place of a word, and the task of the reader was to revive the sound of that word as he or she read.

Once the image is associated with the sound of a word, it can be used wherever that sound occurs in the language. By the rebus principle, more complex words can be spelled out by combining word signs. (See Fig. 4.2.) The word signs then function as syllabic signs: their sound is detached from the original visual meaning. The visual character of the sign begins to seem arbitrary, and writing becomes a secondary system depending upon spoken language for its meaning. Reading becomes, at least in theory, a double process, in which the visual signs recall the appropriate sounds and the sounds recall words in the language. Reading and writing then require a detour through spoken language. At the same time writing becomes a closed system. In preliterate picture writing a new sign could always be added to include in the message some new worldly detail. If the sign follows the conventions of representation, the reader has a good chance of figuring out what is meant. In a word-syllable system of phonetic writing, it is more difficult to add signs. Signs are added principally to cover words or sounds not already in the system and must obtain the consent of a community of writers and readers. The spoken language now asserts control over the visual system, and writing, like language itself, becomes a matter of consensus.

The process of phonetization and abstraction continued with the development of syllabic writing, in which individual words are broken down into clusters of consonants and vowels. Egyptian hieroglyphics and Sumerian cuneiform used syllabic signs together with logograms, but there have been many pure syllabic systems, which contained no suggestive pictures to complicate the scheme. Unlike logograms, syllabic signs mean or refer to nothing but sounds; they form a small, closed system of perhaps 50 or 100

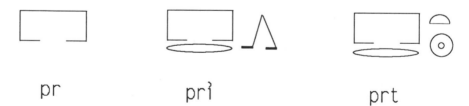

FIG. 4.2. Egyptian hieroglyphics embodied various stages of picture writing and phonetic writing. For example, the floor plan of a house became the symbol for the Egyptian word "house," *pr.* The symbol was then used in other words where the pr sound occurred, such as *pri,* "to go forth," and *prt,* "winter." But the Egyptians continued to use silent ideograms as well: the word *pri* included a pair of legs to indicate a word of motion; *prt* included the ideogram for the sun. (See Davies, 1987, p. 31 and Gardiner, 1927, p. 541.)

signs. The most abstract, and apparently final, stage in the development of writing was the alphabet, invented by Semitic peoples and perfected by the Greeks, in which 20 or 30 signs served to record the whole range of words in a language.

All these are writing systems of the second order. Alphabetic, syllabic, and word signs are all visual images of spoken language, and they need to be revived by a human reader, translated back into speech. This translation was obvious in the ancient world and the early Middle Ages, when readers customarily read aloud. There is evidence that even today silent readers, even readers at the computer keyboard, vocalize their texts mentally if not physically, so that a whisper of the spoken word remains. (On vocalization in reading, see, for example, Crowder, 1982, especially Chapter 8.) In reviving spoken language, the reader is turning discrete images into continuous sound. All systems of phonetic writing are analytic: they divide the flow of spoken language into a sequence of signs. The division becomes less intuitive and more technical as the units become fewer. Word symbols are units of sound and meaning. Syllables are units of sound only, but they are still sounds that we can hear in isolation. Alphabetic symbols stand for sounds that in general do not occur in isolation: the alphabet is therefore the most abstract system of all, the system farthest removed from a speaker's immediate, intuitive knowledge of his or her language.

In the history of writing, the transfer of control from image to sound was not immediate and will perhaps never be complete. Even in alphabetic cultures the letters and other elements in the writing space continue to influence the reader directly, as visual signs. The visual influence was much stronger in early word-syllable systems such as hieroglyphics. The Egyptian signs were masterful little pictures, reflections of the Egyptian natural and cultural world rendered in a few simple strokes. And even after centuries of phonetic writing, hieroglyphs retained their power as images, elements of the world taken into writing. The elements possessed a magical animism:

> In [Egyptian] burial chambers, signs designating animals or potentially hostile beings were modified—mutilated or pierced with knives—so that the subjects of the images would not harm the dead person. (Vernus, 1982, p. 102)

Even in Egypt, however, the need for efficiency eventually distorted these beautiful and dangerous picture signs into more cursive forms, where the original image was no longer recognizable.

AFTER PHONETIC WRITING

The phonetic principle completely reformed the writing space. In hindsight, all picture writing before that discovery appears innocent, prelapsarian.

Although picture writing with its peculiar powers did not disappear after the invention of phonetic writing, its status was radically diminished. Picture writing survived only for special purposes: to communicate to people without a common language, to catch the reader's notice, to make a public display, and conversely to keep a secret. Picture writing survived in religious symbols, such as the Egyptian cross, the star of David, and the several varieties of the Christian cross, and in magical symbols such as the signs of the zodiac and of alchemy, some of which have been borrowed by modern astronomy and chemistry. Heraldry in medieval and modern Europe has constituted an enormously complicated system of picture writing. Traditional trade signs and trademarks have existed for thousands of years and are now more important, or at least more prestigious, than ever. A company may now spend millions of dollars developing or changing the picture sign by which it will be identified to tens of millions of consumers. Then there are airport signs, road signs, and a variety of public warning signs, which may combine words and images. (See Wills, 1977.) Picture elements in such systems as these are designed to identify objects (restaurants, bathrooms, gas stations) and situations (slippery when wet) rather than convey a discursive message: that task is left to phonetic writing. Modern examples of picture writing are in fact simpler in intent, though more sophisticated in execution, than Shahâsh'king's preliterate Ojibwa text.

The case of electronic writing is special: the computer makes possible a picture writing as sophisticated as the writing of Shahâsh'king, though for a different purpose. By combining alphabetic writing with images and diagrams, the computer medium fosters a writing that vacillates between intuitive and highly abstract modes. An electronic text may be a scattering of alphabetic signs among picture elements with various sizes and functions, elements that address the writer and reader without reference to speech. Furthermore, these images and diagrams can move. The computer can be programmed to draw a graph from numerical data in a file: that is, the computer can serve as a scribe giving visual expression to the information in "real time," as the reader looks on. In the animated visual space of the computer, the verbal text must compete for the reader's attention with a variety of pictorial elements, any or all of which may be in motion. While pictures and verbal text have been combined in previous technologies of writing, the spoken word has not faced such determined visual competition since the introduction of the phonetic principle.

We can see the eclectic and animated qualities of the computer's picture writing in the now familiar example of the Macintosh desktop. (See Fig. 4.3.) The controlling metaphor here is the business office. It is with the help of this metaphor that the user manages files and activates programs. Files take the shape of sheaves of paper; files are contained in libraries that are represented as folders. A program for word processing may look like a hand writing on a piece of paper. When the user wants to get rid of a file, he or she drops it

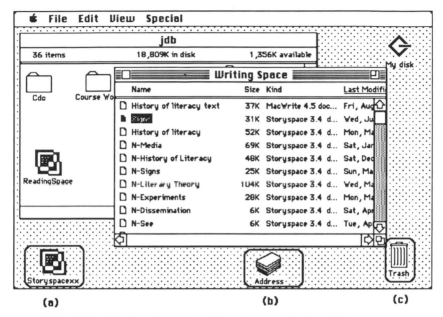

(a)   **(b)**   **(c)**

FIG. 4.3. The Macintosh desktop. Three icons are circled. (a) A program: clicking on this icon will activate the program. (b) A file containing data: clicking will display the file by activating the program to which it belongs. (c) The "trash can," which permits the user to throw away unwanted files and programs. Reprinted with the permission of Apple Computer Corporation.

into a metaphorical trash can. Every image is the reification of some aspect of information processing. We noted that Shahâsh'king's picture writing was generic and presented to the reader the conceptual world of the Ojibwa Indian. The Macintosh desktop is similarly generic. It gives us the world as an information processing environment—an efficient office in which documents and data are effortlessly produced and digested.

As a static image, Fig. 4.3 cannot show the animation of the Macintosh desktop. In fact, everything in this picture world moves under the direct or indirect control of the computer user. With the help of the mouse, the user positions the arrow over particular images, clicks, and then drags. If the image is a file, it follows the user's dragging motion and moves to another folder or copies itself onto another disk. If the image is a program, then clicking twice will activate the program and change the screen accordingly. In other words these images are symbolic elements in a true picture writing. They do not merely remind the user of documents and programs: they represent documents and programs. Reorganizing and activating these elements *is* writing, just as putting alphabetic characters in a row is writing.

These elements are called *icons*, and they constitute the computer's original contribution to our writing system. Although an icon may have a name, it is above all a picture that performs or receives an action, and that action gives the icon its meaning. The word "icon" is more appropriate than programmers may realize. For like religious relics, computer icons are energy units, which focus the operative power of the machine into visible and manipulable symbols. Computer icons also remind us of the use of Hebrew letters in the Cabala or the use of alchemical and other signs by Renaissance magi like Giordano Bruno. (See Frances Yates, *Giordano Bruno and the Hermetic Tradition*, 1964.) Such magic letters and signs were often objects of meditation (as they were in the logical diagrams of Raymond Llull); they were also believed to have operational powers. But electronic icons realize what magic signs in the past could only suggest, for electronic icons are functioning representations in computer writing. The function of icons is to tie together elements in the computer's writing space: that is, they show how documents are grouped, and they connect documents to the program that creates them. As in the old Ojibwa picture writing, the spatial relationship of the icons is significant; it may show, for example, which documents are stored together on the same disk. The Macintosh desktop is a representation that takes full advantage of its two-dimensional surface. Even the words on the screen serve as visual units and enter into the larger spatial structure: the words, usually names, are set above, beside, or beneath images, and their placement is meaningful. Such spatial arrangement of words has always been a feature of diagrams in printed texts, but while diagrams are the exception on the printed page, they become the rule in electronic writing. The whole computer screen is a moving, evolving diagram.

PICTORIAL SPACE

In all picture writing, before and after literacy, the elements exist at the margin between linguistic and pictorial meaning. Sometimes, particularly when the picture text is a narrative, the elements seem to aim for the specificity of language. Sometimes, these same elements move back into the world of pure form and become shapes that we admire for their visual economy. The elements oscillate between being signs and being images. More properly, it is the reader who oscillates in his or her perception of the elements. When readers find themselves admiring the simplicity of the Macintosh icons or the childish character of the Ojibwa figures, they have ceased to examine these elements as signs in a text. That same distancing also occurs in using computer icons and graphics, when the user begins to attend to the technical quality of the bitmap. In the next instant the user may resume the role as reader and treat the elements as arbitrary signs, just as he or she does letters of the alphabet.

In the representational art of the West, the space of a picture is formal, but it is not codified. The picture pretends to be a reflection of the visible world. At least from the Renaissance to the 19th century, artists and their viewers assumed that a picture should be a mirror of nature. Therefore the space of the picture should reflect the space of nature, and the picture's elements should be arranged as they appear in nature. In a verbal text the space is wholly conventional, and learning to read means learning the conventions of the space. Pictorial space and textual space are therefore apparent opposites: the one claims to reflect a world outside of it, and the other is arbitrary and self-contained. The situation becomes particularly complex when painters put words into the space of their pictures (or when writers put images into their texts). This was an intermittent practice in Western art, but both Chinese landscape and ancient Greek vase painting introduce writing into their pictorial space. The juxtaposition creates a pleasing tension. The words seem to be trying to transform the world of the picture into a writing space; at the same time, the picture invites the viewer to consider the words as images or abstract shapes rather than signs. In Chinese writing the word signs are themselves beautiful shapes whose function is to decorate as well as signify.

The space of picture writing has always carried this ambiguity between the written and the pictorial, or the conventional and the natural. Modern systems seem more conventional and arbitrary, whereas in preliterate systems the conventions are often less obvious because there is less technical refinement. In the Ojibwa text, Shahâsh'king drew his camp where it was in fact located and tried to make his picture correspond to the geography of the battlefield. However, he also expected his readers to see that the picture elements constituted a message and to understand textual conventions in his writing. Every element in the picture was a sign, but many of the elements were drawn, however crudely, to be pictures as well. In computer picture writing the messages conveyed by the images (icons, diagrams, graphs) are much more precise, but even here the images are often interesting as pure forms. A defining quality of picture writing is its capacity to combine two radically different spaces.

A pictorial space is always open, capable of receiving new images, whereas a writing space may be open or closed. Ojibwa picture writing, for example, lacks closure: it does not present a finite set of alternatives by which to divide experience. Although there were conventional elements in Indian writing (see Mallery, 1972, pp. 649ff), new signs could surely be introduced, as long as they suited the representational conventions of the previous signs. We can easily imagine a female stick figure, a baby, a horse, a string of beads, and so on. All the elements of the Ojibwa cultural and natural world could be included in such a message, and we would never be surprised to see a new element. The same is not true of road signs and other pragmatic, modern uses of picture writing: these are closed systems with a more or less fixed number of elements. The system is a code whose elements could be replaced with words or even numbers. Modern picture writing is in fact patterned on the closed system of the alphabet.

Computer writing is more complex, for it includes in its space a number of systems, both open and closed. Phonetic writing, graphs, diagrams, and icons can exist side by side on the computer screen, as they often do in Macintosh programs. The computer space is always ready to incorporate new signs. Each Macintosh program has its own icon. To receive a new program is to receive a new icon, a new element with which to write. And every sophisticated program presents its user with a new vocabulary of data elements that have their own visual expression. These elements become topical units that the user combines to construct meaningful texts. For example, in a spreadsheet program the elements are cells, which the user replicates and fills with numbers and formulae. In a graphics program, the elements are circles, squares, and other geometric figures that the user can create, move, resize, and distort. Within each program such elements may form a closed and articulated code. But the computer system as a whole is a constantly expanding repertoire of such codes. While each such code is well-defined and stable, the collection is not. The elements of writing in the computer are always in flux.

WRITING IN THE MARGINS

As we have noted, at any moment in the history of writing, one material and technique dominates, while others exist for marginal or special uses. The Greeks and Romans continued to write on stone after they had papyrus; indeed, we continue to write on stone and parchment today, although paper is our dominant material. The same holds for the elements of writing. The alphabet has been dominant since the time of the Greeks, and yet other writing systems have been and continue to be used. The computer itself is still a marginal technology, but, as it challenges and disrupts our current economy of writing, it compels us to reexamine the margins of writing that the alphabet, pen and paper, and printing have established.

We have seen how electronic writing incorporates picture writing, which was made marginal thousands of years ago by the invention of phonetic systems in Egypt and Sumeria. Outside of the computer, picture writing today is public and functional. We do not allow picture writing into "serious" private communication, and no one tries to write a formal essay or scientific report in pictures. While picture writing in the form of charts and diagrams is permitted and even encouraged in technical literature, such diagrams are not thought to constitute part of the text. They are instead doublets, visual reflections of the verbal (or mathematical) text. In the electronic writing space, however, picture writing moves back toward the center of literacy.

The computer may also change our attitude toward technologies for ephemeral writing. In the age of print, it is permanence and fixity that is valued. The printing press permits works to survive indefinitely. In fact, the ability to survive in faithful reproduction is both the reward and the proof of an author's value: we honor important texts by putting them into a medium that will guarantee their survival. Eraseable, temporary writing surfaces, such as chalkboards or pencil and paper, are obviously secondary in status. No one would bother to write a whole novel on a blackboard or to copy it in pencil in a notebook. Conversely, we assume that what is written only on a blackboard or in a notepad must not be as important as a text that has been set in type. Even today, the goal of every serious writer is print, and ephemeral media simply help the writer reach that goal.

We cannot, of course, preserve and transmit our literature on blackboards. On the other hand, an eraseable writing surface has advantages that writers have never been able to exploit. There may be texts that can only exist on blackboards, texts that are meant to be erased and modified repeatedly. On a blackboard or with pencil in a notebook, writers maintain the tentative quality of their work; they know that they can reconsider and rewrite. In the ancient world and in the Middle Ages, writers often wrote on waxed boards or dictated to a slave who wrote on wax. Their words were then edited and transferred to papyrus or parchment. Only the writer and the scribe, then, had the experience of the ephemeral medium and understood the contrast between the freedom of the wax and the relative constraint of ink on the page. In the age of print, authors wrote their drafts on paper in longhand: the permanent medium of the Middle Ages had become an ephemeral medium. (See Rouse & Rouse, 1989.) Today, when many authors type or compose at their word processors, the contrast between the changeable and the permanent (between the draft and the published copy) remains important. Every author knows both the terror and the satisfaction of seeing his or her words frozen into print. Writers who work at a word processor on texts destined for print know the opposite terror: that they may erase their text by accident before they can freeze it in hard copy.

In the eras of the manuscript and the printed book, if writers wanted to maintain the tentative quality of the text for their readers, they had to resort to a trick. They pretended that their writing was not writing at all, but rather conversation. Plato's dialogues were early examples of this ruse, and many writers since Plato have used it to emphasize the immediacy and flexibility of their writing. In the age of print, which conspicuously lacks immediacy, authors have used every imaginable literary resource. The history of both ancient and Western literature would have been inconceivably different, if writers could have given their readers notepads and waxed boards instead of or in addition to finished books. And now with the electronic medium, writers can do just that. The new medium combines the qualities of the printing press and the blackboard. It can transmit perfect copies of texts, yet it offers the author and the reader the opportunity to modify the text at any time. In electronic writing the ephemeral is no longer marginal: durability simply provides another dimension by which the text can be measured. A text that changes repeatedly to meet changing circumstances may now be as compelling as one that insists on remaining the same through decades or centuries. Moreover, such a text reminds us of writing on the "original" writing surface, human memory, where the inscribed text changes so quickly and easily that we are not aware of writing at all.

The Greeks, who devised the first modern alphabet, also possessed a picture writing that did not require papyrus, paper, or any material surface— a mnemonic system that came to be called the "art of memory." The art consisted of establishing in the mind vivid images as visual equivalents of ideas or names to be remembered. The practitioner of the art then imagined a building or garden and put vivid images down in it. To recall the images and associated ideas, one imagined oneself walking through the building in a predetermined order and examining each image as it appeared. Although the technique seems strangely elaborate to us, it worked for Greek and Roman orators, who delivered long speeches without notes. (See Frances Yates, *The Art of Memory*, 1966, Chapters 1-4.) The art was in fact a method for turning the mind itself into a writing surface, for engraving in the mind a message in pictures. Cicero himself drew the analogy, when he wrote that in the art of memory "... we use [memorized] places for wax [writing boards] and images for letters" (*De oratore*, 2.354). Images supplanted letters as the units of writing, images that stood for discrete topics. The art was also called "topical memory."

It is significant that topical memory developed in Greece after the introduction of alphabetic writing. The art of memory always existed in relationship to writing, as an alternative way of maintaining a store of information for ready use. We commonly regard writing itself as a supplement to human memory, a means of improving on this "natural" human capacity. In this case, however, the reverse was true: the art of topical memory was designed to supplement writing. And yet topical memory supplemented alphabetic writing in a curiously subversive way—by reverting to picture writing. It wrote at a coarser grain than the alphabet and moved its user back into a silent and evocative world of images. The meaning of its elements varied from specific words in the language to whole abstract ideas, and eventually in the Middle Ages the elements took on a moral significance that is not easily expressed in any number of words. In all its forms, the art of memory was a niche in which picture writing could continue and even flourish after the coming of alphabetic literacy.

Like the ancient art of memory, contemporary electronic writing is the art of encompassing ideas and setting them down in a writing space. As we have seen, electronic writing is topical, encouraging the writer to define and write with units larger than or different from the individual word. The computer is also a fluid writing space that can plausibly rival human memory in composing and decomposing such units. Electronic writing is a new art of memory. As we shall see in a later chapter, the computer promises to redraw the margin between writing and memory—to reshape, though not to replace human memory. The computer can take into itself a dynamic network of elements that before lived only in the writer's or reader's mind. It can embody the topical memory envisioned by Cicero or Giordano Bruno and become a reflexive possession of the human writer and reader. The writer's memory then forms a continuum with the electronic writing space, as it previously formed a continuum with the printed or written page. And navigating through the electronic writing space will place new demands on human mental capacity and imply a new definition of memory itself.

WRITING ON THE WIND

In many cultures, there have been forms of storytelling and poetry that do not rely upon writing for production or presentation. This so-called "oral literature" is in some sense the antithesis of writing. However, like writing, oral literature does require a technical attitude toward the acts of composition and performance, a sense of difference from everyday speech. The writing space for storytelling and oral poetry is the space between the speaker and his or her audience, and that space is available in any culture. Oral literature can flourish before writing and may continue apart from or in conjunction with the art of verbal/visual writing. Storytellers remain today throughout the developed world: all parents tell stories to their children, and there are even those who make this kind of storytelling a hobby or an occupation. In the third world, where literacy is often partial, storytelling, oral poetry, and communal plays and ceremonies are still central to cultural life.

The term "oral literature" covers an enormous variety of such performances and texts. There are the Zulu and Xhosa praise poems of southern Africa, the songs of medieval troubadours, 17th-century Irish poetry, Indonesian shadow theatre, and Homeric poetry. (See *Oral Poetry* by Ruth Finnegan, 1977.) Perhaps no one definition can contain this variety. Oral poets in some traditions, for example the Irish bards, memorized their poems before their performances and recited them from memory. They used their minds, then, as a writing surface, in order to separate the two halves of communication, composing and hearing the message. (See Nagy, 1989, pp. 143-144.) In other traditions the poet or storyteller has engaged the audience in the process of composition: the presence of the audience was necessary for the story to proceed. This has always happened in informal storytelling for children: the children are asked to name characters or decide the fate of the monster. Such was also the case with the famous oral poetry, the Homeric epics of the eighth and seventh centuries B.C. Homer and his fellow bards apparently composed their songs spontaneously before their audience. (See Lord, 1968.) But Homer had to make careful preparation. In order to compose metrically and grammatically correct verses, he had available an elaborate system of ready-made phrases, now called "formulae." Every reader of Homer notices the formulae, in particular the descriptive epithets: Achilles is "swift-footed"; Odyssey is "wily"; Athena is "gray-eyed"; Zeus is the "son of Kronos." These Homeric formulae constitute a writing system in which the unit is the phrase rather than the word. Paper or papyrus was not needed for formulaic composition. Like a jazz musician, the Homeric poet would improvise in traditional phrases on traditional themes. And like the jazz musician, the poet was reminding the audience of what they already knew.

The Homeric system, the common property of the poet and the audience, controlled the reading as well as the writing of the poem. Just as the poet learned to sing epics through repeated attempts under the direction of a mentor, the audience came to understand epic songs through repeated hearing of one or more poets. The audience learned the special vocabulary and the repeated phrases, and it learned the fund of mythological stories upon which every poet relied. Repetition built in the listeners' minds a network of associations including the characters of the various gods and heroes and all the adventures in which they took part. Because of these associations, each epic performance became a peculiar transaction between poet and audience, a kind of writing and reading in which each phrase and line would recall and reinforce the whole system. Homeric poetry is unusually economical in its repetition of phrases and lines. But repetition is a feature of many traditions of oral literature. Repeated elements create a system, and wherever there is such systematic repetition, there is a kind of writing. Oral poetry is a writing that travels through the air as "winged words," but conveys to the listener by long repetition a complex network of verbal elements, a network as sophisticated but different in character from the structures of handwriting or print. The network grows slowly but indefinitely as new poets continue to add nuances.

The contrast between oral and written texts is important for an understanding of electronic writing, because in some ways the new medium more closely resembles oral discourse than it does conventional printing or hand-writing. (See Noblitt, 1988.) Homer's repetitive formulaic poetry is a forerunner of topographic writing in the electronic writing space. The Homeric poet wrote by putting together formulaic blocks, and the audience "read" his performance in terms of those blocks. The electronic writer and reader, programmer and user, do the same today. Like oral poetry and storytelling, electronic writing is a highly associative writing, in which the pattern of associations among verbal elements is as much a part of the text as the elements themselves. Just as the ancient Homeric audience built up associations around the characters of Greek mythology, so electronic readers rely on an interplay between the structures that the author has created and their own associative structures. The electronic reader plays in the writing space of the machine the same role that the Homeric listener played as he or she sat before the poet.

Electronic text is, like an oral text, dynamic. Homeric listeners had the opportunity to affect the telling of the tale by their applause or disapproval. Such applause and disapproval shared the aural space in which the poet performed and became part of that particular performance, just as today the applause of the audience is often preserved in the recordings of jazz musicians. The electronic writing space is also shared between author and reader, in the sense that the reader participates in calling forth and defining the text of each particular reading. The immediacy and flexibility of oral presentation, which had been marginal in ancient and Western culture for over two millennia, emerges once again as a defining quality of text in the computer. However, there remains a great difference between oral poetry and the silence of electronic writing. With electronic text both writer and reader are aware that they are manipulating signs within a sophisticated visual writing system. The responsiveness of the computer medium is balanced by the distancing and abstracting qualities of visual writing itself.

CONSTRUCTIVE WRITING

Some writing systems operate simultaneously under conflicting principles. Hieroglyphics and cuneiform combined word signs, syllable signs, and even pure picture signs that had no phonetic value. Japanese writing is still today a complex system including word and syllable signs represented in several different scripts. True phonetic writing, at least as embodied in the Greek alphabet, is remarkably uncomplicated. It subordinates writing to a single principle, and it seeks to drain the pictorial meaning from the written sign. The Greek alphabet aimed at creating a uniform system of writing, in which there was nothing beyond a phonetic transcription of the spoken word. In this respect the Greek alphabet has been our model of writing for 2,700 years. The alphabet defines text as the phonetic transcription of prior speech and moves everything else away from the center of the writing space. Perhaps no writing system in human use can remain purely phonetic or even purely alphabetic. Even our alphabet is contaminated with word symbols such as "1," "2," "3," and "&." Nevertheless, the goal of alphabetic writing is to simplify by exclusion.

Electronic writing by contrast is inclusive, and for that reason it resonates with and reminds us of the earliest forms of writing. Electronic writing is more like hieroglyphics than it is like pure alphabetic writing. The computer welcomes elements that we in the West have long come to regard as inappropriate to writing: electronic writing is a continuum in which many systems of representation can happily coexist. On the other hand, this new technology, like all its predecessors, does have margins. Such forgotten or demoted technologies as picture writing, mnemonics, and oral poetry gravitate back toward the center of electronic writing. What in turn becomes marginal is precisely that quality that has been central for the last 500 years: the fixed and monumental page of print, the book that exists in thousands of identical copies and heroically resists change.

Electronic writing is not only inclusive; it is also constructive. (See Joyce, 1988.) It enables the writer to build new elements from traditional ones, as we have seen in the examples of hypertext in the preceding chapter. Hypertext depends on the computer's capacity to designate any unit of text as a new element in an expanding vocabulary of signs. The writer of a hypertext designates these signs in the act of creating connections. The writer draws a link from one paragraph to another paragraph that explains or elaborates it. He or she links a graphic (say, a Renaissance portrait) to an explanatory text (on technique in Renaissance portraiture). By connecting two paragraphs, the writer is in effect defining two new writing elements. Each paragraph has become a unitary sign. Whatever else the first paragraph means as prose, it now has an added meaning as the source of a textual connection, and the second paragraph now takes on the meaning of destination. The connection forms these two signs into a new sentence, which reads: "This paragraph leads to that one." The reader comes to understand the sentence by activating the link and moving from one to the other. That movement, mediated by the computer, is the reading of the sentence. The same is true when the writer links a graphic with a paragraph of explanation. If the reader chooses to follow the link, he or she expects that the paragraph of prose in some way comments upon or explains the graphic. George Landow notes that:

> Designers of hypertext and hypermedia materials confront two related problems, the first of which is how to indicate the destination of links, and the second, how to welcome the user on arrival at that destination. Drawing upon the analogy of travel, one can say that the first problem concerns exit or departure

information and the second arrival or entrance information. (Landow, 1989, pp. 188-189)

Landow points out that departure and arrival have a rhetorical dimension; the presence of a link from element A to element B causes the reader to assume that B somehow explains A. Like a sentence of prose, the movement itself from A to B is taken by the reader as a rhetorical gesture. The movement is a meaningful juxtaposition of the two elements, which have become symbols in the hypertext. There are as many new symbols in each hypertext as there are sources and destinations for the links. Writers of hypertext create the elements of their writing system in the act of writing— by adding new composite elements to the alphabet, graphics, and icons available on the computer. Writing in the electronic medium is challenging precisely because writers are compelled to define their own system as they proceed. Reading in the electronic medium is challenging as well, for readers must decipher the system as they read. It is as if a reader found it necessary to relearn the alphabet for each printed book he or she read, and in the very act of reading.

5

Seeing and Writing

A generation ago, the classical scholar Eric Havelock could still claim that "[the] visual development of the written signs has nothing to do with the purpose of language, namely instantaneous communication between members of a human group" (Havelock, 1982, p. 53). This attitude was appropriate to the age of print because printing reduced each letter in a text to a visual minimum. Unlike the calligrapher, the typographer's art was to make the letter unobtrusive, to convey the various letter shapes without distracting the reader. And typographers have been so effective that we as readers hardly notice the subtle differences that exist among the various typefaces used in books today. As children we are trained to read silently and quickly, looking through the printed page rather than at it.

As we now move beyond the technology of printing, it is no longer appropriate to dismiss the visual history of writing—the changes in both the written signs themselves and their deployment on the page or screen. No writing system is static. Even the letters of our alphabet have continued to develop since Roman times. In the Middle Ages there was an elaborate and ever-changing population of scripts throughout Western Europe. The age of print has been unusually conservative in character, but even it has not been immune to change. And the computer now promises to accelerate the development again, as it offers writers the opportunity both to create their own character fonts and to deploy pictorial elements in new ways.

The layout of the text (the surface of the roll, the page of the book) has always developed along with the individual elements. When the writing space became conceptually narrower in the shift from picture writing to phonetic writing, the layout became narrow and cramped as well. Early Greek writing was linear in concept and appearance, while all the subsequent development in papyrus and parchment manuscripts and in printed books has served to reestablish the second dimension in the visual structure of the text. In later antiquity, writers regained their interest in the diagram or illustration placed beside or incorporated into the space of the text. Since that time our writing space has been a hybrid of verbal and pictorial elements. Even the conservative technology of print has permitted pictures and more recently mathematical graphs and diagrams to flourish. The computer now adds the capability of animation and so combines pictorial, alphabetic, and mathematical writing into one dynamic whole.

MECHANICAL LETTERS

Early printed books attempted to replicate manuscripts both in letter form and in layout. In cutting his type, Gutenberg copied the Gothic script of his day, including all the ligatures and abbreviations, altogether about 300 different elements. (See Steinberg, 1959, p. 31.) It took several decades for printers to realize that there was no need to use abbreviations and ligatures that rendered the text easier to write (by hand) but harder to read. Each letter of the same type could now be identical, guaranteed by the method of production (casting lead in copper matrices). The precision of the machine now replaced the organic beauty of the handwritten page.

Mechanization did not eliminate human craftsmanship from the process of writing. Instead, it deferred the craftsman from the final product of ink on paper. Letters were still handmade: a craftsman fashioned a set of steel punches that embodied the design for a typeface. These punches were pressed into matrices to serve as molds for the lead type itself. Some early punchcutters actually cut more than one form of the same letter in order to imitate the variation of the scribe, but this practice was clearly misplaced in a technology whose purpose is identical reproduction. Letter forms evolved much more slowly in the age of print than in the previous age of manuscripts. The gradual trend was to pare down the visual form of the letters—in effect to define the writing space with progressively less ink and more white space. Serifs became straighter and thinner, and there was greater contrast between thick and thin strokes. The whole typeface betrayed less and less the hand of the craftsman. The trend reached an extreme in the late 18th century with the designs of Didot and Bodoni.

In the 19th century, mechanization intensified with the development of steam-driven printing presses and the Linotype. Yet in the design and use of typefaces and in the appearance of the printed page, the result was not greater standardization, but greater variety, a sense of growing freedom in what could be shown. The pantographic punch-cutter made it possible to cut a new letter in steel simply by tracing an enlarged pattern of the letter (Lieberman, 1978, pp. 54-55). If in the 16th and 17th centuries, most printers were satisfied with some form of Garamond, printers in the late 19th and 20th centuries could choose from hundreds or thousands of faces. They experimented with forms that earlier printers would have considered barbaric or unrecognizable (but that medieval illuminators might have appreciated). Other typographers reacted to this excess by creating faces such as Helvetica and Futura that were free of all unnecessary strokes.

Nevertheless, the printed page has remained a conservative writing space. The thousands of exotic, so-called "display" fonts appear in advertising, but seldom in books. For book production, the typographer may now choose from dozens of book fonts (with names that signify both tradition and innovation, such as Times Roman, Modern, Baskerville, and Garamond No. 3) which his or her trained eye can distinguish for readability, "color," and "tone." But such distinctions are so subtle that the average reader cannot identify any of the common book fonts. On the other hand, if **any of the thousands of** display **fonts were used in printing** books, the reader could tell immediately that something was wrong. Printing is a frozen medium in more ways than one: its letter forms stabilized between the 16th and 18th centuries and have since changed only a little. And depending upon its use as an auxiliary to printing or as an alternative writing space, the computer can either reinforce this stability or sweep away the whole tradition of typography.

ELECTRONIC LETTERS

The art of letter design will not be fully understood until it can be explained to a computer ... (Donald E. Knuth, 1982, pp. 5-6)

If the trend in the age of print has been to make the visual symbol simple, unornamented, and mathematically precise, a backlash developed in the 19th century led by William Morris, who distrusted mechanization in almost any form. In England as elsewhere, 19th-century printers had been aiming for quantity rather than quality. The demand for inexpensive newspapers and books was exploding, and inventors were trying to clear the bottlenecks in production by developing mechanical printing presses, new forms of cheap paper, and mechanical typesetting. But when Morris founded the Kelmscott press in 1891, he was not interested in mass production. Instead of industrialized simplicity, he aimed for ornament and organic form, a return to the first century of printing or to age of the manuscript. He modeled his Golden Type on the work of the 15th-century printer, Nicolas Jenson. For his edition of Chaucer, he went further and designed a Neogothic typeface. He chose a hand press and handmade paper. The resulting books were beautiful, but themselves excessive, their pages dense with ink and full of ornamentation— and utterly different in spirit from the early printing that Morris meant to imitate. (See Steinberg, 1959, pp. 29-30.) The irony is that these nostalgic books could only have been produced in the Industrial Age: the precision of his Chaucer was greater than was possible in a Renaissance printed book or a medieval manuscript. It was the advance of technology that permitted Morris to go back in this characteristically Victorian way: Morris took photographic enlargements of printed pages in order to study old typefaces. (See Morris, 1982, p. xxxiv.) Morris' work in printing was a kind of technological nostalgia that celebrated the modern technology it appeared to reject.

A similar nostalgia has been evident in the first decade of word processing. The word processor is an attempt to harness the computer in the service of the older technology of print, and the word processor's presentation of text is nostalgic, in that it looks back to the aesthetic criteria of the printing press. The electronic medium in fact allows complete graphic freedom: the writer may ultimately control each pixel on the screen in representing letters, diagrams, or images. When writers are first given this freedom, on personal computers like the Macintosh, they indulge in greater excesses than Morris, decorating their texts with a variety of type sizes, styles, and fonts. They mix elements from the whole history of typography, often without any sense of propriety or proportion. Professional graphic artists can lodge a similar complaint: bit-mapped personal computers permit untrained users to indulge in a riot of graphic design. Often it is graphic design appropriate to the printed brochure or the billboard rather than the computer screen.

There is an inevitable degeneration in the quality of typography and graphics in the new electronic writing space, because the computer encourages the democratic feeling among its users that they can serve as their own designers. Anyone can experiment with type size or style when the computer provides the fonts and drops them into place at the writer's request. Anyone can create and insert his or her own illustrations with the help of automated drawing programs. The new technology thus merges the role of writer and typographer that had been separate from the outset of the age of print. In the age of print, typographers had access to special tools and the skill to use them, and they made the decisions about page layout. Printers have always understood their role as craftsmen, and their guilds, which served to protect their aesthetic as well as the economic prerogatives, remained strong until the middle of the 20th century. Now the electronic writer and designer can own and use professional tools without bothering to develop professional skills.

However, electronic writers are dabbling in the wrong art, if they worry too much about the typography of their text. The pixels of the electronic medium define a space inherently different from that of ink on paper. At present the electronic space is coarser: it is not possible to create subtly curved or bracketed serifs in letter forms or finely organic lines in drawing. The computer screen will continue to improve in this respect: pixels will grow smaller and create a denser space. But the discrete character of computer graphics will not change in the foreseeable future and must always remain in tension with the continuous character of ink on paper, parchment, or papyrus. The impermanence of the electronic image also discourages an attention to fine visual detail. Electronic writers sense that their writing and therefore their typography is always subject to recall and change. The traditional typographer has exactly the opposite impression—every letter must be in its place, because there is no way to recall 1,500 printed copies if an error is discovered. In this sense, even the humble word processor operates in a visual space different from that of the printing press and the typewriter. Typographers and graphic designers who complain about the mess that naive users make on their terminal screens are themselves children of a different technology and are apt to judge the computer's writing and drawing space in the wrong terms.

Professional typographers also use the computer. Just as the word processor has replaced the typewriter, so computer editing and photocomposition now dominate professional book production. Most books today are published by electronic photocomposition; metal type has almost disappeared, even for fine book production. The computer introduces a new degree of mathematical rigor in the design of letter forms themselves. One way to produce electronic fonts is to trace and digitize enlarged photographs of the letters. The other, more intriguing method of computer design is not to copy old letter forms point by point, but rather to generate new letters mathematically. The computer scientist Donald Knuth has used parameterized equations to define the curves of the letters. The computer generates the points by working out the equations. What Knuth has done is to throw the alphabet into the space of analytic geometry. The idea of geometrically defined letters is an old one: it dates back to Renaissance typographers, calligraphers, and artists, including Pacioli, Albrecht Dürer, and Tory. (Lieberman, 1978, p. 41). But rather than using compass and straightedge, the computer specialist creates letter forms by numerical analysis, precisely the task for which the electronic computer was originally developed. Computer typography reduces the writing space to a Cartesian plane, in which every letter is determined by a set of numbered lines or points. It is the triumph of the mathematization of writing that never quite succeeded in the era of mechanical printing.

On the other hand, the use of the computer to mathematize printing is also an example of technological nostalgia. It turns our attention back to the medium of print, applying mathematical precision in order to perfect the appearance of text on the page. Perfection is still defined in terms established by printers in the 15th and 16th centuries—as the clean, crisp, static image that occupies the monumental writing space of ink on paper. Work on computer typography directs our energies away from appreciating the electronic space in its own right—a space in which the subtleties of type size and style may no longer be important to the writer's or the reader's vision of the text.

THE ELECTRONIC PAGE

Typography in print begins with the letter and never goes much further. A glance at the typographer's handbooks shows how much importance is placed on the choice of the typeface itself. Indeed, once the typefaces and styles (and perhaps colors of ink) have been chosen for a book, there are very few decisions left to be made. Each page will be a rectangle of text with some white space around it. Illustrations will occupy blocks reserved for them within the rectangle or on separate pages altogether, and in any case illustrations are relatively rare in "serious," discursive books. Advertising and magazines present many more possibilities for creative design, but the layout of a book is as conservative as the choice of fonts appropriate to the book. And many typographers would agree that the decisions of layout all flow from the letter. The printing press is really a letter processor.

In some ways the earlier handwritten page offered more freedom of design than the printed page. Already in the Carolingian period, scribes used a different script (uncial) to indicate titles and demarcate sections. The word "rubric" comes from rubrication, the medieval technique of beginning a text with a large red capital, often elaborately decorated. By the 13th century scribes had developed a number of visual cues to help the reader locate text and keep his or her orientation. Different styles and sizes of letters, different colors of ink, section numbers—all these devices were pioneered in the Middle Ages and then standardized in the age of print. Probably the most important visual structure in the medieval codex was the marginal note. Medieval texts were often arranged into two or more layers on the page. The center of the page contained the more ancient and venerable text, while the margins offered explanation and commentary added by one or more scholars. This structure helped to orient the reader. It was relatively easy to move back and forth between text and notes, certainly much easier than it was for the reader in the ancient world to juggle several rolls of papyrus. Marginal notes told readers what to look for and provided constant support in the task. Many Renaissance or later readers found these notes to be a hindrance, the weight of centuries of misreading of the text, and printers began to clear the page of this interpretive material, allowing the text to occupy the whole of the writing space and therefore to speak for itself. Notes moved to the foot of the page and eventually to the back of the book. But in banishing the notes modern printers have sacrificed both the immediacy of reference and the sense of visual and intellectual context that marginal notes provided to their medieval readers. (It is only in electronic text that we can recapture both immediacy and context.)

In the modern printed book, the space is simple and clean. Different texts do not compete in adjacent spaces for the reader's attention, as they still do in a magazine or newspaper. In a magazine the text is divided into blocks of varying shapes and sizes, and readers find themselves pulled back and forth among the blocks. The page layout reflects the topical nature of the material—a combination of advertisements, notices, and long and short articles. A magazine or newspaper is in this respect closer in spirit to the topographic writing space of the computer, where the "typography" also mirrors the topical nature of the text itself. (For an example of a complex electronic typography, see Fig. 5 in Chapter 2.) Larger units of text together with images can be isolated on the computer screen. The screen becomes a magazine page in which units even rearrange themselves to meet various needs.

In the current generation of machines, for example, the so-called "window" is the defining feature of computer typography. A computer window is a framing device: it marks out a space for a particular unit of verbal text, graphics, or both, and it frames the writer/reader's view of that space, which is an indefinite two-dimensional plane. The window may show only a portion of the plane at a time, but often the view in the window can be adjusted or scrolled to reveal other parts. In some computer systems windows can be "tiled"—set side by side so that the writer/reader can look onto two or more planes at once. In other systems the windows can be "stacked," so that the planes of text and graphics pile on top of each other, again without really touching. The whole electronic writing space becomes a stack of two-dimensional writing surfaces. Of course, a printed book is also a stack of two-dimensional planes or pages, but the great difference is that printed pages stay in one order and, except in novelty books for children, each page completely obscures all the pages underneath it. Working at the computer, the writer/reader can move one window aside in order to view parts of the windows below; he or she can reorder the stack by plucking one window from below and placing it on top. If the windows contain different texts, say two chapters in a book, the reader can move back and forth adding to and cutting from each. This new typographical space is sometimes said to have two and a half dimensions, because the writer looks straight down on the stack of planes. The writer cannot move around or behind the planes in a full third dimension, although this may well be possible in the next generation of computer software. (See Levy, Brotsky, & Olson, 1988, especially pp. 3ff.)

No previous writing technology has offered anything quite like the windowed typography of the current microcomputer. Switching between windows is in some ways like shuffling papers in a notebook, but nothing in previous technology corresponds to enlarging the size of the window (the text immediately rearranges itself to fill the gap) or scrolling through text in a window. These operations show that the text is not pasted to the window, as it is to the printed page. In fact, both the window and the text may change at any time. The window may fly like a helicopter over the textual plane, or the text may realign itself to suit the dimensions of the window. Visible windows or portions of windows compete for the reader's attention and actively change shape and status when they succeed in attracting attention. (See Fig. 5.1.)

If we are viewing a hypertext, the windows take on a structural significance. In a hypertext there are operational links between units: text in one window can be linked to text in another. Following a link can make windows appear, disappear, or rearrange themselves so that the destination text comes to the front of the screen and captures the reader's attention. This animation becomes an element of electronic typography. It is as if in a printed book the

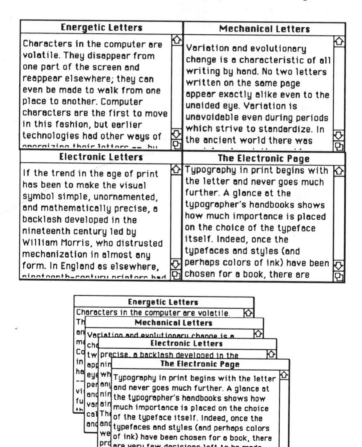

FIG. 5.1. (a) Tiled windows simply divide the screen into two, four, or more rectangles; all are in the same plane. (b) Stacked windows occupy different planes or levels closer to or further from the reader.

pages reordered themselves to put the next interesting paragraph before the reader's eyes.

Even within a single window, objects (images and verbal text) can be stacked: text can slide underneath a graphic, or the graphic itself may be moved to reveal another graphic. The layout of the screen may always change, and the reader may participate in those changes. Like the text itself, the typography is not determined prior to the reading, but is instead a manifestation of the act of reading: it is one aspect of interactive text. The screen enters into a series of configurations, and that evolving series is the visual expression of a particular reader's journey through a textual structure. No one configuration is likely to be as attractive as a page that a professional typographer can produce for print. But no one configuration lasts very long, and it is the movement from one configuration to the next that carries much of the meaning of an electronic text. In a conventional printed text or manuscript, the reader's eye moves along the letters, and possibly back and forth among images, whereas the letters and images themselves are static. In electronic text both the reader's eye and the writing surface are in motion.

Computer animation can take a variety of forms. It is not only a matter of programmed motion pictures, still images shown one after another to give the illusion of a continuous scene. Computer text and graphics can be animate in the sense of having their own organic impulse, of appearing to move or change according to their own logic and in their own time. Even alphabetic texts can appear at various locations on the screen and change or disappear at intervals. (See Nishimura & Keiichi, 1985.) Such animation requires a peculiar reading technique in which the text moves under the eye rather than the reverse. Yet this kind of reading is already common in electric and now electronic billboards that deliver news and advertising. Audiences have been reading unstable text for decades in the form of the subtitles in motion pictures. The difference is that the computer allows any writer to play with the movement of text and gives the writer a freer space for such experimentation.

Reading the complex electronic page demands an attention to text, image, and their relationships. Readers must move back and forth from the linear presentation of verbal text to the two-dimensional field of electronic picture writing. They can read the alphabetic signs in the conventional way, but they must also parse diagrams, illustrations, windows, and icons. Electronic readers therefore shuttle between two modes of reading, or rather they learn to read in a way that combines verbal and picture reading. Their reading includes activating signs by typing and moving the cursor and then making symbolic sense of the motions that their movements produce.

PICTURES IN THE TEXT

Moving pictures into the computer's writing space is remarkably easy. But the electronic space demands a translation: the image must be digitized, all continuous lines and shadings must be transformed into a binary coding. It is possible to feed a picture taken by a video camera into the computer—to capture a portion of the continuous spectrum of the visible light, transform that portion into a series of bits, and save those bits as a picture in the machine's memory. A graphics program can then isolate a portion of the picture, shrink or enlarge it, produce a mirror image or a negative copy. But the program can work all these further transformations only because the picture has been encoded. And in general, the computer can combine words and pictures so easily because both are represented in the same binary code. The digitization of images inevitably strips away their context and allows the machine, or rather its programmer, to define new contexts. The further step is to turn some pattern of bits into an operational symbol or icon. An icon, we recall, is an image that stands for a document or a program in exactly the same way that one pixel pattern stands for the letter "A," another for "B," and so on. (See Fig. 3 in Chapter 4.)

In electronic writing, then, pictures and verbal text belong to the same space, and pictures may cross over and become textual symbols. The unified character of the electronic space is unusual, though not unprecedented in the history of writing. The development of phonetic writing, while it did not eliminate pictures altogether from the writing space, did create a dichotomy between image and phonetic sign. Phonetic writing pulls the writer and reader toward the pure linear space of spoken language, whereas pictures, diagrams, and graphs pull them back toward a pictorial space, which is at least two-dimensional and whose meaning is not strictly codified. Different writing technologies have responded to this tension in different ways.

In Egyptian writing, for example, there was an intimate relationship between pictures and text, both in wall-painting and on papyrus. Hieroglyphs were themselves little pictures, and so both visually and conceptually Egyptian writing could blend smoothly with illustration. (See Weitzmann, 1970, pp. 57-69.) The Greek and Roman writing space was not as friendly to pictures. The ancients regarded writing as an instrument for holding spoken words in a fixed form until they could be revived by the voice of the reader. Book decoration was, therefore, an insignificant art in antiquity. (See Nordenfalk, 1951, pp. 9-20.) From the pure alphabetic space of early Greek inscriptions, it took several hundred years for the Greeks to readjust and admit pictures and diagrams fully into the writing space. (See Weitzmann, 1970, pp. 97ff.) The growing importance of pictures in late antique books formed a link with the Middle Ages. Medieval manuscripts presented a complex space of words, pictures, illustration, and ornamentation—the most complex prior to the electronic medium. In medieval books, pictures were often separated from the text and given prominence as full-page miniatures. But there was also a new impulse to decorate the writing space—to create the illuminated letters that were unique to the medieval writing.

Like computer icons, medieval illuminated letters functioned simultaneously as text and picture. In fact, medieval illumination threatened to turn letters back into images or abstract designs and sometimes made the letters all but impossible to read. (See Alexander, *The Decorated Letter*, 1978, p. 8.) Perhaps the best-known example is to be found in the Book of Kells, where the Greek letters chi-rho-iota (standing for "Christ" in Matthew 1.18) occupy a whole page. The design is so intricate that the shapes of the letters are almost completely obscured. Yet these illuminated letters remain part of the verbal text: they have to be included in order to read the verse. They constitute the perfect interpenetration of picture and word space. The Book of Kells is abstract illumination, but medieval illuminators could also transform an individual letter into a miniature picture with recognizable human or animal subjects. Sometimes the letter was distorted to contain its subject; sometimes the humans or animals were elongated or distorted to fit into or around the letter. The initial letter was often out of proportion to the rest of the text and could encompass almost anything in its luxuriant growth—fantastic creatures as well as elements of the natural world. It is as if the illuminator were trying to absorb the whole visual world into the letter, which itself had grown enormously large in order to receive the world. Medieval illumination embodied a dialectic between writing and the world; it was a means by which writing could describe or circumscribe the world—not symbolically through language, but visually through the shape of the letter itself.

The technology of print favored a stricter separation of the verbal and pictorial writing spaces. Diagrams and illustrations were as popular as ever. But for technical reasons, these images were not as well integrated with the words, as they had been in the best medieval traditions. (See Tufte, 1983, pp. 181-182.) Woodcut illustrations were segregated from the printed text as a product—the wood betrayed much more the hand of the craftsman. Many printed books have contained no illustrations at all, just as many medieval manuscripts contained none. The ideal of the printed book was and is a sequence of pages containing ordered lines of alphabetic text. When the woodcut was replaced by the copper engraving, more elaborate and finely drawn images became part of the printed book. Printers and authors became more ingenious in putting words and images together. The 17th and 18th centuries were the age for allegorical frontispieces and illustrations. (Perhaps the most famous example is the crowded frontispiece in Vico's *New Science*, which Vico patiently explains in his introduction embodies point for point the substance of his interpretation of history. See Vico, 1948, pp. 2-23.) Today it is technically possible to place pictures and illustrations in and around text, and even to superimpose images upon the text.

Photolithography allows any image to be taken onto the page. Some books (especially those designed for young children or for coffee tables) are mostly pictures. Yet the pictorial and verbal spaces are still not as subtly combined as they were in medieval illuminated manuscripts. Most books for adult readers still segregate blocks of text from blocks of pictures, and pictures or plates are often gathered together in the middle of the book to lower production costs. On the other hand magazines, newspapers, advertising tabloids, and billboards all tend to subvert the primacy of linear verbal text in our culture. They work against the ideal established by the printed book.

So, from the nadir of early Greek writing, in which there was no room for pictures, the writing space of the papyrus roll, the codex, and the printed book have permitted a variety of relationships between picture and text: pictures have been decorative, explanatory, allegorical. They have commented on the text; the text has commented on them. But only in the medieval codex were words and pictures as unified as they are on the computer screen. On the screen, as on medieval parchment, verbal text and image interpenetrate to such a degree that the writer and reader can no longer say where the pictorial space ends and the verbal space begins.

DIAGRAMMATIC SPACE

The diagram is a kind of picture writing that can only exist after the invention of phonetic writing. It is a codified picture, in which each element has a well-defined reference: it is verbal writing with picture elements. Allegorical pictures are diagrams, whose elements are images that recall the world. They now seem quaint precisely because we expect diagrams to consist of abstract rather than iconographic elements. There is in fact a surprisingly long tradition of abstract diagrams as aids to exposition. Plato used a line diagram to explain his epistemology in the *Republic*. The tree diagram, so important for computer structures, is very old: there survive early medieval manuscripts that display hierarchical information as a tree. (For example, there are trees in the manuscripts of Cassiodorus; see Mynors, 1937, pp. xxiii-xxiv.) Because of the tradition of illumination in which writing and drawing coexist in the same writing space, medieval writing was receptive to both allegorical and abstract diagrams. Among the most famous and elaborate diagrams were those of the 13th-century theologian, Ramon Llull. (See, for example, Llull, 1985, pp. 105-109 and plates 12-13.) Diagrammatic representations of thought continued in print, and diagrams, like illustrations in general, flourished after the shift from woodcuts to copper engravings. Giordano Bruno and other Renaissance magi, influenced by Llull, produced books of the greatest visual interest, filled with abstract and allegorical representations of thought. (For a discussion of Giordano Bruno's work and influence, see Yates, 1964.) More sober writers also used diagrams. Tree diagrams were particularly popular for displaying a ramified subject matter.

All diagrams in manuscripts or in print are of course static representations. The writer and the reader have to activate these diagrams mentally, just as they activate the verbal text. For the first time in the history of writing, electronic technology now offers its writers and readers fluid text and truly

	May	June	July	Quarter
Sales	$1000	$800	$1000	$2800
Taxes	$50	$40	$50	$140
Total	$1050	$840	$1050	$2940

(a)

	May	June	July	Quarter
Sales	$1200 ----------$800----------$1000----------▶ $3000			
Taxes	$60	$40	$50	$150
Total	$1260	$840	$1050	$3150

(b)

FIG 5.2. In this spreadsheet, the first three columns each record one month's activity. The fourth column (Quarter) is automatically keyed to be the sum of the first three. The first row represents sales, the second row (Taxes) is automatically set to be 5% of the first row, and the third row (Total) is the automatic sum of Sales and Taxes. Now if the user changes the figure for Sales in May from $1000 to $1200, the change automatically propagates to recompute the other underlined cells. Spreadsheet a becomes spreadsheet b. The cells in this spreadsheet are thus linked together to form a numerical hypertext.

animated diagrams. The animation is no mere gimmick. It reveals again the hypertextual character of electronic writing in which distant elements can be linked together and these links can be conceptually active.

The popular computer spreadsheet is an example of an active diagram and indeed of a hypertext. The spreadsheet enables the user to display and modify relationships among numerical entries, usually budgets or accounts of some kind. The user sees a grid of cells on the screen and fills the rows and columns of cells with appropriate numbers, just as an accountant would do with pencil and paper. For example, if the spreadsheet represents the income of a small business, its columns might be months of the year, and its rows might be sales, taxes on sales, and so on. (See Fig. 5.2.) The electronic spreadsheet is far more flexible than a sheet of paper, making it easy to copy, modify, and rearrange the values. An electronic spreadsheet is also a text, not simply because there may be verbal labels for the columns and rows, but because its cells hold the values of interrelated variables. The spatial relationships of the cells define relationships among the variables. The diagram, like a verbal text, is a symbolic structure and is open to symbolic manipulation. Thus, a column or row of figures can be added automatically; an entire row can be reduced by a factor of three; two columns can be switched. Individual cells can also be linked together. If the value of cell C is defined as the sum of the values of A and B, then each time the user changes A or B, C will change automatically. An accountant can link together dozens of cells with intricate calculations; as he or she alters figures, the changes propagate automatically throughout the grid. The speadsheet becomes a dynamic tool for seeing the effect that one change in a budget will have on other items. Its power is due to the fact that it is hypertextual: each of the cells is a unit, and the cells are interconnected in a network of dependencies. Before the computer, a diagram that was interconnected and active in this sense existed only in the imaginations of Llullists and Hermetists of the Renaissance.

NUMBERING SPACE

A spreadsheet in fact lies halfway between a verbal text and a true mathematical diagram or graph. For in a graph the writing space itself is numbered. The graph has long been an important form of picture writing and has gained steadily in status since the 18th century, as it has been applied to data from experimental science. (See Beniger & Robyn, 1978, pp. 1-11.) It comes as no surprise that the computer is the ideal space for drawing and analyzing graphs.

Diagrams were important even in ancient geometry: the *Elements* of Euclid contained proof after proof describing how to construct geometrical objects with straightedge and compass. But the writing space of Euclidean geometry was a synthetic space in which numbers themselves were conceived in geometrical terms. The situation changed with the development of Cartesian geometry in the 17th and 18th centuries. The Cartesian writing space is numbered. The points of a line can be set into correspondence with real numbers, and two perpendicular, intersecting lines can mark out a grid so that every point in their plane has a unique numerical identity. These lines or axes indicate the scale by which the writing itself (the data points) is measured. The modern graph, therefore, belongs to a space different from the verbal space of a printed or handwritten book. In the verbal space the rows of letters mark out a horizontal scale, but only a very coarse one. If one letter is a bit higher or lower than the others in the same line, only the attractiveness of the line is affected; the meaning of the sentence does not change. But in a Cartesian graph, a raised or lowered data point may change the meaning of the whole mathematical text. Here spatial relationships are precise and always significant, because they represent numerical relationships among the data. In fact in a Cartesian graph, *only* the spatial relationships between elements have meaning. The elements are points that have no characteristics other than position on the plane.

A scientific graph is an utterly systematic form of picture writing. The scientist may see in the graph an organizing principle that was not apparent in the column of numbers from which the graph was generated. It may seem obvious that a graphic representation reads more easily than a column of numbers, but experimental scientists in the 17th and 18th centuries came to this realization more slowly than Descartes himself might have hoped. A number of mechanical devices were invented—weather clocks, automatic barometers, tide recorders—that produced line graphs as they measured. Yet scientists often took these graphs and converted them back into numerical tables for analysis. (Beniger & Robyn, 1978, p. 2) The late 18th and the 19th centuries saw the first systematic use of graphs to represent and analyze data from the world.

Today the graphic writing space is fully established: there is often no quicker or more reliable way for a scientist to examine intelligently (that is, to "read") the massive number of measurements that his or her computer-controlled instruments can record. The drawing of these diagrams is itself automated: computers collect the data and then plot them according to the viewer's requirements. In examining these graphs, scientific readers are looking for both patterns and exceptions, and the trick is to make both visually apparent. Thus computers can be programmed automatically to reduce "noise" or to produce maps in exaggerated colors to give a clearer sense of contrasts.

Such automated graphs and maps in the computer have readers, but no single, identifiable writer. The plotting programs are written by human beings, but the data are supplied by instruments whose function is to record such natural events as electromagnetic radiation, sound or pressure waves, and temperature. Often the instruments are attached directly to computers that record and store the measurements. No doubt many scientists believe that their graphs are natural writing or nature's writing—that human beings are reading what nature itself has produced. Human scientists can read nature's writing because they have mastered the mathematical language of nature. Without the numbered writing space, this natural writing cannot be recorded or understood. But it is precisely that requirement that makes the human scientist more than a passive reader. The scientist not only reads the graphic results; he or she also determines the variables to record and the way in which those variables will parameterize the writing space. Even in the simplest graph the scientist determines what the x and y axes will mean and what scale each will have.

Scientific picture writing is itself a process of discovery. The writer determines the parameters of the space and then lets the instruments do the writing. And even with the most sophisticated program, some human writer, programmer, or scientist must still decide how the writing space will be numbered. He or she may renumber the space many times to see the data from different perspectives. Scientists do not in general know what pattern their data will produce, and in fact they change perspectives in order to see something they have not anticipated or could not see clearly from another view. The computer can be effective here precisely because it allows rapid reworking of the space. In scientific graphing, the writer and reader are often the same scientist or team of scientists, and the irony is that such writers do not know in advance what they will be giving themselves to read. Here the scientific picture writer resembles the verbal writer, who may also be surprised by the text he or she produces. Scientific graphic writing, particularly with the aid of the computer, distances writers from their writing (data) in such a way that the writing no longer seems to belong to them at all. We might compare this situation to the automatic or trance writing practiced at various times in history, most recently by the surrealists. But in those cases the goal was to lose control, to annihilate the conscious censor and allow unconscious images and ideas to pour forth. In the automatic writing of science, a layer of computerized control is imposed between the world and writing space. The space itself is disciplined by the numbering scheme imposed on it.

GRAPHIC RHETORIC

Although the numbered graph was and is an alternative to verbal writing, the barrier between the graph and the textual writing space has never been absolute. Even a pure Cartesian graph has its axes labeled with letters of the alphabet. The history of graphic design and typography shows that in the best graphs the numbered space and the verbal space not only coexist, but also interpenetrate. The statistical graphs of the 18th and 19th centuries contained a fair amount of writing, which served to anchor the graph to the verbal writing space. Edward Tufte, a contemporary writer on graphics, still advises that graphs should be combinations of words, images, and numbers and adds that "[d]ata graphics are paragraphs about data and should be treated as such" (Tufte, 1983, p.181). He means that graphs should be integrated into the text so that the reader's eye moves easily from a paragraph of words to the graph and on to more words. The free combination of words, numbers, and images that is characteristic of the electronic writing space did not begin with the computer; it has been a feature of the best graphics of the last two centuries.

Scientific graphs combine the oldest and the newest of languages—picture writing and modern mathematics—and the result is a rhetoric that our culture finds most convincing. To make modern science palatable to a general audience, it seems that most of the mathematics must be translated into words or pictures. One pretty result is the mathematically defined pseudopicture, in which equations rather than tangible objects create the lines and shadings. Thus, mathematical objects called Mandelbrot sets can be made in surreal landscapes—a mountain lake or steep cliffs beside a placid sea. The point is to trick the viewer into putting the image in the wrong category, regarding it as an object in pictorial space drawn after nature, rather than as a graph. Programmers play this game perhaps out of a concealed desire to demonstrate that mathematics underlies the world. The Pythagorean impulse to construct the world from numbers comes naturally to anyone who builds or programs computers.

Experts in computer graphics have learned how to generate all sorts of recognizable forms mathematically and to give their forms a three-dimensional presence. Their aim is to enable the machine to create images that look as if they came from the world of light. For example, the images in Fig. 5.3 were generated from a data structure that was itself based on a series of photographs. Once the computer has turned these photographs into a mathematical structure of points and shadings, it can manipulate that structure to generate a variety of images with different lighting and from different perspectives. The machine can create an animation in which the viewer's perspective changes as he or she walks through the building. Computer graphics such as these are vivid examples of the computer's ability to mathematize space: to bring numerical and pictorial space together.

Even without the computer, however, contemporary graphics seems dedicated to combining the picture with the scientific graph. One unhappy result is the pseudograph that is now common in newspapers, magazines, and television. Here the numbering of the space is so reduced that it becomes a decoration for rhetorical effect, and the graph resolves itself into naturalistic forms, like a degenerating tradition of art or architecture. A graph showing the increase in airline ridership over the past ten years will feature a passenger jet zooming up to the right over a Cartesian grid, its exhaust trail defining the increase year by year. A bar chart of industrial pollution will have colored smoke stacks to indicate the values of each pollutant. A pie chart on snack food in America will take the form of a real pie. These are graphs seeking to return to their roots as pure iconic picture writing, in which images float free in a continuous and unnumbered space. Perhaps the descent from the great visual rhetoric of the 19th century to the pseudographs of today's newspapers mirrors the decline in verbal rhetoric in the same period. In any case, in this final era of print technology, designers of books, journals, and newspapers mix words, images, and diagrams without restraint. The result is sometimes successful, sometimes a parody. Graphs take on grotesque shapes in order to reflect their subject matter. Diagrams sometimes intrude in the verbal text itself, as illustrations did with greater artistry in the Middle Ages. Conventional lined text is superimposed on diagrams, so that the diagrams seem to be a prisoner of the text to which they refer. The pure verbal writing space, the implicit ideal of print technology, now penetrates or is penetrated by the pictorial space of the image and the numerical space of the graph.

At its worst, the printed page often seems exhausted—as if it were trying to convince itself of its own vitality with riotous displays of color and form. At its best, however, print is anticipating the new visual rhetoric of electronic

FIG. 5.3. Two computer-generated images from the UNC Walkthrough project. Reprinted with the kind permission of Frederick P. Brooks, Jr., principal investigator, and John Airey, team leader. Orange United Methodist Church fellowship hall design by Wesley McClure, FAIA, and Craig Leonard of Böhm NBBJ.

writing, in which words, images, and numbered elements easily occupy a single space. On a bit-mapped computer screen, every pixel is an element in a two-dimensional Cartesian graph: letters of the alphabet are themselves graphic lines and curves. The whole visual space of the screen is numbered by its x and y coordinates, and the computer can draw text at any coordinate position. It can also give over any position to a graphic. It is therefore natural to include numerical graphs on the screen along with the text, just as it is natural to include digitized pictures and icons. Sedate rows of linear text are becoming the exception rather than the rule. Instead alphabetic text may be anchored anywhere on the screen—beside, above, or below picture elements. The numbered space also serves as a grid to control the movement of graphs and diagrams. The computer can plot lines of data before the reader's eyes. It can present, for example, political maps that change to reflect the passage of years or centuries—a technique that until recently was limited to film or video with hand-drawn animation. The computer makes possible a kind of historical atlas in which invasions and battles, colonization, and the growth of populations and cities are shown in time as well as space.

The authors of such an atlas will have to learn to work in a new dimension. Designing for the printed page, they must consider how to turn historical change into a readable, static picture—how to place timelines, lines of march, and dates on the map in a readable way. An electronic map will have to be readable even as it changes; the authors must conceive of their map as a temporal experience for their readers. The same holds for writers who seek to animate any verbal or graphic text in the computer. They must envision what the reader will see at each moment and how that view will accord with what comes before and after. Authors in print or manuscript must also conceive of their text as unfolding in time, but they have little control of the reader's pace. The electronic author who chooses to animate must bear greater responsibility for the reader's temporal experience, because he or she can regulate the flow of text and images on the screen.

The Conceptual Writing Space

6

The Electronic Book

THE IDEA OF THE BOOK

Every written text occupies physical space and at the same time generates a conceptual space in the minds of writers and readers. The organization of writing, the style of writing, the expectations of the reader—all these are affected by the physical space the text occupies. Above all, the physical space of a writing technology defines the basic unit, the volume of writing. So for centuries in the ancient world, the papyrus roll, about 25 feet long, constituted a written volume. (Our word "volume" comes from the Latin *volumen*, which means roll.) The codex, which replaced the roll, was more effective in enclosing, protecting, and therefore delimiting the writing it contained. The writer was and still is encouraged to think of his or her codex as a unit of meaning, a complete verbal structure. The physical book has fostered the idea that writing can and should be rounded into finite units of expression: that a writer or reader can close his or her text off from all others.

The papyrus roll was poor at suggesting a sense of closure. In the ancient world, authors would often perform their works before an audience of listeners who would not have their own copies. The writing on the roll served as a script, to be consulted when memory failed. The character and the length of these ancient texts were not determined by the size of the roll, but rather by the needs of performance. Since Homeric poets were probably illiterate, their poetry was not determined by writing at all. The *Iliad* and *Odyssey* were far too long to fit on one papyrus roll. In a sense these poems were unbounded; they were fragments of a network of stories that could be extended indefinitely. Each Greek tragedy, on the other hand, was too small to fill up one roll, because its length depended on the conventions of the Greek dramatic festivals. The tragedian did, however, have to write down his play in order to convey it to the actors, so that tragedy remained halfway between orality and full literacy. Even when writers like Plato wrote for individual readers, the oral character of ancient writing remained strong. Perhaps for that reason the ancients were content with the papyrus roll, which was adequate for reading aloud, but not for silent reading and study. The papyrus roll was certainly too short to serve as a grand unit of expression: each major work by a philosopher, historian, or poet must have occupied several rolls. It is no coincidence that many ancient poetic and historical texts do not have climactic endings. They simply fall silent, leaving the impression that there is always more to say. It is perhaps characteristic of a primarily oral rather than written culture, that its texts are often incomplete.

A codex could hold several times as much text as a roll. The early Christians apparently preferred the codex, because one codex could hold all the New Testament writings. Pagan texts followed in being transferred to the new medium. (See Reynolds & Wilson, 1978, pp. 30-32.) The physical presence of the book also began to matter more, as public performance was replaced by individual study. Silent reading became common by the later Middle Ages, but long before that books were set before individual readers—monks in their monastic libraries, for example. (See Saenger, 1982.) Writers and readers were encouraged to identify the physical book, which they held in their hands, with the text and so to see the end of the book as the end of the text. The importance of the book as an object reached its zenith in the Middle Ages, when illuminated manuscripts were examples of multimedia writing at its finest, in which all the elements functioned symbolically as well as aesthetically to create a network of verbal-visual meaning. In this one sense, printing was not an improvement: it destroyed the synthesis that medieval manuscripts had achieved. On the other hand, printing strengthened the impression of the book as a complete and closed verbal structure. Although in medieval codices and early printed books, unrelated texts were often bound together, standardization and economies of scale eventually encouraged printers to put one text in each volume.

In the centuries following the invention of printing, then, writing become synonymous with producing a book. It became the goal of every serious writer to add another volume to the world's library. The paged book became the physical embodiment, the incarnation, of the text it contained. Incarnation is not too strong a metaphor. Through printing, we have come more and more to anthropomorphize books, to regard each book as a little person with a name, a place (in the library), and a bibilographic life of its own. Modern printing includes the making of the binding and dust jacket, so that every copy of an edition looks the same inside and out. Today you can tell a book by its cover. This was not the case in early printing, however, when books were often bound after they had been transported and sold (Febvre & Martin, 1971, p. 159). Children in elementary school learn to draw books with smiling faces, to personify each book with the voice of its text. And books not only talk to us; they also talk about each other. Each strives to assert its identity, while at the same time entering into a cascade of relationships with other books. The relationships are attractive and repulsive, as the book refers the reader to some books and warns against others. Each book must be different enough from all other books to deserve its own place in the library, and it should be complete in its own terms. Many texts in the age of print have required more than one volume—English novels of the 19th century were often published in three volumes even when one would have sufficed, apparently to give the readers the sense that they were getting what today is called "a good read." But the set of volumes simply became a larger book and was often eventually bound as one.

While electronic technology does not destroy the idea of the book, it does diminish the sense of closure that the codex and printing have fostered. The imposing presence of the book is gone. Instead of a binding that the reader can grasp and pages that the reader can turn, the computer uses storage media that must be hidden away in elaborate electro-mechanical devices, such as disk players or printed circuit boards. A CD-ROM disk is shiny and thoroughly appropriate as a futuristic technology of writing, but it offers the reader no visible cue to the beginning or end of a recorded text. The technology of computer storage may well change several times in the coming decades, but it will evolve toward greater information density, keeping the text remote from the reader. The electronic book therefore is not available as an object for decoration in the medieval tradition. Instead, the book is abstract—a concept, not a thing to be held. The writer's and reader's attention is focused on the text as a structure of verbal and visual ideas that may be realized on the computer screen. In these (admittedly early) days of electronic writing, the reader seldom has a sense of where he or she is in the book. The reader does not know whether there are hundreds of screens yet to read or just a few. There are ways of orienting the reader in an electronic document, but in any true hypertext the ending must remain tentative. An electronic text never needs to end. It is a simple matter to branch to a new text or to break into the middle of a text, read a few screens, and then leave. If readers add to the text as they read, their additions may have the same status as the original. An electronic book is a structure that reaches out to other structures, not only metaphorically, as does a printed book, but operationally.

An electronic book does not join itself to other books end to end, as printed books do when we set them on a shelf. Instead, the electronic book can merge into a larger textual structure at a thousand points of contact; it can dissolve into constituent elements that are constantly redefining their relationships to elements in other books. An electronic book is not as vigorous in asserting its identity over against all others in the world's libraries. It invites exploration as part of a vast network of writings, pointing the reader both to itself and to other books. Electronic writing therefore breaks down the familiar distinctions between the book and such larger forms as the encyclopedia and the library. It is this breakdown—the coming together of the book, the encyclopedia, and the library—that we will explore in this chapter.

GREAT BOOKS

The book in any technology is a receptacle, a place to put verbal ideas. Once a culture has books, it is perhaps inevitable to dream of putting down all verbal ideas in one place, of creating a "great book." The desire to make a great book was shared by medieval writers, by the Greeks and Romans, and perhaps even by the scribes of the Assyrian library at Nineveh. In the age of the papyrus roll or the codex, that desire expressed itself in two contrasting forms: the library and the encyclopedia. A library amasses books; an encyclopedia condenses them. Both seek to organize and control books in order to make them available to the reader.

The encyclopedic impulse was strong in later antiquity, when editors produced handbooks or miscellanies on subjects important to them, such as rhetoric, poetry, natural history, and medicine. The impulse was also strong in the era of Byzantine scholarship, and it was particularly strong at times during the Middle Ages in Western Europe. Because medieval scholars attached great importance to authoritative texts (the Bible, the Church fathers, later Aristotle), they felt the need to collect and summarize those texts in handbooks of their own. The most influential encyclopedias (by Martianus Capella, Isidore of Seville, and later Vincent of Beauvais) became authoritative texts themselves. These compilations were great books, and they encouraged philosophers and even poets to produce their own great books in response. Philosopher/theologians produced *summae*, which were encyclopedic in ambition—attempts to join the major philosophical and theological traditions into a convincing whole. This joining and reconciling of written authorities was the central task of medieval scholarship, as Ernst Curtius points out:

> For the Middle Ages, all discovery of truth was first reception of traditional authorities, then later—in the thirteenth century—rational reconciliation of authoritative texts. A comprehension of the world was not regarded as a creative function but as an assimilation and retracing of given facts; the symbolic expression of this being reading. The goal and the accomplishment of the thinker is to connect all these facts together in the form of the "summa." Dante's cosmic poem is such a summa too. (Curtius, 1973, p. 326)

The encyclopedic impulse diminished somewhat in the age of print. As books multiplied, it became harder to aspire to the goal of a book that would encompass all important works, even in a single field. Although more encyclopedias and handbooks were produced than ever before, the aim of the encyclopedists became more utilitarian: to generate more accurate information rather than to synthesize all knowledge. The French *Encyclopédie*, whose first volume appeared in 1751, was both the last successful encyclopedia in the medieval sense and the first modern encyclopedia. It was a statement of the ideals of the Enlightenment as well as a compendium of technical information. In the 19th and particularly in the 20th century, making encyclopedias became a business rather than a philosophical endeavor. The major encyclopedias now maintain permanent editorial staffs, which revise the volumes continuously to furnish up-to-date information in a convenient package. Their concern is to provide information on subjects of popular interest, not to demonstrate the interrelations of all subjects. Yet even today, the ideal of the encyclopedia as a synthesis of knowledge has not completely vanished. The introduction of electronic technology may even reawaken that ideal. For the computer always encourages writers to make new texts out of old ones, and electronic texts naturally join themselves into larger and larger structures, into encyclopedias and libraries.

ENCYCLOPEDIC ORDER

Prior to the invention of printing, the population of books grew and declined along with the associated culture. In some periods manuscripts were plentiful; in other periods few manuscripts were read or copied, and many works were lost altogether. The great period of loss of ancient texts, for example, occurred from the sixth to the eighth centuries—both in the Latin West and in the Byzantine East. (See Reynolds & Wilson, 1978, pp. 47-48, 75-76.) Each period of sustained growth created a "textual overload," when there were many more books than a reader could afford to own or had the time or the dedication to read. The opposite problem was a lack of books during periods of cultural decline. Whenever texts become inaccessible—either because the available technology is too successful at producing texts or because the culture goes into decline—readers have turned to encyclopedias and handbooks. At the time of Pliny the Elder's *Natural History*, in the first century A.D., readers had to confront an enormous quantity of scientific and literary texts produced by the Greeks of the classical and Hellenistic periods. By the time of Martianus Capella's allegorical encyclopedia of the liberal arts in the fifth century or Isidore of Seville's *Etymologies* in the seventh, the problem was paucity. Vincent of Beauvais' *Speculum* appeared in the 13th century, when the already large medieval library was again being supplemented by

Aristotle and other ancient texts. And 300 years of printing created a vast textual space for the French *Encyclopédie*. Indeed, printing has made textual overload a permanent condition: more books have been produced in each succeeding century, and new editions have succeeded in preserving most important books from the past. (Eisenstein, 1979, vol. 1, pp. 181ff.) The "information revolution" ushered in by the computer is only the most recent manifestation of a problem that is now 500 years old.

The encyclopedia offers a solution for both glut and famine. When there are too many books, it offers to control information that has gotten out of hand. When books are not available, the encyclopedia summarizes information that the reader cannot get from original sources. In either case, the encyclopedia puts textual elements in a place where the reader can be sure to find them. In this sense the encyclopedia performs a therapeutic as well as a bibliographic function: it reassures the reader that the texts in the contemporary writing space are under control. A great encyclopedia performs this function for a whole culture. The key to any encyclopedia is therefore its organization, the principles by which it controls other texts. And the choice of organizing principles depends upon both the contemporary state of knowledge and the contemporary technology of writing.

The ancient and medieval encyclopedias were organized at first simply by association and then by progressively more elaborate hierarchies of topics. Pliny the Elder constructed his *Natural History* on what we would call naive principles of association. He began with the stars and planets, then moved to the geography of the earth, then to humans, animals, plants, and finally minerals. In presenting animal life he began with land animals, then described sea creatures and then birds. This intuitive approach was appropriate for his Roman readers, who were not scientifically sophisticated. It was also appropriate to the highly linear papyrus rolls upon which his work was recorded. After the invention of the codex, encyclopedists gradually developed more elaborate categories and deeper hierarchies. Martianus Capella fit his small encyclopedia into the framework of the seven liberal arts (grammar, rhetoric, dialectic, arithmetic, geometry, astronomy, and music). Isidore of Seville appealed to etymology as well as the seven liberal arts for his organizing principles. In the 12th century, Hugh of St. Victor included the mechanical as well as liberal arts in a scheme that had half a dozen levels. (See Châtillon, 1966.) Vincent of Beauvais used, in addition to other traditional schemes, the seven days of creation from the Old Testament. (See Lemoine, 1966.) The motive in all cases was to provide a framework that would be familiar or accessible to an educated reader. The codex with its "random access" made the reader's work easier and allowed the author to develop a more elaborate outline of knowledge. The outline in turn solved the problem of textual overload by providing categories for all the elements of learning: it showed that one book could indeed encompass the textual world.

Hierarchies continued to be used in the Renaissance and after, but the cumulative medieval systems became less and less appropriate for categorizing new scientific knowledge. Francis Bacon responded by trying to derive his topics from first principles. In the second book of the *Advancement of Learning* he offered a system based upon three mental faculties: memory, imagination, and reason. To the faculty of memory belonged historical experience and writing. Imagination gave us art; reason gave us philosophy and natural science. Bacon went on to elaborate these categories and include the traditional disciplines in this new hierarchy. But the printing press and scientific discovery continued to generate information that needed to be accounted for in any great book. And so there was a growing trend toward neutral methods of "information processing"—alphabetization and indexing, which unlike topical outlines did not presuppose a shared body of knowledge or world-view among the readers. The shift from hierarchical to alphabetic organization in dictionaries and encyclopedias was an admission that such systems as the seven liberal arts, which could be possessed by all educated readers, could no longer accommodate specialized knowledge in physics, anatomy, geography, and mathematics. Most encyclopedias from the 18th century through the 20th have been alphabetical, because access to information, understood in an increasingly technical sense, has become more important than philosophical vision. A good contemporary encyclopedia exploits every technique of print technology to help the reader find the relevant articles, paragraphs, and even finer units of text. These techniques include tables of contents, indices, headnotes, sidenotes, and various type styles, all of which are in the service of alphabetically ordered articles. Printing, which had created a new degree of textual overload, also offered the solution of alphabetical order and precise indices.

Editors of encyclopedias, however, have never been entirely happy with this solution. Those who set out to make encyclopedias are writers who want to impose an intellectually satisfying order upon the world of texts. And alphabetic ordering does not do this: it does not define a writing space in which relations among topical elements are made clear. In an alphabetic encyclopedia, "Bantu" may come after "Banque de France" and before "Baptism, Christian," and the sequence means nothing. The editors of the *Encyclopédie* printed their articles alphabetically, but they did not wish to deny the philosophical value of a hierarchical arrangement of knowledge. D'Alembert wrote in the "Preliminary Discourse" that such an arrangement

... consists of collecting knowledge into the smallest area possible and of placing the philosopher at a vantage point, so to speak, high above this vast labyrinth, where he can perceive the principal sciences and the arts simultaneously. . . . It is a kind of world map which is to show the principal countries, their position and their mutual dependence, the road that leads directly from one to the other. (D'Alembert, 1963, p. 47)

Diderot and D'Alembert included in their preface a tree of knowledge based on Francis Bacon's. Articles in the *Encyclopédie* contained references to indicate their place in this tree, although readers could not easily use the tree to organize their reading. The *Encyclopaedia Metropolitana* (1849) in the 19th century also tried to have it both ways: it was a "Universal Dictionary of Knowledge on an original plan, projected by the late Samuel Taylor Coleridge, comprising the twofold advantage of a philosophical and an alphabetical arrangement." Coleridge himself saw the encyclopedia as an educational tool: the reader should be introduced to all knowledge through the proper method, which consisted "in placing one or more particular things or notions, in subordination, either to a preconceived universal Idea, or to some lower form of the latter ..." (p. 22). Coleridge seems to have imagined the ideal reader starting at page one of the encyclopedia and working straight through. So, while he believed strongly in the topical arrangement that goes back to the Middle Ages, Coleridge's encyclopedia was a clear product of the technology of print, in which the text is laid out in one ideal order.

The 15th edition of the *Encyclopaedia Britannica*, first issued in 1974, was another curious hybrid. It was a good printed encyclopedia, but it was also a book straining to break free of the limitations of print. Mortimer Adler gave the *Britannica* both a topical and an alphabetic arrangement. The main articles were printed alphabetically in volumes called the *Macropaedia*. A separate volume, the *Propaedia*, was a vast outline, in which all knowledge was arranged into ten parts, the parts into some 140 divisions, the divisions into sections, and so on. The *Propaedia* outline was not adventurous or idiosyncratic: it was "constructed and corrected in the light of detailed recommendations, directions, and analytical contributions from scholars and experts in all the fields of knowledge represented" (*Encyclopaedia Britannica*, 1974-1987, vol 1, p. 6). It divided knowledge into categories suggested by the current sciences: Matter and Energy (Physics and Chemistry), The Earth (Geology), Life on Earth (Biology), Human Life (Anthropology and Sociology), and so on. The most original aspect of Adler's outline was that it was meant to be a guide for reading the *Macropedia* articles. The reader who pursued topics through the outline was eventually referred to pages in the *Macropaedia*. The *Propaedia* therefore served to reorder the articles of the *Macropaedia*: to show their relationships in Adler's structure of knowledge. There might be no single extended essay in the *Britannica* on creation myths in various cultures or on French tragedy or on the world's rain forests, but the reader could construct such an essay by finding that topic in the *Propaedia* and following the references. The *Propaedia* referred the reader to paragraphs, sections, or articles in the *Macropaedia* from which the essay could be fashioned. In other words, the *Propaedia* turned the encyclopedia into a hypertext whose parts could be assembled and reassembled by the reader.

The problem was that the references were hard to follow in a printed work of 30 folio volumes. Most readers of the *Britannica* were not willing to go to the trouble: they were content to read the articles in the conventional way. In any library that displayed the *Britannica*, the *Propaedia* could immediately be identified as the shiny new volume among the well-used and worn ones. This was not due merely to laziness on the part of the readers. In fact, the *Britannica* was trying to deny the defining qualities of the printed book—its fixity and its linear order. If an encyclopedia is to be an alphabetical sequence of articles, the reader expects that each article will be a self-contained essay. The *Britannica* tried to create both a sequence of articles and a set of instructions for dismantling and reassembling those articles to make new readings. Eventually, the editors of the *Britannica* decided to add a conventional index and take most of the references out of the *Propaedia*. The *Propaedia* remains an outline of knowledge, but is no longer a blueprint for alternate readings of the rest of the work. Since the mid-1980s, the *Britannica* has become again a conventional printed encyclopedia.

THE ELECTRONIC ENCYCLOPEDIA

In spite of or indeed because of its inconsistencies, the *Britannica* points the way to a new kind of encyclopedia. The complex system of references in the *Propaedia*, which seemed irrelevant to readers of a printed book, would make good sense in an electronic edition. The computer would facilitate the task of moving through the encyclopedic outline and among the various articles. It would take over the mechanical aspects of consultation: by getting the reader to the article and letting him or her read, by transferring the reader from one text to another, and by keeping the reader aware of his or her current position within the structure of the encyclopedia. In general the structure of an electronic encyclopedia can be both deeper and broader than that of its printed counterpart. A printed book is generally divided into chapters or headings within chapters, but in the electronic medium the visible and useful structure may extend to the paragraph, the sentence, or even the individual word. The computer can permit the reader to manipulate text at any of these levels.

In this way the computer restores the legitimacy of topical arrangements for great books like the encyclopedia. It answers the modern objections: that the world of textual knowledge is now too complex to be organized by topics; that any topical outline may be arbitrary or confusing; and that the reader will not be able to find elements because he or she will not know their place in the editor's outline. All this is true for a printed encyclopedia but not an electronic one. The problem of finding information in an electronic encyclopedia is facilitated by the fact that searching can be partly or wholly automatic. Readers can ask the machine to take up the search wherever their own knowledge fails them. And such searching can cut across any categories established by the editor. The title and even the text of every article can be stored in an electronic index, so that the encyclopedia is always in alphabetical order. The difference is that the alphabetical order is not the single canonical order of the text, as it is with a printed encyclopedia. Outlines or other topical arrangements can coexist with the alphabetical order. An electronic encyclopedia can be organized in as many ways as the editors and the readers can collectively imagine.

It is true that any topical outline today must seem arbitrary, because it reflects one editorial view of the organization of knowledge, which the reader may not share or even comprehend. The problem was less serious in the Middle Ages, when there was much broader agreement about the available structures of knowledge. But by the time of the *Encyclopédie*, D'Alembert recognized that there were many possible stuctures. When he compared the encyclopedia to a world map, he went on to say that ". . . one can create as many different systems of human knowledge as there are world maps having different projections. . . . There are hardly any scholars who do not readily assume that their own science is at the center of all the rest, somewhat in the way that the first men placed themselves at the center of the world" (D'Alembert, 1963, p. 48). The encyclopedists were forced to choose one map, and they picked the one based on and therefore validated by Francis Bacon. And in the recent *Britannica*, as we have seen, Mortimer Adler felt compelled to defend himself against this charge—by pointing out that his *Propaedia* outline was certified by scholars and experts. Adler's other defense was that his outline was not rigid: the topics could be displayed in a circle around which the reader could move associatively. However, the circle as a structure is the antithesis of the printed book, which is linear in presentation and hierarchical in organization. In a printed book, the reader is not invited to begin anywhere and move to any related section. By allowing multiple organizations, the *Britannica* has anticipated an attitude toward knowledge that belongs to the new medium, where the circle and the line are equally at home.

Because it was a printed book, the *Britannica* could only present one outline (which itself occupies a whole volume), and that outline had to be a consensus. An electronic edition can be more daring, precisely because it does not impose upon the reader a single fixed view. The electronic encyclopedia could offer Mortimer Adler's outline, along with Coleridge's, Bacon's, or the outline of Hugh of St. Victor. It could offer a variety of contemporary views—one by a physicist, one by a historian, and so on. Each outline would be a distorting lens (or as D'Alembert suggested, a different projection) in which some areas of knowledge occupied the foreground while others were in the distance. But the reader would not be permanently constrained by any one view: he or she could shift back and forth among outlines. Or the reader could reject the very idea of a rigid outline. For the outlines themselves float on top of a network of elements, and the electronic medium can present these elements as a hypertext without imposing a strict hierarchy. The editors of an electronic encyclopedia can insert explicit references at any point in any article. In print such references interrupt the visual flow of the text; furthermore, the reader must activate them by hand. In the electronic medium the references can be invisible until the reader asks to see them and can be followed automatically at the reader's request. The editors are therefore free to create a referential network that functions underneath and apart from their topical outlines. All texts in all technologies of writing are bound together by an indefinite number of implicit references, echoes of words and phrases. But only the computer allows the reader to track such echoes—in an encyclopedia as in any electronic book. The computer permits many structures to coexist in the same electronic text: tree structures, circles, and lines can cross and recross without obstructing one another. The encyclopedic impulse to organize can run riot in this new technology of writing.

Readers themselves participate in the organization of the encyclopedia. They are not limited to the references created by the editors, since at any point in any article they can initiate a search for a word or phrase that takes them to another article. They might also make their own explicit references (hypertextual links) for their own purposes, and these new references can be stored as part of any reader's copy of the encyclopedia. The reader might even be permitted to alter one of the encyclopedic outlines or create his or her own. Readers who are writing their own essays may include their text in separate notefiles and link these files into the encyclopedia. In other words, readers may personalize their own copy of the encyclopedia so that the structure and even the prose reflect their reading of the world of texts. As we have emphasized, it is always a short step from electronic reading to electronic writing, from determining the order of texts to altering their structure.

Some electronic encyclopedias are already commercially available, including Grolier's *Electronic Encyclopedia* (1988). These are not true electronic books, but rather printed books that have been transferred to the computer. In some cases articles conceived and written for print have been put in machine-readable form (Grolier's is an electronic version of the *Academic American Encyclopedia*) and made available with conventional search programs. That is, the reader types in a word or phrase to search (say "whales" or "Russo-Japanese War") and is presented with articles that contain the word or phrase in their title or body. Grolier's does allow the reader to leave beyond hypertextual bookmarks in order to collect articles of interest. But in general, although readers can search for topics in a number of ways, they cannot intervene in the structure of encyclopedia or build new structures. Most of the electronic encyclopedias currently available do not reflect the power or the limitations of the new medium, but rather the

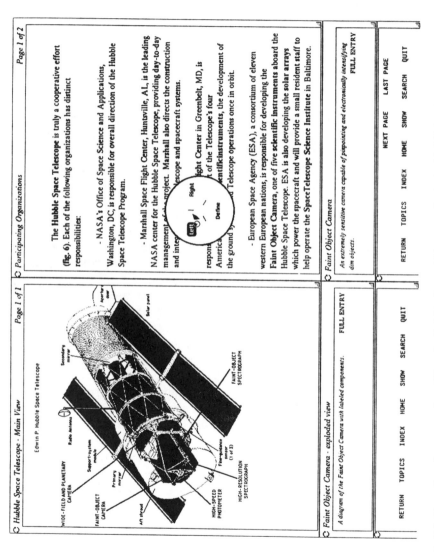

FIG. 6.1. In this Hyperties document describing the Hubble Space Telescope, both the highlighted phrases on the right and portions of the illustration on the left serve as hypertextual links. ©1988 IEEE. Reprinted with kind permission from *Computer* and the authors: Marchionini and Schneiderman,1988, p. 75.

conservative character of the publishing industry, which is bound inevitably to the technology of print. They only begin to suggest the flexibility that the computer can bring to the organization of a great book.

An exception is the system called Hyperties. It also presents images and text on the computer screen, but in this case both the text and the images are animated. When the reader points to a highlighted phrase or to a graphic element, a window pops up to provide an explanation or elaboration. The reader reads by following links from window to window: a text in Hyperties is a network of such links and therefore a true hypertext. (See Fig. 6.1.)

The flexibility of hypertext together with the enormous capacity of electronic storage changes the scope of the encyclopedia. The encyclopedic vision has always been that the great book should contain all symbolic knowledge. This vision has always been utopian: the making of such a great book is impossible because of the human limitations of the editors as well as the limitations of the available technology of writing. Thus, editors of encylopedias have always made explicit or implicit exclusions: the mechanical arts, for example, were not represented in the early medieval encyclopedias of Martianus and Isidore; biographies were not included in the first *Britannica*. Encyclopedias in the Middle Ages were often statements of high learning: the utilitarian value of encyclopedias has been emphasized only in the last 200 years. In this century American encyclopedias have cut out scholarly subjects in favor of articles of popular interest in order to maintain the largest possible readership. The electronic encyclopedia seems to be following the American trend, although perhaps only because the current examples are often American. In any case, the computer can hold so much information that there is little need to be selective: the reader need only look at a tiny portion at any one time. The attitude toward the knowledge contained in electronic encyclopedias will be opportunistic, almost irreverent, because of the temporary character of electronic information. This was not the case for an encyclopedia in manuscript or in print, where the technology encouraged more or less permanent structures of knowledge. Today we cannot hope for permanence and for general agreement on the order of things—in encyclopedias any more than in politics or the arts. What we have instead is a view of knowledge as collections of (verbal and visual) ideas that can arrange themselves into a kaleidoscope of hierarchical and associative patterns—each pattern meeting the needs of one class of readers on one occasion.

ELECTRONIC ENVIRONMENTS

We need to consider how digitized images and sound should be integrated into an electronic encyclopedia. In more than one proposal for the encyclopedia of the future, the pictures, sounds, and even smells and tastes seem to overwhelm and replace verbal text. The result would be not principally a hypertext, but instead a multimedia presentation in which the computer addresses all the reader's sense and puts the reader into the situation described. Readers do not read about the French Revolution; they visit Paris in 1789. They do not read about the chemistry of rubber; they take part in an experiment. They do not read about Jupiter, but instead board a simulated spacecraft heading for the planet.

Such multimedia displays would seem to expand the range and the power of the encyclopedia, to be the computer's equivalent of the diagrams or pictures common in printed encyclopedias since the 18th century. (Along with its 17 volumes of prose, the *Encyclopédie* consisted of 11 volumes of plates, of which its editors were justifiably proud.) But there is a danger in such an encyclopedia of losing the symbolic character of reading and writing. As an encyclopedic computer program grows more elaborate, it may make more decisions for the reader and present these decisions in a perceptual, rather than symbolic form. The reader becomes a mere viewer, and the encyclopedia becomes interactive television, or what is now sometimes called "virtual reality." Here is one description of an encyclopedia as a simulation, a guided tour through a world of the editor's making:

> A *tour* is a particular path through some information (the model). . . . A *filter* is the logical analog of an optical filter. Placed between a model and an observer (the user), it can mask out detail, add emphasis, combine information from several sources, and help determine presentation style. . . . A *guide* is the user's personal (electronic) agent in the encyclopedia system. The guide sets up tours, explains, helps select filters, points out interesting topics, and provides help when requested. The guide also builds up a description of the user's preferences to better tailor the tours that the encyclopedia provides. Guides might have different personalities and styles; the user could pick a guide according to his or her tastes, for example, the Renaissance balance of Leonardo da Vinci or the novelty of the latest rock star. In terms of the models-tours-filter-guides metaphor, using this future encyclopedia bears little resemblance to reading through a set of tomes, but is better viewed instead as a conversation with a guide or tutor who accompanies us during our learning adventure in an electronic amusement park or interactive science museum. (Weyer & Borning, 1985, p. 65)

Such a computer program, if it were ever possible, would be a kind of anti-encyclopedia, just as computerized simulated environments are in general anti-books. Entering into an environment is the antithesis of reading, because in place of a symbolic structure of words, equations, graphs, and images, the program offers the user the illusion of perceptual experience. An encounter with texts is replaced by perceptions, and the distancing and abstracting quality of text is lost. A simulated rock star or even Leonardo da Vinci as the personified voice of an encyclopedia is no solution at all to the problem of encyclopedic organization. To the extent that the persona is a convincing personality, it merely gets in the way. If we were to meet such a person who knew everything, the question would still be how to learn anything from the encounter—how that person would convey structures of knowledge to us. To structure knowledge, we need a book: in the electronic medium the computer as hypertext, not as superhuman. An electronic encyclopedia may certainly combine several media. The defining quality of the electronic medium is its ability to interweave words, pictures, video images—any material that can be represented as bits. All such material can be formed into an electronic book; it can be treated textually or hypertextually, as a network of elements through which readers can travel. But to clothe a hypertextual network in the persona of a rock star is to obscure the purpose of hypertext itself.

THE ELECTRONIC LIBRARY

The library as a great book adopts a strategy opposite to that of the encyclopedia. While the encyclopedia absorbs and digests other books, the library attempts to control knowledge by collecting as many books as possible within one conceptual and physical structure. The library is the physical realization of a culture's writing space of books. In medieval and early modern libraries, books were often chained to their shelves. Such libraries did not merely contain books; the books became part of the furniture and walls. What the reader does metaphorically in the encyclopedia, he or she can do literally in the library—move into and through a textual space.

The space of the library has evolved along lines similar to those of the encyclopedia, but the principles of organization for libraries have generally been more utilitarian. Ancient Greek and Roman libraries of papyrus rolls were arranged by subject and then by author (Jackson, 1974, p. 23). In the later empire period, the Romans also divided their collections by language: one for Greek and one for Latin. It was common in the Middle Ages and even later to divide the books by university faculty: law, medicine, theology, and the arts. Within each division the organization was roughly alphabetical. However, unlike modern encyclopedias, modern libraries never adopted a completely alphabetical arrangement. They continued to classify books by topic, and, as we would expect, the classifications became more complicated and more ad hoc. When Conrad Gesner published his *Pandects* in 1548, he still suggested classing books under the seven liberal arts as well as by university faculty (Jackson, 1974, pp. 128ff). But by the end of the 19th century, the founders of modern classification, C. A. Cutter and Melvil Dewey, claimed to reject anything but utility as their criterion. Describing his system, Dewey wrote: "[t]he impossibility of making a satisfactory classification of all knowledge as preserved in books, has been appreciated from the first, and nothing of the kind attempted. Theoretical harmony and exactness have been repeatedly sacrificed to the practical requirements of the library..." (Jackson, 1974, p. 388). The Library of Congress call numbers, by which books are now shelved, follow a topical system that few users bother to learn. Apart from knowing that books on psychology or books on German literature are shelved together, the user simply treats the call number as a street address, a means of locating the book.

The call numbers in fact constitute a vast system, a mapping of the conceptual library onto the building, which is itself a physical hierarchy of floors, stacks, and shelves. At the same time the library's card catalog provides three different conceptual views of the library: a list of authors' names, one of titles, and one of subjects. The library is a single physical hierarchy that is reorganized or "written over" in three ways by its catalog system. In current libraries the catalog is often computerized, making it easier for the user to jump back and forth among the three views and to search for keywords in titles or subjects. The user can therefore rearrange the conceptual library with relative ease. But the books themselves are still printed, and the user must eventually leave the electronic world and set out on a physical journey among the stacks. In a fully electronic library, the books themselves would be stored electronically; the library would no longer be a building that the reader had to visit. The computers, storage devices, and communications equipment must be housed somewhere, but the reader has no need to see the equipment, any more than he or she needs to see the physical plant of the local telephone company. In such a library, the books could rearrange themselves at the reader's request. The same book could in effect appear on different shelves: for example, a book on the history of theories of mind could appear in the psychology section and in the philosophy section. It is often claimed that a principal advantage of a physical library is that the reader can browse and come across interesting books by chance. But an electronic library could give the reader the same opportunity. A graphic videoscreen could even display the spines of the books on shelves and allow the reader to reach in and open the books, if that is really the best way for the reader to browse.

A major library of printed books is always changing: new books come in, and the physical shelving is expanded or redone. But the ideal of the library is not change, but preservation. Libraries have seemed venerable because they preserved what was created by past writers and valued by past readers. Francis Bacon called libraries "... shrines where all the relics of the ancient saints, full of true virtue and that without delusion or imposture, are preserved and reposed" (Bacon, 1955, p. 233). The English poet George Crabbe called them the "tombs of those who cannot die" (1966, p. 9). No one would apply this funerary rhetoric to an electronic library that reorganizes texts as readily as it preserves them. Electronic libraries will no doubt preserve the books of the past, although in a transcribed form. But the reverence accorded to the traditional library of manuscripts and printed books came from the fact that the building itself was a kind of monumental writing, a writing and reading space in stone. In the age of print the library itself became the replacement for Victor Hugo's cathedral: the entry hall or reading room of more than one great library was built to resemble the nave of a cathedral, with the circulation or information desk as the altar. There is nothing monumental about an electronic library, which might appear to users as a CD-ROM or simply as a code number that they select on their university's communications network.

FROM PERSEUS TO XANADU

When we look for examples of electronic libraries, we find the same situation as with electronic encyclopedias. There are modest systems already in operation and others in progress, and then there are proposals for a utopian future. In one sense the electronic library is already decades old, for there have been bibliographic and textual databases since the 1960s. At first these databases were expensive and were therefore restricted to industry and medicine, law, and the physical sciences. But now all kinds of information are being put into commercial and private databases: newspaper articles, airline schedules, census data, scholarly bibliographies. Some of the commercial databases already constitute electronic almanacs, indicating the eclectic tastes that the electronic medium both serves and fosters. Other databases are forerunners of an electronic research library. Not only the bibliography of many fields but also the texts of Greek and Latin literature, important poets in various modern languages, and the *Oxford English Dictionary* (1987) have been converted into electronic form. We already see the impulse to create "universal" databases: to have all U.S. Court decisions, all archaeological data from pre-Columbian America, all medical bibliography, or all medieval English literature in one electronic place. There is already underway a project called Perseus whose goal is to assemble an electronic library of materials for classical studies: millions of words of ancient texts in Greek and translation with grammatical notes, a 30,000-word Greek dictionary, an historical atlas, diagrams, and even pictures (stored on videodisk) of archaeological sites. The Perseus project seeks to place before the reader all the materials of a small research library, and also to make the materials interconnected or hypertextual: "Put an atlas, a dictionary, and a collection of texts onto a single compact disk, and you have done more than make three kinds of reference work available. Each affects the form of the other" (Crane, 1988,

p. 40). The result will be a universal database, a new space for reading and for writing, since Perseus will also allow the reader to take notes or make excerpts for his or her own purposes.

The universal electronic database may be individual or collective. The individual writer dreams of recording all his or her essays, notes, and jottings in one systematic form, while scholars and scientists imagine vast collective repositories of information available immediately to any user in the nation or the world. For some, these two visions coalesce: each writer's database is absorbed into the universal network, until all writers occupy a single vast space in which all previous literature has been recorded. In this ultimate electronic library, as on a smaller scale in Project Perseus, the distinction between private and public writing breaks down. The computer makes all public writing available to each reader, at the same time permitting the individual to externalize all of his or her own writing.

This utopian (for others, dystopian) vision lies somewhere in the background of all proposals for the electronic collection of text. The desire is always to extend the collection, to incorporate new texts, to bring the whole of a field into the same electronic structure. And this passion is a familiar one: what other goal have librarians ever had than to bring all books under their systematic control? The goal of a universal collection goes back at least to Alexandria, where the Ptolemies apparently ordered that rolls found aboard ships entering the port were to be seized for their library. The modern equivalents of the Alexandrian library are the great national collections, such as the Library of Congress and the British Library, which receive by law copies of all books printed in their respective countries. There are already proposals for universal electronic libraries. One of the earliest has the appropriate visionary name "Xanadu"—it is a proposal by Ted Nelson, who as we have noted also coined the name "hypertext." Xanadu is to be an electronic subscription library: users pay to participate, but the expectation is that everyone will see the value of participation, and the library will become the universal writing space. Nelson has labeled his project: "A Piece of Software that Proposes a New Era of Computers, a New Form of Instant Literature and a Whole New World." The Xanadu system structures information in the computer in such a way that any text can be referenced by any other, these references can in turn be referenced, and so on. Nelson explains that "[b]y using links to mark and type data elements, and to represent typed connections between the data elements, the Xanadu system provides A UNIVERSAL DATA STRUCTURE TO WHICH ALL OTHER DATA MAY BE MAPPED . . ." (Nelson, 1987, p. 1). But the developers have much more in mind than a computer data structure. They see writers and readers throughout the world working in the same conceptual space. Xanadu is "a plan for a worldwide network, intended to serve hundreds of millions of users simultaneously from the corpus of the world's stored writings, graphics and data" (Nelson, 1987. p. 1; see also *Literary Machines* by Nelson, 1984). Xanadu is a vision for the macrocosm: millions of texts are to be managed and ultimately joined into one world network. The result would be a larger library by far than any ever realized in print or manuscript.

Others have preferred to imagine the microcosm—how such a vast writing space might appear to an individual writer or reader. An example here is a proposal called "Tablet." This Tablet would be a computer the size of a notebook—it looks rather like the old Etch-a-Sketch toy—which delivers text (as well as graphics and video) with clarity equal to the printed page. The writer can record words or draw on the screen with a stylus. Tablet is also the outlet for a worldwide system, in which all users can read and many can write:

> Imagine a tremendous hypertext encyclopedia where every expert in every field maintains his or her knowledge online. Such a document can only keep growing and assimilating more and more information, pushing older and less popular information to lower levels while maintaining a hierarchical structure. (Young et al., 1988, p. 12)

Tablet is portable—the writer can work under a (natural) tree—but portability does not mean that the writer will be disconnected from the network of all other texts and writers. The network follows the writer wherever he or she goes.

> ... Tablet integrates a cellular telephone link. This will not only support voice but data communications as well ... Tablet will have a GPS (Global Positioning System) receiver as a built-in component. GPS is an existing satellite-based system which enables objects to locate themselves in the world to within a few meters. (Young et al., 1988, pp. 9-10)

Every carrier of every Tablet will not only be in contact, but his or her position in the global library will be registered. In earlier times, as we have noted, books were chained to shelves in order to guarantee that patrons would not smuggle them out of the library. The Tablet cannot be taken out of the library, because the world has become the library and the chaining is now electronic.

Neither Tablet nor Xanadu is likely to perform as advertised: besides the technical problems, there are insurmountable political and social obstacles to a universal system. But the image of the electronic library as a community of writers in instant and effortless communication—this image will persist, and it will define the next age of writing. Working libraries will continue for some time to be hybrids: combinations of machine-readable materials, computer services, and familiar printed books and journals. But the emphasis will gradually move from the physical to the electronic components. The library as an idea will become as ephemeral as electronic technology itself; it will no longer be a building or even a fixed conceptual structure, but instead a constantly evolving network of elements. To write and to read in this library will be to move through the network examining and altering elements. Writer and reader will be "connected," and each act of writing and reading will leave a trace for future writing and reading. In at least one sense, the goal of all previous ages will be realized: the library will finally be nothing other than a great book, a larger structure composed of the same elements in the same writing space as the book itself.

THE BOOK OF NATURE

> I saw buried in the depths, bound with love in one volume, that which is scattered through the universe. (Dante, Paradiso, XXXIII, 82ff)

The electronic writing Tablet is an attempt to break down the limits of the conventional book—to put the whole world of writing into one book. Yet the Tablet also takes the book out into the world. Writers carry their Tablets everywhere. When they write on (or talk to) their Tablets, the information moves back and forth through a network that blurs the distinction between the world of nature and the symbolic world of the library. For writers seated under the trees beaming information to all other interested writer/readers, the world has become an enormous volume in which they can leave their electronic marks. Like many similar proposals Tablet is a technology for writing *on* the world.

The metaphor of the world-book is not peculiar to the computer age. Throughout the history of writing, the book has served as a metaphor for nature as a whole and for the human mind in particular. Scholars such as Ernst Curtius have traced a series of analogies among the ideas of mind, book, encyclopedia, library, and the world of nature. We shall examine the metaphor of the book as mind in a later chapter, but here we can say something more about the book of nature. The metaphor appealed to the Middle Ages, precisely because of the importance of venerable texts and textual authorities for the medieval mind. For the medieval scholar, the world was made intelligible through such key works as those of Augustine and Aristotle. The very structure of the world was supposed to be mirrored in such books, and conversely the universe itself came to be viewed as a great book—hence the importance of encyclopedias and summae that brought the whole textual world under control. The ambition of encyclopedists and theologians was nothing less than "...to gather all strands of learning together into an enormous Text, an encyclopedia or summa, that would mirror the historical and transcendental orders just as the Book of God's Word (the Bible) was a speculum of the Book of his Work (nature)" (Gellrich, *The Idea of the Book*, 1985, p.18). As Curtius has argued, the poet Dante could invoke the same metaphor. At the end of the *Paradiso*, Dante's ultimate vision is of the universe as an enormous book that has finally been put together properly: "... all that has been scattered throughout the entire universe, that has been separated and dissevered, like loose quaderni [quires], is now 'bound in one volume.' The book—[in which all is contained]—is the Godhead" (Curtius, 1973, p. 332). Dante's poem itself has been called a summa, an attempt to encompass all knowledge between two covers.

The time for writing theological summae is long past, but the *Encyclopédie* or the 15th edition of the *Encyclopaedia Britannica* can be understood as modern secular attempts to encompass the book of nature in the technology of print. We recall that D'Alembert described the *Encyclopédie* as a world map (D'Alembert, 1963, p. 47). And now proposals for hypertextual encyclopedias and libraries (Xanadu, the Tablet, and many others) translate this vision into the electronic medium. However, the metaphor has changed in response to the new technology. In the age of the manuscript and especially in the age of print, the book was valued for its capacity to preserve and display fixed structures. It was a technological reflection of the great chain of being, in which all of nature had its place in a subtle, but unalterable hierarchy. The hierarchical divisions of knowledge by Hugh of St. Victor or even Francis Bacon belonged on the written or printed page. Even as late as Coleridge, an encyclopedist thought that the purpose of his great book was to demonstrate how each notion is subordinated "to a preconceived universal Idea" (*Encyclopaedia Metropolitana*, 1849, p. 22)—in other words, to present hierarchies of knowledge. The passion for hierarchy finds its purest expression in the elaborate table of contents of modern encyclopedias and other great books in print. The table of contents is both hierarchical and linear: it shows subordination and superordination, and it also shows the reader the order in which he or she will encounter these ideas in reading from first page to last.

There is nothing in an electronic book that quite corresponds to the printed table of contents. Menus in an electronic book can indicate a hierarchy of topics, but there is no single, linear order of pages to determine how the reader should move through the hierarchy. In this sense, the electronic book reflects a different natural world, in which relationships are multiple and evolving: there is no great chain of being in an electronic world-book. For that very reason, an electronic book is a better analogy for contemporary views of nature, since nature today is often not regarded as a hierarchy, but rather as a network of interdependent species and systems. The biological sciences dispensed with the great chain of being over a century ago—long before the advent of the electronic computer. More recently, but also long before the computer, physics rejected simple hierarchical views of matter and energy. In fact the metaphor of the book of nature has long been moribund. But with the coming of the computer, we have a writing technology that suits a contemporary scientific conception of the world, and the metaphor of the world as a hypertextual book can now be explored. We can expect contemporary scientists and scholars to come more and more to the conclusion that the book of nature is a hypertext, whose language is the computational mathematics of directed graphs. This is an intriguing prospect. For if scientists are studying the interdependencies of nature, while humanists are reading hypertexts, then our vision of nature can be reunited with our technology of writing in a way that we have not seen since the Middle Ages.

7

The New Dialogue

THE READING PATH

A written text is a structure in space that implies a structure in time: writing turns time into space. In this respect a verbal text is like a musical score. The score is a visual pattern of barlines, notes, rests, and dynamic markings, but the pattern only makes sense when read as a sequence of measures. Most of us can read music, if at all, only by playing it on an instrument, but a good musician can read the score directly, activating the musical signs in his or her head. Those who can only read music by playing it are like people who read verbal texts by saying the words aloud: they are almost entirely absorbed by the unfolding temporal structure of the music. The good musician, however, can appreciate the second dimension, the "vertical" structure of the score as well. A thorough reading of text or music requires attention to the space as well as the time of the writing. And once again, the particular relationship between the time and space of the text depends on the writing technology used. In a medieval codex the spatial structure is the pattern of rubrication and various sizes of letters; in a printed book it is the arrangement into paragraphed pages; in the computer it is the pattern of textual windows and images on the screen. The temporal structure of a text is created by the reader's moment-by-moment encounter with these elements.

If the reader is reading a story or an essay, the words create a rhythm of expectations. One word alludes to something earlier in the text or looks ahead to something to come. Expectations, explicit references, and allusions are also part of the purely oral arts of storytelling and public speaking. But the important difference between listening to a story and reading a book is that, while listeners simply allow the words to come to them, readers must themselves make the words move. What the reader sees on the page is a pattern of signs, and he or she takes in some portion of the pattern in each glance. Practiced readers of printed books take in whole words or phrases at a glance: their eyes make jumping movements that psychologists call "saccadic." It is in the pauses between such jumps that a span of letters is viewed and recognized. (See, for example, Levin & Addis, 1979.) Beginning readers today (like most readers in the ancient world and early Middle Ages) focus on single letters and clusters and spell their way through each line. But whether the working unit is a single letter or an entire phrase, the reader's task is to thread these units into a sensible order: to read is to activate verbal elements in time. The English "read" comes from the Anglo-Saxon *raedan*, which also means "to give counsel, to interpret." This etymology reflects a belief that reading is a derived form of speech, that the reader is an intepreter who can make mute texts speak. The Latin word *lego*, which gives the Romance languages their words for reading (*lecture* in French, *lettura* in Italian), has a more interesting etymology. *lego* literally means "to gather, to collect," while one of its figurative meanings is "to make one's way, to traverse." By this etymology, reading is the process of gathering up signs while moving over the writing surface. The reader on a journey through a symbolic space—this image, which fits all technologies of writing, is particularly appropriate to electronic writing.

To read is to choose and follow one path from among those suggested by the layout of the text. In confronting an ancient papyrus roll, the reader had few choices. The earliest ancient writing was strictly linear: it was simply a concatenation of letters that the reader turned back into sound. In fact, some early Greek inscriptions were written in a style called *boustrophedon* ("as the ox turns"), in which the line ran from left to right, bent around, and then continued from right to left with individual letters also drawn backwards. The technique was perfectly linear: the text defined letter by letter a continuous path for the reader to follow. At the other extreme are the numerous paths offered by the modern newspaper, in which several stories are laid out on each page and therefore compete for the reader's attention. A printed encyclopedia lies between these extremes, since each article is meant to be read linearly, but the alphabetized articles themselves can be read in any order.

The codex and the printed book both allow the writer to suggest many paths through the same work. But in most paged books as in the papyrus roll, one path dominates all others—the one defined by reading line by line, from first page to last. The paged book has a canonical order. However, once that order is established, the writer may want to suggest alternatives. The writer may incorporate in the text references and allusions that cause the reader to jump back and forth, at least mentally, as he or she reads. The printed book makes these acts of reference easier through the use of footnotes and page references. A writer using a papyrus roll was more likely to repeat himself just because it was hard to refer the reader back to a previous passage. In each writing technology and in each text, the question is: how and to what extent does the writer control the reader's experience of reading? To what extent does the reader actively participate in choosing his or her path through the text?

The question of control can also be posed in the absence of writing—in purely oral forms of storytelling and poetry. The Homeric poems, which we discussed as examples of oral composition in Chapter 4, have sophisticated structures of expectation and fulfillment. But, like all oral texts, they have no visible structure; nothing in Homer depends on holding a text in one's hands and moving back and forth through the copy. Homeric poets and modern storytellers do not create books. This means, above all, that there is no canonical order to the story. The storyteller's tale is strictly linear, although it need not be fixed from one telling to another. The teller is free to deviate from the storyline without the fear that a written text will prove him or her wrong. There may be, as in Homeric poetry, a network of established heroes and their adventures, but that network can allow for additions and deviations. In fact, "deviation" is the wrong word: it is impossible for the oral poet to deviate from the path, because the poet makes the path as he or she goes. The story still has a temporal structure, a rhythm of expectations and fulfillments. The poet can digress from the main story and hold the audience in suspense, but the awareness of a tension between the fixed, visible text and the flow of spoken language is not available to oral poets or their audience. For example, there is nothing in storytelling that quite corresponds to the reader's sense that in turning the pages he or she is coming to the end of the book.

The Homeric storyteller chooses what events to tell and the pace of the telling, and the storyteller can adjust the tale in order to suit what he or she conceives to be the wishes of the audience. Since the storyteller and the audience are in immediate contact, the audience too has a measure of control over the telling of the tale. We cannot say how Homer's original audience exercised that control: they may have shouted advice, or they may simply have shown greater or less interest as the performer proceeded. We know how modern children express their approval or disapproval of the way a story is told. In any case, writing changes the intimate relationship between the creator and the audience. It is no use shouting at a novel whose plot is heading in a direction we do not like: the book cannot adjust itself to our wishes as readers. In that sense the reader loses control. In other ways the reader is more powerful than the listener, since each reader determines the pace of his or her own reading and can at least try to change the path through the text by scanning or skipping a paragraph, a page, or a whole chapter. In nonfiction or anthologies of stories, readers can read the chapters or sections in orders other than the one suggested. (However, they do so at their peril; they must always be conscious that the book itself defines the preferred reading order.) In general it is harder to hoodwink a reader than a listener, because the reader can stop at any time, reflect, and refer to a previous section of the text. The difference becomes obvious whenever we have the chance to compare oral and written presentations of the same material. When a politician or a scholar speaks (reads a speech), it is harder to find the flaws. If we later read the text in a newspaper or in a journal, we may see nothing but flaws in the argument. Whenever we do have both the written text and an oral performance, we become aware of a tension between the two.

PLATONIC DIALOGUE

Plato was acutely aware of the tension between oral and written discourse, and he created a genre of writing that both embodies and profits from that tension. Plato's dialogues combine the permanence of writing with the apparent flexibility of conversation. Each is the record of an impossibly artful philosophical discussion, and whatever its proposed subject, each dialogue is also about the difference between philosophy as conversation and philosophy as writing.

Plato's Socrates prefers conversation to writing. In the *Phaedrus*, he tells a story that seems to condemn writing as a vehicle for any true philosophy. Socrates and Phaedrus have been examining the nature of rhetoric and public speaking. Toward the end of the discussion, Socrates tells the story of the Egyptian god Theuth, a great benefactor of the human race. Theuth was an avid inventor, who gave us arithmetic, geometry, astronomy, draughts and dice, and the alphabet. The king of Egypt was another god named Thamus, and so Theuth took his inventions to the king and explained the purpose and value of each. Of the alphabet, Theuth said, "this invention... will make the Egyptians wiser and will improve their memories, for it is an elixir of memory and wisdom that I have discovered" (See *Phaedrus*, 274E in Plato, 1919, p. 563). But the king replied that writing would have just the opposite effect: "...this invention will produce forgetfulness in the minds of those who learn to use it, because they will not practise their memory. Their trust in writing, produced by external characters which are no part of themselves, will discourage the use of their own memory within them. You have invented not an elixir of memory, but of reminding; and you offer your pupils the appearance of wisdom, not true wisdom" (275A, p. 563). Socrates goes on to explain that written words on a page are dead things. They cannot, as he puts it, answer questions we pose of them; they cannot explain themselves or adjust themselves to various readers. The process of adjustment and explanation is possible in philosophical conversation, the kind of questioning and answering that Socrates himself practices. The best writing, Socrates tells Phaedrus, is that of the living word, written in the mind of the student by a wise teacher, for this word is active: "it knows to whom it should speak and before whom to be silent" (276A, p. 567).

The ultimate failure of writing did not prevent Plato himself from becoming one of the most influential authors in the ancient world. However, it is true that Plato's dialogue was a nostalgic form looking back to a time when Greek culture could do without writing. Plato lived in a period of transition in the history of literacy. Alphabetic writing was not new, but literacy had taken centuries to work its way into the fabric of Greek culture. By Plato's time, children were going to school principally to learn to read and write, and the lawcourts were beginning to rely on written documents rather than hearsay. Plato understood that a whole way of life was finally passing, a way of life based on the spoken rather than the written word. (See Eric Havelock, 1982.) Nostalgia, however, is not the key for Plato: the key is rather the question of control in the new space that writing creates.

Platonic dialogue is a consciously literary attempt to imitate philosophical conversation. As the *Phaedrus* points out, such conversation is spontaneous, capable of going in any direction in order to pursue a problem. And the dialogue itself seems to share that spontaneity: Plato appears to abdicate control of his text by reporting conversations between Socrates and his followers. Yet this apparent abdication gives Plato a subtler control over his reader. Plato leads and instructs his readers in the same devious way that Socrates leads and instructs his partners in the discussion—by getting them to acquiesce until they are too deeply involved in the argument to reject it. Still Plato the writer seems to envy Socrates the oral philosopher, because Socrates can adjust his questioning to his audience. He can guide his interlocutor along the proper path, securing agreement at each step. Plato as writer sets up his path, but he cannot be sure that the reader is following. The reader is free to make all sorts of misunderstandings that the text separated from its author cannot correct. The text cannot ensure that it will be read properly (in accordance with the author's wishes), because the text no longer belongs to its author. For Plato, then, writing is both too rigid and too free. Readers too may feel the limitation of the dialogue: that they cannot truly enter into the staged conversation. They may be exasperated as Socrates brings his audience to some particularly outrageous conclusion. Readers may want to break in and change the course of the discussion, but they would only be shouting at a text. What is true of all writing is painfully obvious in a dialogue: the form invites the reader to participate in a conversation and then denies him or her full participation.

FROM DIALOGUE TO ESSAY

A Platonic dialogue is a hybrid, a compromise between oral and written controlling structures. Such hybrids were common in ancient writing, where many genres were intended for oral performance—including speeches, dramatic and lyric poetry, and perhaps highly rhetorical history. Writers in these genres used structures that could be appreciated in reading aloud or in reading to others who do not have their own texts. So, for example, such early prose authors as Herodotus made use of a technique called "ring composition." Herodotus would proceed to tell a story, then digress on an interesting detail, and then notify the reader/listener that he was resuming the original storyline. The narrative proceeded as a straight line with occasional digressive loops. In early ancient works of fiction and nonfiction, the dominant structure was usually the line. Plays took the reader step by step through events; history was written chronologically (with digressions). Early writing was paratactic; later, rhetorical writing became periodic, favoring elaborate sentences with many subordinate clauses. But both the paratactic and periodic styles were oral, not visual: they depended for their effect on hearing rather than seeing the text. Gradually in the ancient world, forms developed that were remote from the oral performance: the treatise, the encyclopedia, the handbook. Poets began to offer books of short poems that could be sampled; historians and academics began to write essays on scholarly subjects. But, except perhaps in some branches of philosophy, ancient texts continued to be strongly linear. And the papyrus roll with its simple visual layout suited this linear structure.

After the invention of the paged book, linear structure of course survived. People still wrote narratives to be read straight through. The oral character of the text waxed and waned throughout the Middle Ages depending upon the genre. Heroic and lyric poetry was destined for performance; medieval encyclopedias, like their ancient counterparts, were designed to be consulted by single readers. In general, however, the new form of the book placed greater emphasis on the second visual dimension. It became more common to make hierarchical structures visible on the page by using different letter sizes and forms as well as different colors of ink. The invention of printing reinforced this trend. Printing standardized the table of contents, which is a hierarchical description of the contents of the book. As we saw in Chapter 2, hierarchy can be expressed in a tree diagram, and such diagrams appeared frequently in printed books from the 16th century on. (See Ong, 1958, pp. 74-83, 199-202, 314-318.) In the centuries following the invention of printing, the paragraph assumed its modern form both typographically and conceptually. And today all our major forms of nonfiction—the essay, the treatise, the report—are expected to be hierarchical in organization as they are linear in presentation. This is the paradigm for scholarly and scientific as well as business and technical writing. A scholarly essay should lead the reader step by step through its argument, making clear how each piece of evidence is relevant. The backbone of a technical report should be a careful outline of topics. Such an outline not only shows how each piece fits, but also directs the reader's movement through its parts. Whether we are told to write deductively or inductively, the result is still supposed to be a hierarchy of ideas and a carefully controlled reading.

This need to establish a hierarchy and to direct the reader is more than a matter of style; it now defines the professional activity of all academic writers. All scholarly research is expected to culminate in writing. The historian or scholar does research not for its own sake, but in order to have something to write. The same can be said of many of the social and even the hard sciences. And in order to be taken seriously, both scholarly and scientific writing must be nonfiction in a linear-hierarchical form. The historian's task, for example, is to establish causes and effects: to provide the reader with a consistent, analytical path through some aspect of history. The historian would not be allowed to offer two or more explanations that bore no relation to one another. An historian might argue, say, that the Roman Empire fell as the result of a combination of factors (economic stagnation, barbarian invasion, Christianity), but he or she would have to offer a plausible story, showing how each factor lent impetus to the others. Social or physical scientists set up controlled experiments in order to exclude all but one or a few factors. When they write up their results, the goal is to tell a simple story of cause and effect, although in today's complex sciences this ideal is seldom achieved. The point deserves emphasis: only the linear-hierarchical style of argument is permitted in orthodox writing today. And this orthodoxy is approved by and built into our institutions of learning and research.

If linear and hierarchical structures dominate current writing, the computer now adds a third, the network as a visible and operative structure. The network as an organizing principle has been latent in all written texts, and Homeric oral poetry shows that the network is older than writing itself. Established by repetition in the minds of both the poet and the audience, the Homeric network contained all the mythological characters and their stories. The poet drew upon that network to tell each tale. After the invention of writing in the ancient world, it became the writer's task to establish his or her own network comprised of references and allusions within the text and connected to the larger network formed by other texts in the culture. From that time until the advent of electronic writing, the referential network has existed "between the lines" of the text—that is, in the minds of readers and writers. Now the computer brings the network to the surface of the text. The computer can not only represent associations on the screen; it can also grant these associations the same status as the linear-hierarchical order. It is as easy for the reader to follow an electronic footnote as it is to scroll to the next screen. The invisible network of associations becomes visible and explicit to an extent never before possible. (The network can never be fully explicit, however, because the verbal ideas of the text will always reach out beyond any given electronic text to all other texts that the writer and reader know.) The electronic writer still has available all the techniques of hierarchical organization from the technology of print. He or she may still establish subordination and may still seek to define cause and effect. The electronic writer may embed hierarchical structures inside of larger networks, or networks inside of hierarchies. The line, the tree, and the network all become visible structures at the writer's and reader's disposal.

THE END OF THE LINE

> I generally approach a question not like this: x —▸ . but like this x ⟋⟍·⟍⟋ . I shoot again and again past it, but always from a closer position. (Wittgenstein in Baker & Hacker, 1980, p. 23)

Plato was unwilling to set out his philosophy as a treatise, as a linear progression in which the writer assumes overt control of the argument. Today, and for the last 200 years in the mature age of print, academic writers have been reluctant to accept any form other than the treatise. But if the printing press reinforced that attitude, the computer calls it into question. Why should a writer be forced to produce a single, linear argument or an exclusive analysis of cause and effect, when the writing space allows a writer to entertain and present several lines of thought at once? This question was posed before the invention of the computer by writers, who felt constrained by conventional structures in both fiction and nonfiction. Susan Sontag has observed:

> ...a distinctive modern stylistics has evolved, the prototypes of which go back at least to Sterne and the German Romantics—the invention of anti-linear forms of narration: in fiction, the destruction of the "story"; in nonfiction, the abandonment of linear argument. The presumed impossibility (or irrelevance) of producing a continuous systematic argument has led to a remodeling of the standard long forms—the treatise, the long book—and a recasting of the genres of fiction, autobiography, and essay. Of this stylistics, Barthes is a particularly inventive practitioner. (Sontag, *A Barthes Reader*, 1982, pp. xiv-xv)

The French essayist Roland Barthes was indeed inventive in breaking down linear form. At every level, from the sentence to a whole book, his texts were characterized by fragmentation and interruption. His classic *S/Z*, for example, is a commentary on a short story by Balzac. A commentary is by nature a series of interruptions, and in this case Barthes' comments overwhelm the story and pry it apart, both typographically and conceptually. Barthes' writing is decadent in the sense that it is a decline or falling away from an ideal form of writing for the age of print. The great monographs of the 19th-century essayists and historians (Carlyle, Ruskin, Burckhardt) showed what printing could achieve; by comparison, Barthes is intentionally playful and perverse. These are traits he shares with such writers as Kierkegaard, Nietzsche, and Wittgenstein, each of whom in his own way attacked the development of systematic, linear argument.

Wittgenstein is a fascinating case. He was an influential teacher, who through his students defined the next generation of English linguistic philosophy. Like Socrates, he was a kind of antiauthor. Unlike Socrates, Wittgenstein did write, although he published little in his lifetime. At least in his later years, he agonized over the task of writing. He would fill notebooks with short, unconnected paragraphs, but when he sought to put these paragraphs together for what would become his *Philosophical Investigations*, he was stymied. Wittgenstein wanted to produce a conventional treatise. He tells us in his Preface that he had considered it essential to set his ideas "in a natural order and without breaks" (Wittgenstein, 1953, p. ix). But he found that . . .

> my thoughts were soon crippled if I tried to force them on in any single direction against their natural inclination.—And this was, of course, connected with the very nature of the investigation. For this compels us to travel over a wide field of thought criss-cross in every direction.—The philosophical remarks in this book are, as it were, a number of sketches of landscapes which were made in the course of these long and involved journeyings. (p. ix)

Wittgenstein could not cast his philosophy in linear-hierarchical form; it had to remain a journey through a network of interrelated topics. This realization caused Wittgenstein more anguish than his Preface admits, and he often despaired of ever finishing his book (Baker & Hacker, 1980, p. 23). At one point he wrote: "The only presentation of which I am still capable is to connect [my] remarks by a network of numbers which will make evident their extremely complicated connections" (p. 24). Baker and Hacker believe that he actually intended to publish his *Philosophical Investigations* as an interconnected network of entries. That is, he intended to number each entry and to indicate after each entry the numbers of other entries to which it was related (pp. 25-26). When the book was finally published, the entries were numbered, but Wittgenstein had abandoned the scheme of adding what we would call the links. (In writing their commentary on the *Philosophical Investigations*, however, Baker and Hacker have constructed diagrams to mark connections that they find.) At least for a time, then, Wittgenstein had conceived of the *Philosophical Investigations* as a true hypertext. But, unlike Barthes, Wittgenstein was a prose innovator in spite of himself. His notion of a book was still determined by the old model, and he wanted very much to find a perfect order for his ideas.

Wittgenstein and Barthes rejected linear argument, but not the physical form, the "look and feel," of the printed book. The reader picks up their books, opens to the first page, and reads in the conventional way. Some writers have extended their attack to the typography of the book itself, creating antibooks that disrupt our notion of how a book should look and behave before our eyes. *Glas* (1974, 1976a) by Jacques Derrida is such an antibook. Each page of *Glas* is divided into two columns: the left offers passages from Hegel with comments, while the right is a commentary on the French novelist Genet. Paragraphs set in and around other paragraphs and variable sizes and styles of type give the page an almost medieval appearance. There is no linear argument that spans the columns, yet the reader's eye is drawn across, down, and around the page looking for visual and verbal connections. And the connections seem to be there, as words and sentence fragments refer the reader back and forth between Hegel and Genet. Thus, an isolated passage in the right column of the first page seems to be referring both to the text and to the reader's response: "Two unequal columns, they say, each of which—envelops or encloses, incalculably reverses, returns, replaces, marks again, cross-links the other" (Derrida, 1974, p. 7; see also Derrida, 1976a). In *Glas* Derrida lays down a textual space and challenges his reader to find a path through it. Whatever else he is doing, Derrida is certainly writing topographically, as if for a medium as fluid as the electronic.

Seven years earlier, in *Of Grammatology* (1976b), Derrida was already drawing a contrast between linear and nonlinear writing. He argued that linear writing was "rooted in a past of nonlinear writing, . . . a writing that spells its symbols pluri-dimensionally; there the meaning is not subjected to successivity, to the order of a logical time, or to the irreversible temporality of sound" (Derrida, 1976b, p. 85; see also Jasper Neel, 1988, pp. 105-107). Nonlinear writing had been suppressed, though never eradicated, by linear writing. But nonlinear writing resurfaced in the literature of the 20th century, when it seemed that the modern experience could not be recorded in the linear way. Derrida concluded that a new form of nonlinear writing was possible, and this new writing would entail a new reading of earlier texts: ". . . beginning to write without the line, one begins also to reread past writing according to a different organization of space. If today the problem of reading occupies the forefront of science, it is because of this suspense between two ages of writing. Because we are beginning to write, to write differently, we must reread differently" (Derrida, 1976b, pp. 86-87). In all this, Derrida was prescient, but he could not know that electronic writing would be the new writing to which he alluded. Derrida suggested that "[t]he end of linear writing is indeed the end of the book" (p. 86). But instead the new electronic medium redefines the book in a way that can incorporate both linear and nonlinear form.

THE NEW DIALOGUE

A work like *Glas* provokes traditional readers, to whom it seems wrong or simply pointless to distort the printed page. In *Glas* the network of relationships that normally remains hidden beneath the printed page has emerged and overwhelmed the orderly presentation we expect of a printed book. *Glas* belongs in the electronic medium, where such relationships are perfectly at home. In computer writing any relationships between textual elements can float to the surface; the computer invites the writer to reveal the inner structure in the appearance and the behavior of the text. An antibook like *Glas* would no longer be an antibook in an electronic edition, because it would work with rather than against the grain of its medium. *Glas* requires the reader to take an active, even aggressive role in constructing the text, and in this way too it anticipates electronic writing. The computer medium encourages a writer to open a new kind of dialogue with the reader. This dialogue replaces the monologue that is the conventional printed essay or monograph. Like the interlocutor in a Socratic dialogue, the electronic reader assumes at least partial control of the argument. In an electronic encyclopedia, for example, the reader's queries determine what text will be retrieved and displayed: the queries cut a particular path through the network of encyclopedic material. The encyclopedia has always tried to allow for this kind of interaction, but now the electronic medium allows essays and monographs to be structured as dialogues in this same way.

In a traditional essay, destined for publication, the writer speaks apparently in his or her own voice and is expected to take responsibility for a text that will go out to hundreds or thousands of readers under his or her name. Publishing is fundamentally serious and permanent, and it is for this reason that plagiarism in science or scholarship is taken so seriously. A scholar or scientist cannot even retract his or her own previously published argument without embarrassment. By contrast, a dialogue speaks with more than one voice and therefore shares or postpones responsibility. It proceeds by apparent indirection and may gradually zero in on its target. A hypertextual essay in the computer is always a dialogue between the writer and his or her readers, and the reader has to share the responsibility for the outcome. Instead of one linear argument, the hypertext can present many, possibly conflicting arguments. A hypertext on the fall of the Roman empire might include several explanations without seeking either to combine or to reconcile them. Instead of confronting a single narrative, the reader would then move back and forth among several narratives, each embodying one of the explanations. An academic historian would deny that such a hypertext is historical writing at all. But it is important to realize that the historian is judging by the standards of the conventional technologies of manuscript and print. Electronic writing threatens to redefine historiography in a way that reveals what Sontag has called the "impossibility or irrelevance of producing a continuous, systematic argument."

The same redefinition applies to all academic disciplines, in which scholarship is now understood as the producing of systematic argument for publication. There will no doubt be great resistance to such a redefinition, since there is already resistance even to the idea of publishing conventional scholarly journals electronically. In this new form of publication, journals would be offered as diskettes rather than printed volumes. The diskettes would be kept in the library, and printed copies of individual articles would be made locally on demand. No doubt some articles in specialized journals would never be printed at all. Electronic publication would allow the same access to information, but it would destroy the cachet of appearing in print. And traditional scholars rightly sense that the monumental, fixed quality of print is necessary to legitimize their arguments. For popular writing, the change should be less traumatic. Newspapers, magazines, guides, and how-to books are all less wedded to the permanence of printing. The idea of an interactive newspaper or video-magazine no longer seems radical at all. Computer communications services already allow the reader to dial in from a home computer and read articles from various published newspapers.

Eventually, the new dialectic structure of hypertext will compel us, as Derrida put it, to "reread past writing according to a different organization of space." Texts that were originally written for print or manuscript can not only be transferred to machine-readable form, but also translated into hypertextual structures. In some cases the translation would restore to these texts their original, conversational tone. Many of the texts of Aristotle, for example, are notes and excerpts from lectures that the philosopher delivered over many years; they were put together either by Aristotle himself or by ancient editors. For decades modern scholars have been trying to sort out the pieces. Printed editions make each text into a single, monumental treatise, but an electronic edition of Aristotle could record and present all the various chronological and thematic orders that scholars have found. This might be the best way for readers to approach the carefully interwoven philosophy of Aristotle: following the electronic links would allow readers to sample from various texts and move progressively deeper into the problems that each text poses. This moving back and forth is the way that scholars reread and study Aristotle even now. The computer simply makes explicit the implicit act of deeply informed reading, which unlike casual reading is truly a dialogue with the text.

Rather than eliminating works of the past or making them irrelevant, the electronic writing space gives them a new "typography." For hypertext is the typography of the electronic medium. A text always undergoes typographical changes as it moves from one writing space to another. The Greek classics, for example, have moved from the papyrus roll, to codex, and finally the printed book. When we read a paperback edition in English of Plato's dialogues or Greek tragedy, we are aware of the translation from ancient Greek to a modern language. But we should also remember that the original text was without book or scene divisions, paragraphing, indices, punctuation, or even word division. All these conventions of modern printing are significant organizational intrusions into the original work. They make it easier to read Sophocles, but they change the Sophocles that we read. We would find it very difficult to read an English manuscript of the 14th century, or even an early printed book, because of the visual conventions. So it is not as if an electronic version will violate the sanctity of old texts for the first time: these texts have always been subject to typographic change.

When it comes to texts written in and for the electronic medium—and a few such texts have already been written—no translation is needed. The new works do not have a single linear order, corresponding to the pages of the book or the columns of the papyrus roll, and so there is no order to violate. It is precisely the lack of a fixed order and commitment to a linear argument that will frustrate those used to working with and writing for the medium of print, just as it will liberate those willing to experiment with a new form of dialogue. For writers of the new dialogue, the task will be to build, in place of a single argument, a structure of possibilities. The new dialogue will be, as Plato demanded, interactive: it will provide different answers to each reader and may also in Plato's words know "before whom to be silent."

8

Interactive Fiction

Bibliographic databases and technical documents have long been regarded as legitimate texts for the computer: novels, short stories, and poems have not. It is true that many novelists now use word processors to prepare manuscripts for publication as printed books. But very few have attempted to write fiction to be read in the electronic space—that is, nonlinear fiction, which invites the reader to conduct a dialogue with the text. Yet fiction belongs just as naturally in this new technology as all the more pragmatic forms of writing. Fiction, at least modern fiction, is by nature open to experiment, and being open and open-ended is precisely the quality that the computer lends to all writing. The flexibility of electronic text makes for a new form of imaginative writing that has already been named "interactive fiction."

We are just emerging from the nickelodeon era of interactive fiction, and the computer's equivalent of the nickelodeon is the adventure game (which costs rather more than a nickel). In an adventure game the player has a mythical world to explore—a dungeon or an enchanted forest or valley. The computer describes the scene, and the player issues simple commands such as "go ahead," "enter the room," "pick up the dagger," "get gold," and the like. The goal is to amass treasure and dispatch monsters, although sometimes the game is more sophisticated, casting the player in the role of a detective who must solve a murder or other mystery. Even the simplest of these games is a kind of fiction. The computer presents the player with a text, and the player's job is to understand and respond to that text. Depending upon the response, the computer presents more text and awaits a further response. The player, then, is a reader, but an unusually powerful reader, for his or her decisions determine what text will next appear. Admittedly the text of most of the current games is simple-minded, but the method of presentation is not. While a printed novel presents its episodes in one order, the electronic writing space removes that restriction for fiction as it does for the essay. Instead of a single string of paragraphs, the author lays out a textual space within which his or her fiction operates. The reader joins in actively constructing the text by selecting a particular order of episodes at the time of reading. Within each episode, the reader is still compelled to read what the author has written. But the movement between episodes is determined by the responses of the reader, his or her interactions with or intrusions into the text, and the reader's experience of the fiction depends upon these interactions.

In its simplest form, interactive fiction requires only those two elements that we have already identified for electronic writing: episodes (topics) and decision points (links) between episodes. The episodes may be paragraphs of prose or poetry, they may include bit-mapped graphics as well, and they may be of any length. Their length will establish the rhythm of the story—how long the reader remains a conventional reader before he or she is called on to participate in the selection of the next episode. At the end of each episode, the author inserts a set of links to other episodes together with a procedure for choosing which link to follow. Each link may require a different response from the reader or a different condition in the computer system. The reader may answer a question posed in the text; there will be one link for each possible reader response. The computer can also keep track of the previous episodes readers have visited, so that they may be barred from visiting one episode before they visit another. Many other tests are possible, but even with the simple matching technique and the tracking of previously visited episodes, the author can create a fictional space of great flexibility. Readers may be allowed to examine a story in chronological order, in reverse chronology, or in a complicated sequence of flashbacks and returns. They may follow one character through the story, and then return to follow another. A reader might play the role of the detective trying to solve a murder, a role familiar from the computerized adventure games. A reader might be asked to influence events in a novel by choosing episodes that promise to bring two characters together or to punish an evil character for his or her deeds: each choice would define a new course for the story. Such multiple plots, however, are only one possibility for interactive fiction. The electronic writing space can accommodate many other literary strategies. It could offer the reader several different perspectives on a fixed set of events. In this case the reader would not be able to affect the course of the story, but the reader could switch back and forth among narrators, each with his or her own point of view. An electronic text could also establish relationships among episodes that are not narrative at all: a poet could define multiple reading orders for an anthology of his or her poems—according to theme, image, time of the year, or other criteria under the poet's or the reader's control.

It is important to realize that electronic fiction in this sense is not automatic fiction. The computer does not create the verbal text: it presents that text to the reader according to the author's preconditions. The locus of creativity remains with the author and the reader, although the balance between the two has shifted. Nor is electronic fiction necessarily random. The author may put any number of restrictions on the reading order. The extent of the reader's choices and therefore the reader's freedom in examining the literary space depends upon the links that the author creates between episodes. The reader may have to choose from among a few alternatives or may range widely through the work. Each author can relinquish as much or as little control as he or she chooses; the author has a new literary dimension with which to work.

"AFTERNOON"

What the author and reader can do with this literary dimension is shown in "Afternoon" by Michael Joyce (1987), one of the first examples of this new genre of interactive fiction. "Afternoon" combines the literary sophistication of a printed work with the immediacy of a computerized adventure game. "Afternoon" is a fiction and a game at the same time, and yet its visual structure is very simple. The reader confronts a window on the computer screen: episodes of "Afternoon," containing from one to a few hundred words, will appear successively in the window. At the bottom of the screen is a small bar, where the reader types replies in order to move to the next episode; the reader may also initiate movement by selecting a word from the current episode in the window. All the text of the episodes was written by Michael Joyce, but the particular order in which the episodes are visited is determined at the time of reading.

"Afternoon" begins:

I try to recall winter. 'As if it were yesterday?' she says, but I do not signify one way or another.

By five the sun sets and the afternoon melt freezes again across the blacktop into crystal octopi and palms of ice—rivers and continents beset by fear, and we walk out to the car, the snow moaning beneath our boots and the oaks exploding in series along the fenceline on the horizon, the shrapnel settling like relics, the echoing thundering off far ice.

This was the essence of wood, these fragments say. And this darkness is air. 'Poetry' she says, without emotion, one way or another.

Do you want to hear about it?"

If the reader types yes, then a link will flash another episode on the screen, whose first sentences are:

> She had been a client of Wert's wife for some time. Nothing serious, nothing awful, merely general unhappiness and the need of a woman so strong to have friends....

If the reader types no, another episode will appear beginning:

> I understand how you feel. Nothing is more empty than heat. Seen so starkly the world holds wonder only in the expanses of clover where the bees work....

"Afternoon" does not accept no as the reader's last word: instead, it moves the reader along a different path. But the reader has other choices as well: he or she can select a particular word directly from the text (such as "poetry," "winter," or "yesterday" in the first episode). Certain words in each window will "yield" and branch to another episode. If the reader defaults by hitting the Return key, then yet another link will be followed. Many different responses will cause the text to move, but until the reader responds with some action of the keyboard or the mouse, the text of an episode remains on the screen, conventional prose (occasionally poetry) to be read in the conventional way.

One voice in a later episode in "Afternoon" describes the reading experience this way:

> In my mind the story, as it has formed, takes on margins. Each margin will yield to the impatient, or wary, reader. You can answer yes at the beginning and page through on a wave of Returns, or page through directly—again using Returns—without that first interaction.
>
> These are not versions, but the story itself in long lines. Otherwise, however, the center is all—Thoreau or Brer Rabbit, each preferred the bramble. I've discovered more there too, and the real interaction, if that is possible, is in pursuit of texture..."

This is the great difference between "Afternoon" and a fiction written on and for paper. There is no single story of which each reading is a version, because each reading determines the story as it goes. We could say that there is no story at all; there are only readings. Or if we say that the story of "Afternoon" is the sum of all its readings, then we must understand the story as a structure that can embrace contradictory outcomes. Each reading is a different turning within a universe of paths set up by the author. Reading "Afternoon" several times is like exploring a vast house or castle. The reader proceeds often down the same corridors and through familiar rooms. But often too the reader comes upon a new hallway not previously explored or finds a previously locked door suddenly giving way to the touch. Gradually, the reader pushes back the margins of this electronic space—as in a computer game in which the descent down a stairway reveals a whole new level of the dungeon. "Afternoon" is constructed so as to remind the reader of the origins of electronic fiction in the computerized adventure games.

"Afternoon" is metaphorically related to computer video games as well. It is like a video game in which the player pilots a spaceship around planetary obstacles that each exert a gravitational force. Readers of "Afternoon" move along paths with their own inertia, while at the same time experiencing the attraction of various parts of the fiction as they move by. It is easy to fall into an orbit around one set of episodes, one focus of the story. Readers find themselves returning to the same episodes again and again, trying to break free by giving different answers and therefore choosing different paths. When it succeeds, this strategy may then push the reader into another orbit.

The planets in Afternoon's solar system are characters and key events. The characters include a poet named Peter who is working as a technical writer for a software company; his employer Wert, Wert's wife Lolly, and another employee in the company with the unlikely classical name of Nausicaa. Peter's is the narrative voice through most of the episodes, but the reader may follow paths in which each of the two women also narrate. Various paths concern the history of these characters, and the reader can find himself or herself parked in an orbit around one of them. The events in "Afternoon" may be significant in the traditional narrative sense: one is an automobile accident which may have killed Peter's former wife and his son. But one of the most gravitationally powerful events is commonplace: Peter has lunch with his employer. What makes the event important is that it is a structural crossroad: the intersection of many narrative paths. Peter's lunch may be the occasion for him to think about Wert's wife, or about his own affair with Nausicaa, or about the crazy computer project on which he is engaged. The significance of the lunch episode depends upon where the reader has been before and where the reader goes next. In some readings "Afternoon" is a picaresque novel in which the characters seem to stay put while the reader wanders.

Sometimes there is only one path leading from a given episode; sometimes there are several. The author's control of the narrative is inversely proportional to the number of paths and the kinds of responses expected of the reader. A single path gives the author the same degree of control as a printed book—in fact, even more control, because the reader cannot flip pages or turn to the back of the book; the reader must simply hit return and go on. An episode with many paths offers the reader the opportunity to head in any of several directions, although the reader may only be aware of this freedom after he or she has returned to the episode many times. And even after visiting all the episodes, the reader has still not exhausted the writing space. The significance of the episodes changes depending upon the order of reading. At one point several characters are invited to tell about themselves. If they do this early in the reading, then their subsequent words and deeds will be measured against this history. Nausicaa, for example, who seems a benign presence, turns out to have been a drug addict and prostitute. If the reader comes upon the self-revelatory episodes late in the reading, then these episodes must be read as explanation and justification of what went before. In either case, we find ourselves invoking familiar literary structures in the effort to make sense of this electronic fiction. The difference is that both (contradictory) structures coexist in the same electronic space, and, at least after several readings, the reader becomes aware of this double presence, so that he or she must reflect on the difference between the two possible readings.

The presence or absence of paths changes the feel of a particular part of the fiction. Wherever the choices narrow to a single path, "Afternoon" becomes a conventional story: it imitates the narrow space of the printed book before broadening again into its "natural" electronic space. The capacity to imitate the printed book is one important way in which "Afternoon" makes its comment on the nature of reading. Each of its paths seems to be a mixture of the accidental and the inexorable. Paths can have narrative force, as when Peter tries to find out whether his wife and son have been in an automobile accident. Following this trajectory makes the story quite linear. Peter fights his way through various telephone calls, in an effort to get information, at the same time reticent to make the most direct calls, that is, to take the most direct path to the information he anticipates. As readers we must do the same: we must be careful about our answers at the end of each episode in order to stay with this narrative strand. A wrong answer will shunt us to another path from which it may be difficult to return to Peter's frantic calls. This is a perfect example of the way in which electronic fiction can take into itself the experience of reading. The need of the reader to struggle with the story mirrors the struggle that the character goes through. "Afternoon" becomes an allegory of the act of reading. The struggle for meaning is enacted by the characters in "Afternoon," which is by now a conventional theme of 20th-century literature. What is new is that the allegory is played out by the reader as he or she reads. "Afternoon" becomes the reader's story in this remarkable way. Readers experience the story as they read: their actions in calling forth the story, their desire to make the story happen and to make sense of what happens, are inevitably reflected in the story itself.

THE GEOMETRY OF INTERACTIVE FICTION

"Afternoon" is about the problem of its own reading. This will certainly be the problem that confronts us with all interactive fiction, at least in the early days of this new form. As an example of topographic writing, "Afternoon" asks us to consider how we are to appreciate the multiplicity of such writing. The writing space of "Afternoon" can be represented by a diagram with squares for the episodes and arrows for the links between episodes. The whole diagram is vast, since "Afternoon" has over 500 episodes and over 900 connections. A fragment of the space is shown below. (See Fig. 8.1.)

The reader never sees this diagrammed structure: the reader's experience of "Afternoon" is one-dimensional, as he or she follows paths from one episode to another. Instead, the reader must gain an intuition of the spatial structure as he or she proceeds in time. This task is rather like that of a mathematician who attempts to envision a four-dimensional object by looking at several projections in three dimensions. Each projection is a snapshot, and the snapshots must be synthesized to win a sense of the whole. For the reader of "Afternoon," each reading is one projection of the geometry of the whole; the whole is the sum of all the possible ways in which "Afternoon" may be read.

The geometry of electronic fiction need not be defined solely in terms of the plot. In "Afternoon," the important events seldom vary on different readings. Instead, it is the characters' reactions and interactions that vary.

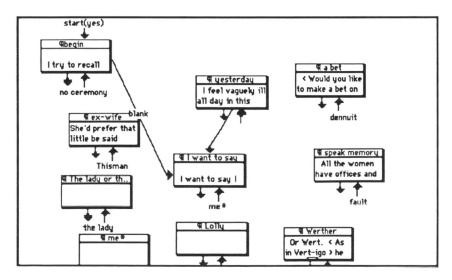

FIG. 8.1. "Afternoon" is a large network of linked episodes.

The electronic writer can exploit other organizing principles of modern printed fiction, such as the stream of consciousness of one character or the points of view of several characters. Linked rings of episodes would be particularly effective for presenting multiple points of view. "Afternoon" has what we might call a subspace in which Lolly and Nausicaa tell their stories, each in several episodes and each ending more or less where she began. There is also the possibility of narrating the same events from different points of view, a technique familiar from Faulkner's *The Sound and the Fury* and Durrell's *Alexandria Quartet*. In the electronic medium the reader can be given more degrees of freedom than is possible in print: he or she may be allowed to flip back and forth among episodes, comparing one narrator's version against the others'.

The author might choose to build a narrative hierarchy by presenting the same events, for example, from three points of view, where the first point of view is in some sense superior to the second and the second to the third. The author might think of these as the divine, the heroic, and the satiric perspectives. From the satiric perspective, events are a confusion, as we normally experience them, making only a provisional sense that dissolves again into chaos. Imagine the dramatic story of Oedipus, told from the perspective of the shepherd who failed to obey the order to kill baby Oedipus and instead gave him away. After many years, this well-meaning shepherd is brought before Oedipus the king, threatened, and made to reveal what he did with the baby. He is then released and left to ponder the horror of Oedipus' crime and his own revelation. From the heroic perspective, events take on greater clarity and urgency, as Oedipus himself would tell the story. The third, divine perspective is omniscient and also detached, for the heroic sense of engagement is lost. It is the story of Oedipus as narrated by Apollo. Our triple structure can be represented in three dimensions. (See Fig. 8.2.)

Each of the levels contains six episodes from one perspective, corresponding to the scenes of the play. The reader begins on the lower (the satiric) level, and the task is to break into a higher realm of understanding. In the preceding diagram, corresponding episodes at each level are linked. Thus, as the reader is visiting one episode on the satiric plane, he or she may succeed in jumping to the heroic plane and instantly see the same event in a new light. The divine level should clearly be harder to reach than the heroic, and yet its presentation of events might be so cold and crystalline that the reader may wonder whether attaining this level was in fact worth the effort. This geometry omits the choral odes which divide the scenes of Sophocles' play. We could include these and have them serve as foci where the change of point of view might occur. The odes, like operatic arias, often take place in a time that is outside the conventional time of the dramatic action, pulling the reader or listener away from the plot to reflect upon the significance of past and possible future action. They provide a perfect moment for a shift in point of view.

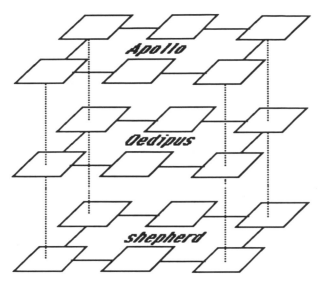

FIG 8.2. The story of Oedipus could be represented as an interactive structure with three levels of narration. Based on a figure from Bolter, 1985, p. 30 ©1985 Topic. Reprinted with permission.

In this Sophoclean structure, each level is in the same narrative mode: each tells a story in the first person. We can also imagine a structure in which each level contains a different mode of discourse—prose, drama, narrative poetry, lyric poetry, and so on. There is no need to limit the modes to fiction: the same experience could also be treated in historical prose and in scientific prose with mathematics. Each level would then be presenting a different aspect of written reality. The fictive level describes a man seated at a mahogany desk writing a letter; the poetic describes the scratch of the quill pen upon paper and the sound of the sand used to blot the ink; the historical discusses literacy in Victorian England; and the scientific explains how ink disperses into the pores of the paper. In the electronic organization the author can refract reality into a series of such perspectives without destroying the rhythm or comprehensibility of the text. Readers do not have to contend with all facets of the event at once; instead, the order in which they examine the various facets determines their experience of the text.

THE GAME OF LITERATURE

The preceding geometries are suggestions; many others are possible. They simply show how we might envision the spatial expression of a multiplicity of temporal experiences provided by any one electronic text. Electronic literature is not static, nor is it "timeless": it exists in "real time," as computer specialists call it, the time that the user passes in front of his or her terminal. The fiction realizes itself on the computer screen and then rolls or blinks out of sight and is gone. The reader might produce the same sequence of screens on the next day, but for any large structure of episodes, exact repetition is unlikely. As readers develop an aesthetic sense for this new medium, they may no longer care about perfect repetition or long preservation.

On the other hand, repetition and return take on new significance in interactive fiction, because in its own way the computer is capable of endless repetition. If the writer is clever, he or she can arrange it so that the reader seldom duplicates a previous fiction, but can always have something like it again. We may judge the success of a work by its ability to adapt to new readings and yet preserve its essence. It may be with readings as with dreams: important ones may not return, but they are never entirely lost either. Conversely we may judge works by their ability to defy categories—to have no essence and so to be different for each reading. In no case can the author in the electronic medium claim to have erected a monument more lasting than bronze; the author must instead delight in writing, like Archimedes, in sand (or silicon).

Playfulness is a defining quality of this new medium. Electronic literature will remain a game, just as all computer programming is a game. We have seen that such literature grows out of the computer games that are popular today. In video games, the kind depicting spacecraft and deadly robots, the player competes against the programmer, who has defined goals and put obstacles in the player's path. The emphasis is on the player, not the programmer, who is an anonymous employee of some software firm. Even in the simplest form of electronic fiction described above, the author/programmer is as important as the reader/player, and the relationship between author and reader may take a variety of forms: they may work cooperatively or competitively. No matter how competitive, the experience of reading in the electronic medium remains a game, rather than a combat, in the sense that it has no finality. The reader may win one day and lose the next. The computer erases the program and offers the reader a fresh start—all wounds healed. Anyone who has written a program knows that the computer has a genius for getting completely and hilariously off track. Fortunately, it is possible to drop everything and start over. This quality will carry over into electronic literature. Every reading of "Afternoon" can be a new afternoon, or the reader can choose to pick up the fiction where he or she left it in the last session. The impermanence of electronic literature cuts both ways: as there is no lasting success, there is also no failure that needs to last. By contrast, there is a solemnity at the center of printed literature—even comedy, romance, and satire—because of the immutability of the printed page.

THE TRADITION OF EXPERIMENT

Interactive fiction is both innovative and traditional. It is certainly new to automate the presentation of text, so that the reader's decisions are automatically registered and cause other words to appear. However, in disrupting the stability of the text, interactive fiction belongs in a tradition of experimental literature (if we may use this oxymoron) that has marked the 20th century—the era of modernism, futurism, Dada, surrealism, letterism, the nouveau roman, concrete poetry, and other movements of greater or lesser influence. (See Lanham, 1989.) The experiments of Dada, for example, were aimed at breaking down all structures of established art and literature, and in that breakdown the Dadaists worked in the same spirit as writers now work in the electronic medium. Jean Arp wrote that in his poems: "I tore apart sentences, words, syllables. I tried to break down the language into atoms, in order to approach the creative" (Grossman, 1971, p. 136). Tristan Tzara proposed a poetics of destruction, when he gave this recipe for creating a Dada poem: "To make a dadaist poem. Take a newspaper. Take a pair of scissors. Choose an article as long as you are planning to make your poem. Cut out the article. Then cut out each of the words that make up this article and put them in a bag. Shake it gently. Then take out the scraps one after the other in the order in which they left the bag. Copy conscientiously. The poem will be like you..." (Grossman, 1971, pp. 124-125).

Dada was an early and influential example of the modern will to experiment. The modern attack was often aimed at the conventions of the realistic novel that told its story with a clear and cogent rhythm of events. In the course of their attack, modern authors found themselves straining at the limitations of the printed page. Because the linear-hierarchical presentation of the printed book was so well suited to the conventions of plot and characters of the realistic novel, to attack the form of the novel was also to attack the technology of print. The French led the way with the nouveau roman and Philip Sollers and the Tel Quel group. From France and elsewhere, we have had programmed novels and aleatory novels. All these were instances of subversion: they worked from within, attempting to undercut the conventions of printed literature while themselves remaining printed books.

Most of the important literature of the 20th century has been accused of subversion. The avant-garde movements like Dada were never so radical as they claimed to be; they were instead extending or perhaps caricaturing the mainstream. Joyce, Virginia Woolf, Pound, T. S. Eliot, and others all participated in the breakdown of traditions of narrative prose and poetry; breaking with such traditions was the definition of being modern. Pound and Eliot set about to replace the narrative element in poetry with fragmented anecdotes or mythical paradigms. Joyce and Woolf devised new ways of structuring their works based on stream of consciousness or on multiple layers of topical and mythical organization. All of these writers were trying to set up new relationships between the moment-by-moment experience of reading a text and our perception of the organizing and controlling structures of the text. The surprising fact is that topographic writing in the space provided by the computer is a natural extension of their work. Topographic writing redefines the tradition of modernism for a new medium. To put it another way, modern authors have already been writing topographically, but they have been using the medium of print, which is not well suited to that mode of writing.

The experimentation with and fragmentation of the form of the novel is certainly older than modernism: it dates back at least to the 18th century. The whole tradition of experimentation needs now to be reconsidered in the light of the electronic medium, since each previous experiment in print suggests ways in which writing may now break free of the influence of print. In another sense all novels embody a struggle between the linear flow of the narrative and the associative trains of thought touched off by the narrative, and the electronic medium provides a new perspective on that struggle. The history of the novel itself will need to be rewritten, so that we understand works by authors from Laurence Sterne to Jorge Luis Borges not only as explorations of the limits of the printed page but also as models for electronic writing. It is as if these authors had been waiting for the computer to free them from print. And in fact, many of their works could be transferred to the electronic writing space and playfully reconstructed there. From this perspective, interactive fiction is the inevitable next step, like the take-off of an airplane that has been gaining speed on the runway. As with the speeding airplane, the moment of take-off for interactive fiction is a matter of definition.

STERNE AND THE NOVEL AS CONVERSATION

Readers have long recognized Sterne's *Tristram Shandy* as an assault on the form of the novel and its conventions of narration. The Russian formalist Victor Shklovsky pointed out more than 50 years ago that "[b]y violating the form [of the novel], [Sterne] forces us to attend to it; and, for him, this awareness of the form through its violation constitutes the content of the novel" (Shklovsky, "Sterne's Tristram Shandy: Stylistic Commentary," 1965, pp. 30-31; see also Rabkin, 1981). Shklovsky saw *Tristram Shandy* as an example of the way in which a novelist dislocates or distorts the order of events in a simple story in order to create a complex plot.

Any reading of Sterne's novel is necessarily a catalogue of the digressions from and dislocations of the events of Tristram's uneventful life. Tristram as narrator seldom lets us alone with the story: he is always breaking in to remind us that he is in fact writing his life story and to point out when he is digressing, omitting, or delaying. He does his best to remove us from the action. There are stories within stories, and characters often read aloud from books and papers. Tristram explains that "... when a man is telling a story in the strange way I do mine, he is obliged continually to be going backwards and forwards to keep all tight together in the reader's fancy ..." (Sterne, 1965, Book 6, Chapter 33, p. 351). In fact, the jumps do not keep all tight in the reader's fancy. The wandering style of narration is reflected in Book 7 in the storyline, when Tristram sets out on a hasty trip through France in his effort to avoid death. The journey is as filled with delays and indirection as the narrative itself. Yet, despite all the obstacles he seems to impose, Tristram is not hostile to his readers. He claims to establish a relationship of equality, to overcome the formal and one-sided relationship between author and reader assumed by the conventional novel:

> Writing, when properly managed (as you may be sure I think mine is) is but a different name for conversation: As no one, who knows what he is about in good company, would venture to talk all;—so no author, who understands the just boundaries of decorum and good-breeding, would presume to think all: The truest respect which you can pay to a reader's understanding, is to halve this matter amicably, and leave him something to imagine, in his turn, as well as yourself. For my own part, I am eternally paying him compliments of this kind, and do all that lies in my power to keep his imagination as busy as my own." (Book 2, Chapter 11, p. 83)

As narrator, then, Tristram pays readers the compliment of expecting them to help construct the novel as they read. The more the narrator digresses and distances us from the story, the closer we feel to the narrator himself, as if we were conversing and not simply reading.

Tristram Shandy is not only an attack on the conventions of the novel as a coherent narrative of events; it is also an assault on the conventions of presentation, on the technology of writing and printing. Sometimes the assault on the book is physical. Chapter 24 of Book 4 is missing: Tristram claims he has torn it out and proceeds in Chapter 25 to tell us what was lost. The pages are misnumbered to indicate the loss. Other characters go further in their mistreatment of the printed page. One learned doctor recommends wrapping a burn in a "soft sheet of paper just come off the press" (Book 4, Chapter 28, p. 246). Later Tristram loses his "remarks" (his manuscript) by leaving them in a carriage that he has sold. He returns to discover that a woman is using the papers to curl her hair, and so his remarks are twisted this way and that. "[A]nd when they are published ...," Tristram adds, "[t]hey will be worse twisted still" (Book 7, Chapter 38, p. 405). Tristram involves his reader not only in the construing of the narrative, but in the very making of the book. Omissions in the text are indicated by asterisks, and Tristram turns the omissions into games. Sometimes he leaves one asterisk for each letter and so creates a code for the reader to decipher. Occasionally he leaves a blank space where the reader may add his or her own words. He challenges the reader to do precisely what a reader can never succeed in doing—to write in the printed text.

It has long been pointed out that *Tristram Shandy* seems to anticipate the work of 20th-century writers who have brought the novel to its end. We can now add that *Tristram Shandy* anticipates electronic writing in important ways. Sterne is a topographic writer, whose achievement is more remarkable because he works in the intractable medium of print. By insisting on a conversation with his reader, Sterne is contravening the natural use of print. In a playful way, he is inviting the reader to give up his or her safe status as reader and to share responsibility for the narrative. Electronic writing puts its reader in the same position. But Sterne can only pretend to offer the reader a chance to participate in the construction of the text. Electronic writing can demand that the reader participate, for, as in "Afternoon," no text may be given until the reader calls it forth. Electronic writing comes much closer to the conversation between author and reader that Tristam imagines. The reason is not that the computer is itself a human partner, but rather that it gives a greater presence to the author than does the printed page. The author is present in the electronic network of episodes that he or she creates and through which the reader moves along associative paths.

Tristram Shandy's conversation too proceeds by association. As Shklovsky puts it,

> [the novel's] diverse material, which is augmented by extensive excerpts from the works of various pedants, would undoubtedly tear the novel to bits were it not drawn together by crisscrossing motifs. A stated motif is never fully developed, never actually realized, but is only recalled from time to time; its fulfillment is continually put off to a more and more remote time. Yet its very presence in all the dimensions of the novel ties the episodes together. (Shklovsky, 1965, p. 40)

Already a large conceptual network, *Tristram Shandy* could in fact be represented as a structure in the computer's writing space, in which each chapter was a topic and in which chapters or runs of chapters were linked according to their several motifs. The reader could then examine the effect of Sterne's digressions by taking alternative routes through the text. The result would be a critical demonstration of the power of association to organize across the linear dimension imposed by the paged book. The network could serve as a critical tool for understanding the novel in a new way. It could also be used to invite the reader to participate in extending the novel, either by adding more connections to the network or by adding chapters to explore motifs that Sterne himself left dangling. *Tristram Shandy* is a fictional structure that is designed to be endless, for the end is death, which Tristram and his author can only seek to postpone by continuing to write. In the electronic writing space, the reader too could participate in that oddly heroic act of postponement.

THE HYPERTEXTS OF JAMES JOYCE

In all modern fiction, there is a tension between the linear experience of reading and the structure of allusion and reference, but critics have recognized that this tension is particularly strong in the later works of James Joyce. Michael Groden explains how *Ulysses* embodies two different conceptions of fiction. The book is a novel, the story of a day in Dublin and the meeting of Stephen Daedalus and Leopold Bloom; it is also a "symbolistic" poem, a pattern of allusions to previous literary and cultural texts. The narrative carries us forward from one incident to the next in that eventful day of June 16, 1904, while the references and allusions pull us away from the narrative flow. According to Groden, Joyce first conceived of *Ulysses* as a more conventional novel, although with an unusual style including both third person narration and first person monologue, a style that would focus upon the minds of Bloom and Stephen Daedalus. Later Joyce began to complicate his text and to expand the style to include the thoughts of other persons as well as omniscient narrative comments. In the final sections of *Ulysses*, Joyce was in fact developing the encyclopedic technique that he would use in *Finnegans Wake*. As Joyce was finishing the last and most allusive episodes, he returned to the first sections and added allusions there too. But he did not completely eliminate the earlier style. He left portions of the earlier novel, perhaps because he wanted the reader to experience not only the finished work but its entire genesis as well. "He only partly reworked the episodes, however, as if to present *Ulysses* as a palimpsest involving all three stages" (Groden, 1977, p. 4).

The word "palimpsest" brings us back to the technology of writing. A palimpsest is a medieval manuscript in which the pages have been whitened and reused, so that one text sits on top of another. In a medieval palimpsest, one text replaces another; the reader is not supposed to see the earlier text. But in *Ulysses* Joyce has written a second text over the first without bothering to white it out: we see and are meant to see both. Moreover, in *Ulysses* it is not clear to the reader which writing is the overlay. Groden can distinguish older and newer layers of text because he has studied Joyce's drafts and letters. The final printed edition is seamless; it may be showing us its entire development, but we cannot read that development.

What the reader finds is a self-referential text. Even without the work of disentangling the genesis, the reader must still move back and forth through the book in order to appreciate the complex relationships of its parts. *Ulysses* is not a book that can be understood by reading straight through or by listening to a sensitive reading. Kenner has argued that Joyce was aware of the technology at his disposal and that *Ulysses* was designed to be read in print:

> ... the text of *Ulysses* is not organized in memory and unfolded in time, but both organized and unfolded in what we may call technological space: on printed pages for which it was designed from the beginning. The reader explores its discontinuities at whatever pace he likes; he makes marginal notes; he turns back whenever he chooses to an earlier page, without destroying the continuity of something that does not press on, but will wait until he resumes. (Kenner, 1962, p. 35)

Kenner is saying that Joyce's writing is topographic and that topographic writing requires a technology that permits the reader to move freely through the text. This is an important insight, although Kenner is too generous in his judgment of print as that technology. Print technology was all that Joyce had available. Joyce, Kenner adds, is careful "to reproduce in his text the very quality of print, its reduction of language to a finite number of interchangeable and permutable parts" (Kenner, p. 36). However, the interchangeable parts of print technology are merely letters, and they are interchangeable only during the production of the text, not during its reading. In print, production is separate from reading. Joyce's topical units range in size from words to whole sections, and the permutations of these units are part of the reader's moment-by-moment experience of the text. How easy is it for the reader to find a reference in a printed edition of *Ulysses*? How can one find all the references to Troy or Tolstoy or Hermes Trismegistus? Flipping through the numbered, standardized pages of the edition is certainly easier than making one's way through a manuscript or a papyrus roll, but it is still a matter of labor and chance. The reader is bound to miss many of the references that Joyce worked into the fabric of his text. Furthermore, there was no convenient way in a printed edition for Joyce to represent to his reader the genetic development of his text, which Groden discovered by patient scholarship.

The question of genesis becomes even more important in *Finnegans Wake*. In its final form, this text is so thick with linguistic distortions and allusions that the novel seems completely lost in the poem. Often we seem to be reading sentences that have a conventional narrative sense, but we cannot see what that sense is. Scholars have been able to chip away layer upon layer of revision and discover that much of the *Finnegans Wake* does have a storyline. Joyce started at least some sections with a kind of prose paraphrase, to which he kept adding greater complexity. Moving backwards through the drafts (as we can do, for example, for the Anna Livia Plurabelle section; see Joyce, 1960) gives us the uncanny experience of watching the text resolve itself into a conventional meaning. But the reader who has only the final printed version cannot imagine this genesis. He is forced to read *Finnegans Wake* along the final temporal layer and then try to work his way down through the layers of allusion.

Joyce places an enormous burden on his reader. The superstructure of the final text alone is taxing; the layers of genesis are even more so. For that reason it is not quite right to claim that Joyce is seeking to reproduce in his text the quality of print. It is true that Joyce employs most every technique available in the repertory of print: like Sterne before him, he experiments with the layout of text, or recapitulates the history of those techniques, by using footnotes, side notes, various styles of type, and even by including musical notation in his text. But Joyce's narrative strategy is too complex and too dynamic for the medium of print.

Joyce could not have anticipated the electronic medium, but his works would be a rich source of experimentation for writers in the new medium. Students of Joyce could, for example, begin to map the network of references in a chapter of *Ulysses* or *Finnegans Wake*. Each sentence or even each word might be made a topical unit in the electronic writing space. These units would first be connected in temporal order, as they appear in print; further links could then be drawn to indicate allusions and parallels. The result would be a massive network that the scholar and even the casual reader (can there be such a creature for *Ulysses* or *Finnegans Wake*?) could traverse in a variety of ways. The reader could begin by reading the text in temporal order and then choose to follow a reference to some other part of the book. As new allusions are discovered, they would be added to the network. This process of discovery would be almost, but not quite, endless. In the theoretical limit, the result would be an interactive text that contained within it all the possible readings of that chapter. Working one's way through this network would not be the same experience as reading a printed edition of Joyce. It would instead be the reading of readings—both watching and becoming the ideal reader of Joyce in the act of reading, a literary and a literary-critical experience at the same time.

BORGES AND EXHAUSTION IN PRINT

Jorge Luis Borges' most famous short piece is perhaps the "Library of Babel" from his *Ficciones*. It is a fantasy in which the human race lives in a gigantic library: the library is composed of an indefinite number of cubicles connected by stairs—something like a drawing by M. C. Escher. The shelves of each cubicle are lined with books that, as the narrator, himself an inhabitant of the library, explains:

> contain all the possible combinations of the twenty-odd orthographic symbols (whose number, though vast, is not infinite); that is, everything which can be expressed, in all languages. Everything is there: the minute history of the future,

the autobiographies of the archangels, the faithful catalogue of the Library, thousands and thousands of false catalogues, a demonstration of the fallacy of these catalogues, a demonstration of the fallacy of the true catalogue, ..., the veridical account of your death, a version of each book in all languages, the interpolations of every book in all books. (Borges, 1962, p. 83)

The narrator goes on to describe the crazy and often desperate reactions of the inhabitants as they come to realize the implications of living in a universal library of random typography. What is this library, after all, but the exhaustion of human symbolic thought? All of the combinations of Gutenberg's letters have been realized and now sit on the shelves waiting for readers. There is nothing left to be written, only discovered, but discovery is impossible because of the crushing number of nonsense books that overwhelm those that are supposed to have meaning. The inhabitants of this world, whom Borges calls "librarians," wander about the cubicles looking for sensible books, but they are helpless before the logic of permutation. Their library is the ultimate static text; the frozen technique of the printed word has become the universe. The exhaustion of writing also means that time has stopped for these readers. The librarians exist in an eschatological moment in which there is nothing left to wait for, because nothing new can be described.

In his other *Ficciones* too, Borges explores worlds of exhausted possibilities or extreme conditions. John Barth has characterized Borges' work itself as the "literature of exhaustion" (see Barth, 1967). The *Ficciones* are tiny pieces without much plot or characterization, pieces that are utterly insignificant by the standards of the 19th-century novel. With Borges we have the sense that a long literary tradition is breaking down, that the novel and perhaps the monograph too are used up. Borges suggests that our culture can no longer produce novels and offers instead anemic book reports and brief descriptions of freakish characters and fantastic worlds. The theme of exhaustion applies not only to literary form, but also to the human condition, precisely because Borges treats reading and writing as synonymous with life itself.

Borges is intrigued by the fact that a frozen text cannot change to reflect possibilities that unfold in time. "An Examination of the Work of Herbert Quain" is the literary obituary of a writer who tried to liberate his texts from linear reading and static interpretation. Quain's novel *April March* is nothing less than an interactive fiction. It consists of thirteen chapters or sections representing nine permutations of the events of three evenings. The novel is therefore nine novels in one, each with a different tone. Borges tells us the work is a game, adding that "[w]hoever reads the sections in chronological order ... will lose the peculiar savor of this strange book" (Borges, 1962, p. 76). He even gives us a tree diagram of the novel's structure.

The longer and more elaborate "Garden of Forking Paths" is a detective story. At its center the story contains a description of a Chinese novel, a novel that seeks to explain and in its way to defy time. It was thought that the author Ts'ui Pên had retired from public life with two objects: to write a book and to build a labyrinthine garden, but the Sinologist Stephen Albert has discovered that these two goals were really one: that the book *was* the garden. The manuscript Ts'ui Pên left behind was not, as it seemed, "a shapeless mass of contradictory rough drafts" (p. 96), but instead a ramifying tree of all possible events. Albert explains:

In all fiction, when a man is faced with alternatives he chooses one at the expense of the others. In the almost unfathomable [work of] Ts'ui Pên, he chooses—simultaneously—all of them. He thus creates various futures, various times which start others that will in their turn branch out and bifurcate in other times. This is the cause of the contradictions in the novel. (p. 98)

Albert goes on to explain that "[t]he Garden of Forking Paths is an enormous game, or parable, in which the subject is time" (p. 99). Ts'ui Pên "believed in an infinite series of times, in a dizzily growing, ever spreading network of diverging, converging and parallel times" (p. 100). Albert does not make clear to us how these multiple versions were organized in manuscript. But the metaphor of the garden suggests a luxuriant growth of textual possibilities. Both that suggestion and the story itself are abruptly closed off as Albert himself is murdered by the narrator of the story. The abrupt ending stands in contrast with the novel as Albert describes it—a novel that refuses to close off its bifurcating paths and come to a single definite end. "The Garden of Forking Paths" suggests that the end of a text is always arbitrary or tentative. As Stuart Moulthrop has put it, "[t]he story could turn out otherwise, and in a sense does—but that sense cannot be realized in a fiction committed to conclusive definition and singular seriality" (see Moulthrop, 1988, p. 7-8; see also *Reading for the Plot* by Peter Brooks, 1984, pp. 317-319).

For Borges literature is exhausted because it is committed to a conclusive ending, to a single storyline and denouement. To renew literature one would have to write multiply, in a way that embraced possibilities rather than closed them off. Borges can imagine such a fiction, but he cannot produce it. The *Ficciones* are themselves conventional pieces of prose, meant to be read page by page. Yet the works he describes, the novels of Herbert Quain or the *Garden of Forking Paths*, belong in another writing space altogether. Borges himself never had available to him an electronic space, in which the text can comprise a network of diverging, converging, and parallel times. He could not see that the literature of exhaustion in print by no means exhausts the electronic medium.

THE NOVEL AS PROGRAM

There are so many experimental novels and novelists today that any choice among them is arbitrary. The will to experiment even extends to children's fiction: books in the series entitled "Choose Your Own Adventure" or "Find Your Fate" offer young readers something like the computerized adventure game. Each book contains a garden of forking paths, from among which the reader must choose. At the bottom of page 18, one may read: "If you choose to risk the curse, turn to page 29. If you press on down the tunnel, turn to page 42" (Wenk, 1984, p. 18). Thus, the book sacrifices the linear order of pages to allow for multiple reading. There are many of these programmed novels, some for adult readers. The novel *Rayuela* by the Latin American writer Cortázar offers two possible reading orders: one a linear narrative and the other a satirical comment on that narrative. Other writers who have experimented with fragmented narrative include Raymond Queneau, Italo Calvino, and Michel Butor. (On Queneau and Calvino as forerunners of electronic writing, see Paulson, 1989, pp. 296-299. On Michel Butor see Grant, 1973, pp. 27-32.)

One experiment seems to have achieved an anonymous notoriety: everyone seems to have heard of this work, although very few know its title or author. Marc Saporta's *Composition No. 1* was published in France in 1962, and the English translation, a work consisting of about 150 unnumbered pages, appeared in the following year. (See Sharon Spencer's analysis in *Space, Time, and Structure in the Modern Novel*, 1971, pp. 85-87, 209-211.) This fiction consists of loose sheets of paper, each containing one or a few paragraphs printed on one side. The sheets (at least in the English version) are somewhat larger than octavo, larger than a deck of playing cards, to which the author compares them. In the introduction, which is printed on the box and also appears as one of the pages, the author explains:

> The reader is requested to shuffle these pages like a deck of cards, to cut, if he likes, with his left hand, as at a fortuneteller's. The order the pages then assume will orient X's fate. For time and the order of events control a man's life more than the nature of such events.... A life is composed of many elements. But the number of possible compositions is infinite. (Saporta, 1963)

Composition No. 1 consists of passages in the story of X, a character we learn about only through his reflection in the events and other characters of the narrative. X, an unsavory figure, is married to Marianne, has a mistress named Dagmar, and also rapes a girl named Helga. He apparently steals to support the compulsions of his neurotic wife, and he possibly dies in an automobile accident. By way of redemption, he seems to have played some role in the French resistance, although this strand in the story is the most obscure.

It is Saporta's tour de force that the reader is able to figure out this much from the experience of reading the pages one at a time. Each page is necessarily only a vignette. Even for a contemporary reader, accustomed to fragmentation and suspension, the natural impulse is to turn the page in order to find out what happens next. But the next page bears no immediate relation to the previous action. This fiction is not static: on most pages there is action or at least dialogue that promises to advance our knowledge of the characters. We get the impression that we are reading pages torn from a conventional novel. We find ourselves searching for their "proper" order—that is, for an order that makes chronological and causal sense. We become literary detectives, since the pieces in this puzzle are topical elements in a written text. Connecting these topics reminds us of papyrology or other scholarly detective work with the fragmentary remains of ancient writings. It is always the papyrologist's hope that newly found fragments will turn out to be part of a known or, better still, unknown, but identifiable ancient work—that both the text and its context will be revealed. We feel that hope as we read Saporta. Indeed, to call the work "fragmented" is to assume that it was originally whole, that the fragments belong in one order.

As 20th-century readers, we are prepared for the focus to shift from one page of a fiction to another. But we want to find a reason for such shifts. Each time we shuffle the pages, some intriguing juxtapositions happen by chance. It is a characteristic of our literary imagination that we can so often provide an interpretation for these juxtapositions. Whatever order falls out is a lesson in the nature of reading. We become active readers, fashioning texts as we shuffle pages. Saporta's trick makes us uniquely aware of the effect of narrative order upon the reading experience, as we see in practice what we are always told in theory. There is not one possible order for the episodes but a broad class of acceptable orders, each producing its own literary effect. Some orders are better than a simple chronological story, and many are worse. The number of reading orders for Saporta's composition is not infinite, as the author claims. If there are 150 pages in the set, then the number of possible presentations is 150!—a number with 263 digits, but still finite. *Composition No. 1* has necessary limits: as Sharon Spencer points out, in every possible rearrangement of its pages we will still have a portrait of X, the silent, second character in each fragmentary scene (Spencer, 1971, p. 211).

Composition No. 1 is an exercise in choice within a large but still limited fictional universe; indeed, it is a tiny universe in comparison to Borges' Library. Saporta's universe is one of French existential romanticism, fascinated by the interplay of chance and fate. Moreover, Saporta seems to be working in a different direction from the one we have been considering for topographic writing in the computer. The author of *Composition No. 1* apparently disavows responsibility for the structure of his work. In seeming to deny form, he displaces the formal responsibility onto his reader. In fact,

Composition No. 1 has form; otherwise, it could not remain recognizable as a work of fiction. There are loose formal relations that exist among the pages when read in any order—relations established, for example, by the comparison of two female characters. Moreover, each paragraph or page is itself a conventional formal structure. Saporta's style is characterized by precise images and rhetorical effects: on each page, not a single word seems out of place. The precision on the page is in marked contrast to the disorder that prevails between pages and requires a different strategy of interpretation. On the page we may assume that the author is in complete control, and we may examine every mark of punctuation for nuances of meaning. Moving between two pages, we can only ask ourselves more general questions: how, for example, did the author arrange the beginning and ending of each page to make them fit together smoothly in any order?

Saporta's experiment in chance fiction seems to be an inevitable step in the exhaustion of printed literature. When all the other methods of fragmenting the novel have been tried, what remains but to tear the pages out of the book one by one and hand them to the reader? From the ideal of perfect structural control, Saporta brings us to the abdication of control. But we can also see in Saporta's experiment, and in others like it, not only the end of printed fiction, but also a bridge to the literature of the electronic medium.

MULTIPLE READING

Composition No. 1 brings us back to "Afternoon," for Saporta's work is an "Afternoon" under the limitations that print imposes. Each page of *Composition No. 1* is a topographic unit, like an episode of "Afternoon" as it appears on the screen. In both fictions, the burden of constructing the text is thrown back upon the reader. And in both cases the reader struggles to make narrative sense of the episodes as they present themselves: to construct from these disordered episodes a story in which characters act with reasonable and explicit motives. In *Composition No. 1* we may resort to stacking the pages in piles. In "Afternoon" the medium itself resists that solution, since we cannot get at the episodes except by typing responses, and even then the episodes appear only one at a time.

If we put *Composition No.1* and "Afternoon" side by side, we see all the more clearly how our desire for a story has been fostered by thousands of years of reading in manuscript and print. When we read and write in these older technologies, we are compelled to narrow the possibilities into a single narrative. We have not yet learned to read and write "multiply," as Stuart Moulthrop has described it (Moulthrop,1988), in part because our technologies of literacy have suggested just the opposite: that we must read and write linearly. To read multiply is to resist the temptation to close off possible courses of action; it is to keep open multiple explanations for the same event or character. It is an almost impossible task for the reader to remain open in a medium as perfected as that of print. Saporta must tear his novel apart in order to resist the perfection of print, and still our first impulse is to try to put the novel back together.

"Afternoon," on the other hand, does openly and with ease what experimental writers in print could do only with great difficulty. It offers a narrative that encompasses contradictory possibilities. In "Afternoon" an automobile accident both does and does not occur; the narrator does and does not lose his son; he does and does not have a love affair. The story itself does and does not end:

> Closure is, as in any fiction, a suspect quality, although here it is made manifest. When the story no longer progresses, or when it cycles, or when you tire of the paths, the experience of reading it ends. Even so, there are likely to be more opportunities than you think there are at first. A word which doesn't yield the first time you read a section may take you elsewhere if you choose it when you encounter the section again; and sometimes what seems a loop, like memory, heads off again in another direction.
>
> There is no simple way to say this.

There is no simple way to say this in the linear writing of print. But "Afternoon" embodies the idea of openness with utter simplicity. What is unnatural in print becomes natural in the electronic medium and will soon no longer need saying at all, because it can be shown.

All our topographic writers in print (Sterne, James Joyce, Borges, Cortázar, Saporta) are "difficult" writers, and the difficulty is that they challenge the reader to read multiply. They call to the reader's attention the painful contrast between the temporal flow of narrated events and the interruptions and reversals that the act of writing imposes upon those events. All their experimental works are self-consciously concerned with the problem of writing. That concern is shown by the difficult relationship between the narrator and text, between the text and its reader, or both. The difficulty in writing (and therefore in reading) appears with Tristram Shandy, who is always getting further behind experience as he writes, and again and again in the 20th century. Saporta and Cortázar must give special instructions to their readers. *Finnegans Wake* may well be the most demanding book that has ever been published and critically received. In each case, the printed fiction must work against its medium in order to be topographic. There is a conflict between the printed volume as a frame and the text that is enframed. The frame is not adequate to contain and delimit the text, which is constantly threatening to spill out of its container.

By contrast, the computer provides a frame that gives way as the text strains against it; the stubbornness of the printed book suddenly disappears. In "Afternoon" the margins "yield" to the reader. The elements of the text are no longer fragments of a prior whole, but instead form a space of shifting possibilities. In this shifting electronic space, writers will need a new concept of structure. In place of a closed and unitary structure, they must learn to conceive of their text as a structure of possible structures. The writer must practice a kind of second-order writing, creating coherent lines for the reader to discover without closing off the possibilities prematurely or arbitrarily. This writing of the second order will be the special contribution of the electronic medium to the history of literature.

MULTIPLE WRITING

The computer gives the reader the opportunity to touch the text itself, an opportunity never available in print, where the text lies on a plane inaccessible to the reader. Readers of a printed book can write over or deface the text, but they cannot write in it. In the electronic medium readers cannot avoid writing the text itself, since every choice they make is an act of writing. The author of "Afternoon" wrote the prose and poetry for each episode, and he fashioned electronic structures of expectation and fulfillment on analogy with the static structures of printed fiction. But in giving the reader a role in realizing those structures, he has also ceded some of his traditional responsibility as author. This sharing of responsibility points the way in which electronic writing will continue to develop: we can envision an electronic fiction in which the reader is invited to alter existing episodes and links and add new ones. In this way the reader becomes a second author, who can then hand the changed text over to other readers for the same treatment. Electronic fiction can operate anywhere along the spectrum from rigid control by the author to full collaboration between author and reader. The promise of this new medium is to explore all the ways in which the reader can participate in the making of the text. Stuart Moulthrop suggests that the reader should be "... invited not just to enter a garden of forking paths, but to expand and revise the ground plan at will. This would cause a substantial shift in the balance of authority, one with enormous implications for the idea of literature itself; but it would nonetheless be a logical development of writing in the electronic medium" (Moulthrop, 1988, p. 16; see also Joyce, 1988).

The reader's intervention may come at any level of the electronic text. We have been considering fixed episodes and their connections, but the reader could also intervene to change the text itself. Such intervention could begin with simple letter substitution and typographic changes, perhaps under constraints programmed by the author. Letter substitutions can change words into other words or into nonsense that may suggest several words at once. Typography can be altered to make the text visually more exciting. Such changes too have been prefigured by writers in print. Mallarmé with his spatial poems such as "Coup de dès" and Apollinaire with his *calligrammes* were followed by the Dadaists, by LeMaître, and more recently by the writers of "concrete" poetry, who deployed letters and words in defiance of the conventions of lines and strophes (Solt, 1970, p. 8; see also Seaman, 1981 and Winspur, 1985). Concrete poetry too was an expression of the growing dissatisfaction with the medium of print in the 20th century. Concrete poetry too belongs in the computer; indeed, the computer makes possible truly kinetic poetry, a poetry in which letters and words can dance across the screen before the reader's eyes.

The poet William Dickey has already begun to create interactive poems. In "Heresy: A Hyperpoem," words, images, and icons compete on the screen for the reader's attention. (See Fig. 8.3.) The poem is a network of many screens, and the reader moves from one screen to others by activating one of the snowflake-shaped icons. Each screen is a different arrangement of verbal text and image; each vigorously asserts its visual identity. The typography of this hypertext encourages the reader to examine and savor each screen before activating an icon to move on. Sometimes the verbal text penetrates the graphic image, as it does in the following example. Sometimes the spatial

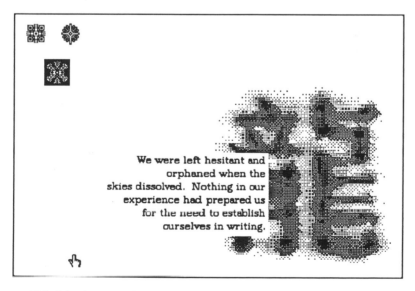

FIG. 8.3. A screen from "Heresy: A Hyperpoem" by William Dickey, reprinted with the kind permission of the author.

arrangement of text against the white background reminds us of the experiments of Mallarmé or LeMaître.

In "Heresy," as in "Afternoon," each textual unit is static; the reader sets the hypertext in motion by moving between fixed units. In future kinetic poems, however, the reader might also intervene to control the speed and direction or the way in which words coalesce and divide. He or she may participate in the reordering of the ultimate constituents of writing—letters, words, and graphic symbols. The reordering of such symbols *is* writing: it is all that any writer can ever do. This insight, which has been laboriously demonstrated and violently contested in the printed literature of the 20th century, becomes a simple and unavoidable fact in the electronic medium. Multiple reading passes inevitably into multiple writing.

Electronic fiction is technologically complicated in that it requires a computer and the sophisticated arrangement of text and graphics on a videoscreen. But it is conceptually simple—simpler than writing for print, where the writer must always force his or her text into a single line of argument or narrative. The computer frees the writer from the now tired artifice of linear writing, but the price of this new freedom for the writer is that the writer must allow the reader to intervene in the writing space.

Chapter
9

Critical Theory
and the New Writing Space

Electronic writing forces us to recast the familiar questions of literary criticism and theory by redefining both the critical object (the text) and the act of reading itself. The coming of the new technology will be felt by all the various communities of readers in our culture: from traditional readers (still the vast majority) to post-modern theorists. In a curious way electronic writing seems likely to end the recent and sometimes bitter debate between traditionalists and contemporary theorists. For the traditional reader electronic writing offers little comfort: it will in fact confirm much of what the deconstructionists and others have been saying about the instability of the text and decreasing authority of the author. Yet electronic writing will at the same time take much of the sting out of deconstruction. As it restores a theoretical innocence to the making of literary texts, electronic writing will require a simpler, more positive literary theory.

TECHNOLOGY AND CRITICISM

Long tradition assigns to good literature the qualities of stability, monumentality, and authority. Works of literature are monuments, and the author who creates monuments is, as the etymology suggests, an authority. If a text is regarded as mimetic, the author deserves credit for the ability to represent nature faithfully. Homer and Shakespeare show us what people were and are "really like" qualities of human nature that have not changed from their day to ours. If a text is regarded as an emotional expression, then the author deserves praise for his depth of feeling, his "lively sensibility," as Wordsworth

147

put it. These literary values date back centuries and are still widely held today: they constitute a status quo from which radical theories of literature diverge. For our purposes, however, it is important to remember that the values of stability, monumentality, and authority have always been interpreted in terms of the contemporary technology of handwriting or printing.

As early as the fifth century B.C., Greek poets and historians stressed the power of writing to fix ideas, to extend human memory. The history of Herodotus would prevent the wars between the Greeks and Persians from being forgotten; a written epic poem would preserve the glorious deeds of Alexander the Great. (Alexander lamented the fact that there was no poet of Homer's authority to sing his story.) The text was regarded as a monument to the deeds and actors it described. And if the Greeks were concerned about the immortality of the subject, the Roman poets seem to have been just as concerned about the immortality of the author. It was Horace who said he had erected a monument more lasting than bronze. Horace's claim was a motif in Latin poetry, and we have embarrassing examples of the claim of immortality made for works that did not survive. Catullus made this claim for the poem of his colleague Cinna: not only has Cinna's work perished, but Catullus himself barely survived the neglect of the Middle Ages. Catullus and Horace trusted flimsy rolls of papyrus to preserve their poems indefinitely. And even this technology showed that text could be preserved indefinitely, although not with complete accuracy, by recopying rolls that had deteriorated.

The Latin language has given us the words "author" and "authority." Certainly in the first century A.D. and later, the Romans regarded their traditional authors (Virgil, Cicero, Livy) with nostalgia and reverence. They studied, excerpted, and imitated these authorities. The appeal to written authority was perhaps even stronger in the Middle Ages with the somewhat more durable technology of parchment, particularly of course the appeal to the Bible and the Church fathers. But the monument could not be perfectly fixed: scribal errors tended to alter the text over centuries. Serious consideration of the transmission of texts began in the Renaissance with scholars like Lorenzo Valla, who were trying to restore authoritative texts of the ancients by separating out interpolations and false ascriptions.

The printing press preserved texts with greater accuracy than before—both ancient texts, as restored by Renaissance scholars, and texts by contemporary authors. The press has also strengthened the author's claim to authority, as the technology and economics of printing helped to widen the gulf between the author and his or her readers. Because printing a book is a costly and laborious task, few readers have the opportunity to become published authors. An author is a person whose words are faithfully copied and sent around the literary world, whereas readers are merely the audience for those words. The distinction meant less in the age of manuscripts, when "publication" was less of an event and when the reader's own notes and glosses had the same status as the text itself. Any reader could decide to cross over and become an author: one simply sat down and wrote a treatise or put one's notes in a form for others to read. Once the treatise was written, there was no difference between it and the works of other "published" writers, except that more famous works existed in more copies. However, there was a great difference between a manuscript and a printed edition of that manuscript. For most kinds of writing, the printed copy had more authority because of its visual simplicity, regularity, and reproducibility. As the author in print became more distant, less accessible to the reader, the author's words became harder to dismiss. In the later Renaissance, scientific writers in print called old authorities into question, and they did so by setting themselves up as new authorities. They published works meant to replace the outdated works of their predecessors: Vesalius sought to be the new Galen, Copernicus to replace Ptolemy.

The audiences for popular and "elite" literature both expanded gradually in the first 300 years of printing, and then rapidly in the last two centuries. This expansion, together with the abolition of patronage, has further enhanced the authority of the author. Today, a successful author's readers are dispersed throughout his or her country or indeed throughout the world and so have a variety of cultural backgrounds. At least since the 18th century, successful authors have been celebrities, whom we honor not simply for their power to entertain, but also for their presumed insight into the human condition. It is a curious notion, but one that we take for granted today: an American novelist is allowed, indeed expected, to pronounce on, say, race relations in her country; a German on the dangers of right-wing extremists in his; a Latin American author on the repressive governments in that region. Part of the explanation is that 19th-century critics believed that poets had special vision-ary powers: that belief carried over into our times, and the poet's vision is now supposed apply to important social and political questions. The technology of print helps to sanction this belief. Well-known writers can get their opinions on almost any topic into print, and the act of printing itself makes those opinions worthy of our attention.

The technology of printing has changed our view of the poem as well as the poet. In the first half of this century, the influential New Criticism conceived of a poem in terms appropriate to a printed text—self-sufficient, perfect, and untouchable. In a good poem not a word or comma should be out of place, just as a good typographer insists that a page be perfect before it is printed. What the New Criticism made explicit was an implicit assumption of all writing in the age of printing. Through the technology of printing, the author and the editor exercise absolute control over the text: nothing they do can be undone after publication. Since everything on the page is part of the author's design, it is natural to assume that even the smallest details are part of the poem's meaning.

TECHNOLOGY AND THE LITERARY CANON

It is still popular in this late age of print to believe in the enduring, "timeless" quality of great works of literature—to believe that such works define our cultural ideals and therefore to argue in a favor of a canon of such works. Literary theorists have recently made an issue of the canon, examining how canons have formed in the last few hundred years of Western culture and why certain works and authors have been included or excluded. In general, these theorists dislike the idea of a canon, and they particularly dislike recent Western canons because of the alleged bias against minority and third-world writers. (See, for example, the special issue of *Critical Inquiry* edited by von Hallberg, 1983.) Traditionalists defend the canon as containing the best work of a tradition with which every educated reader should be familiar. What they approve of is exactly what the critics decry: that the canon tells us whom we must read and whom we can read for pleasure or omit altogether. For the traditionalist, authors in the canon are central to our culture; other authors are relegated to the margins.

This debate over the canon is really a debate over the purpose and nature of reading. In 1984, William Bennett, then Chairman of the National Endowment for the Humanities, defended the idea of grounding education in the reading of works sanctioned by tradition. He took it that "[m]ankind's answers to compelling questions are available to us through the written and spoken word—books, manuscripts, letters, plays, and oral traditions—and also in nonliterary forms, which John Ruskin called the book of art" (Bennett,1984, p. 5). This language sounds inclusive, but Bennett went on to offer a rather exclusive list of great books that should form a core for teaching in the humanities: works by Homer, Dante, Shakespeare, Dickens, the predictable American authors, and so on. "Why these particular books and these particular authors?" Bennett asked. "Because an important part of education is learning to read, and the highest purpose of reading is to be in the company of great souls . . ." (Bennett, 1984, p. 11). Throughout his report Bennett emphasized that student readers should be "in the company of" or "confront" the great minds of the past through the books that they have left.

Bennett's notion of reading as communion with great souls is in fact borrowed from the theory and practice of the Romantics: it is now a traditional view, although at the beginning of the 19th century the Romantics were of course radical. It was radical for them to insist that a work of literature was above all the manifestation of the author's creative personality—that poets were not simply skilled craftsmen, but different and greater souls than the rest of us. Romantic critics fashioned a religion of art to supplement or replace the truths of revealed religion (either consciously as in the case of Matthew Arnold or more tentatively as with Schlegel, Coleridge, or Shelley); they compared poets to prophets and indeed even to God in their creative powers. Some began to treat literature as biography, reading Shakespeare and even Homer in order to peer into the souls of these great artists. Carlyle was a good example, whom M. H. Abrams calls "king among those who read an author not for what he made, but for what he was." (See Abrams, 1953, pp. 248-249. Also for Keble's reading of Homer, pp. 256-262. Abrams' book, *The Mirror and the Lamp*, the definitive study of Romantic theories of literature, has itself become canonical.) But how can an ordinary reader hope to hold a conversation with a great soul? The more the Romantics and their contemporary followers like Bennett emphasize the greatness and uniqueness of the authors of the canon, the less accessible these authors become. Critical reading becomes more difficult, criticism necessarily muted. The conversation becomes a kind of worship, again in keeping with the attitude toward literature in the nineteenth century.

On the other side are those who disagree that we can and should establish a timeless list of great works. Robert Scholes (1986) wrote in reply to Bennett that:

> The purpose of humanistic study is to learn what it has meant to be human in other times and places, what it means now, and to speculate about what it ought to mean and what it might mean in the human future. The best texts for this purpose should be determined locally, by local conditions, limited and facilitated by local wisdom. Above all, they should not be imposed and regulated by a central power. (p. 116)

This reply too has Romantic roots; it suggests the Romantic revolt against authority and tradition. In fact Scholes does not merely distrust centralization; he denies the idea of a center or a mainstream, which necessarily pushes some texts and authors to the margins. No text should be "outside the bounds of humanistic study" (p. 116). At the same time Scholes attacks Bennett's proposal for worshipful reading, reading as a respectful approach to the monuments: "[t]his soulful rhetoric is guaranteed to drain the life out of the texts studied, because it permits only worship and forbids all criticism" (p. 114). Scholes calls into question the whole complex of assumptions of Bennett and the traditionalists: the belief that there is a center to our culture, that great works are unchanging in their message and importance, that great authors are authorities, and so on.

Clearly, these traditional views of the canon and of reading were born of the technology of handwriting and matured in the technology of printing. If handwriting already suggested the goal of fixing the text, printing achieved a true cultural fixity, allowing texts to survive unchanged for centuries. The idea of declaring authors canonical is much older than print. Greek scholars of the Alexandrian period, for example, compiled their canons of epic, lyric, and tragic poets. Our modern notion of canon has as its paradigm the Christian canon of sacred writings, which developed in late antiquity, a relatively sophisticated age of handwriting. The New Testament canon apparently formed in association with the technological breakthrough of the codex. But throughout antiquity and the Middle Ages, copying by hand continued to expose canonical texts to errors. Printing encouraged the making of canon in at least two ways. It ensured far more effectively than handwriting that a work could be "timeless"—in the sense that it could survive for centuries without substantial change. And it provided dignity and distance for works of the canon: it made authors special by providing them with a writing space not available to other literate men and women.

It is no accident that the age of printing became obsessed with assigning authorship and verifying texts. Such scholarship, called "textual criticism," began in the Renaissance and reached its zenith in the 19th century. The goal of this exacting scholarship was to determine letter by letter what Plato, Euripides, or the Church fathers "really" wrote: to apply the standards of printed accuracy to the manuscript tradition of ancient and medieval authors. Textual criticism set out to establish a little canon for each author: a definitive list of works and a definitive edition of each work in which all scribal deviations were relegated to the footnotes. Printing also fostered the ideal of a single canon of great authors, whose works should be distributed in thousands of identical copies to readers throughout the world. By its technique of mass production, printing has helped to make such texts available to every reader in a culture. At the same time, by ensuring that the reader cannot enter into the space that the text occupies, printing encouraged worshipful reading.

The idea of a canon of great authors inevitably suggests a set of beautifully printed, leather-bound volumes chronologically arranged on a shelf in one's study. No conversational, informal approach to such volumes is possible; a reader would be unlikely to make notes in the margins. The reverence or reticence of the reader in fact appeals to supporters of the traditional canon. If reading the canon puts the reader in the company of great souls, it is company that the reader visits only on his or her best behavior. So printing aids in the making of the canon, yet at the same time recent developments in printing technology have also undermined the canon. In the 20th century so many books have become available in inexpensive editions that readers are in danger of losing their attitude of reverence. A great book is less likely to be worshipped when it can be bought in paperback for a few dollars and when it is so flimsy that the pages come away in the reader's hand as he or she turns them. The critics of worshipful reading are still reading books in print, but their attitude is appropriate to paperbacks rather than editions bound in leather. Indeed, the radical literary theories we shall discuss in this chapter, including reader-response criticism and deconstruction, still assume that readers will be reading printed books. But in fact, the electronic medium is a more natural place for the irreverent reading that they suggest.

A canon is by definition a linear-hierarchical structure: it is a list of the most important authors and works, by which other, subordinate works can be measured. Again, the alternative structure is the network. All texts are joined by a rich texture of allusions and references. Some texts are perhaps more richly connected and therefore more rewarding than others, but in principle a reader could begin anywhere and move by allusion and reference through the entire literary tradition. For that reason Scholes can claim that ". . . no text is so trivial as to be outside the bounds of humanistic study" (Scholes, 1986, p. 116). But it remains hard work to read printed books subversively, as Scholes would wish, because the technology itself works against the reader's aggressive appropriation of the text. Thus, the assumptions behind Bennett's statement are still probably shared by the vast majority of readers, who have taken the line of least resistance in the age of print. On the other hand, aggressive, active reading is clearly the kind that the computer fosters. In reading a fiction like "Afternoon," the reader is forced to reflect on the choices he or she makes, because these choices become part of the text itself. The story comes to include the reader. This brand of active reading leaves the reader much less inclined to worship the author.

THE END OF AUTHORITY

As long as the printed book remains the primary medium of literature, traditional views of the author as authority and of literature as monument will remain convincing for most readers. The electronic medium, however, threatens to bring down the whole edifice at once. It complicates our understanding of literature as either mimesis or expression, it denies the fixity of the text, and it questions the authority of the author. The author is no longer an intimidating figure, not a prophet or a Mosaic legislator in Shelley's sense. The author's art is not a substitute for religious revelation, and authors do not lay down the law. The electronic author assumes once again the role of a craftsman, working with defined materials and limited goals. In constructing an electronic text as a network of related episodes, the author comes to emphasize the formal qualities of art, rather than the inspiration that transcends form. And as the Greeks understood, a sense of form is a sense of one's limits. Electronic authors work with the necessarily limited materials provided by their computer systems, and they impose further limitations upon their readers. Within those limits the reader is free to play. The text is not simply an expression of the author's emotions, for the reader helps to make the text. Two subjects, author and reader, combine in the text. Thus, Wordsworth's definition of poetry as a "spontaneous overflow of powerful feelings" does not easily include electronic poetry. First, the overflow is not wholly spontaneous: it must be planned and structured by the author before it can undergo spontaneous transformation by the reader. Second, we have to ask whose powerful feelings the poetry expresses—the author's or the reader's. One Romantic view is that the poets are talking to themselves and that we as readers are eavesdropping. But in the electronic writing space the reader is no eavesdropper; he or she is a necessary element in the conversation.

The reader may well become the author's adversary, seeking to make the text over in a direction that the author did not anticipate. Adversarial reading is not new. One of the great advantages of writing in any medium is that readers can stop, reflect on a passage, and disagree. They can deliberately misread the text in the sense of imposing their own constructions that forcefully contradict the text. Harold Bloom has claimed that misreading is an essential part of the poetic tradition: each poet must misread his or her predecessors in order to create a new text under their otherwise crushing influence (see Bloom, *The Anxiety of Influence*, 1973). The computer makes concrete the act of reading (or misreading) as interpretation and challenges the reader to engage the author for control of the writing space. This engagement is apparent in "Afternoon," where the reader must make an effort to find and stay on the path he or she wishes to travel. In "Afternoon" as in all electronic writing, the control of the presentation of text becomes part of the text itself, because the text consists not only of the words the author has written but also of the structure of decisions that the author creates and the reader explores.

The computer therefore makes visible the contest between author and reader that in previous technologies has gone on out of sight, "behind" the page. The author has always before had the upper hand, although each previous technology of writing allowed for a different kind and degree of control. With the purely linear presentation of the papyrus roll, neither author nor reader had many choices. Since there were very few visual cues, the author had to build all textual structure into the words themselves; the reader could hardly move back or forward without losing his or her place in the structure. Gradually the structure became externalized through the development of the paged book, marginal notes, use of various scripts, and other techniques culminating in modern printed typography. Although it is still fundamentally linear, the printed book is quite sophisticated in its visible structure of chapters, sections, paragraphs, and, for nonfiction, indices—all available to the author to delimit the reader's experience of the text. Yet that same structure makes it possible for the reader to exert some control. There is no convenient way for the author to prevent the reader from skipping over one chapter or turning to the back and reading the last page first. Umberto Eco's *The Name of the Rose* does describe a codex that prevents its own reading: the pages are poisoned so that readers receive a dose if they put their fingers to their lips before turning a page. No one succeeds in getting very far into this book, although even this drastic method cannot prevent the reader from examining pages in an arbitrary order—at least for the few minutes granted him or her. In general, authors in the age of print have exerted their authority in subtler, but still effective ways. The electronic medium challenges all such attempts to circumscribe the reader's participation.

The traditional view of literature as mimesis (imitation) is also troubled by electronic writing and for the same reason, the active participation of the reader. Because the text changes with each reading, the electronic author cannot simply capture a replica of nature in his or her text and offer that replica to the reader. Perhaps the text becomes a more accurate reflection of nature because it now includes the reader in the process of reflection. But in any case the relationship between author, text, and nature is made more complicated by the addition of the reader as an active participant. Rather than envisioning an electronic text as a reflection of our world, we might think of it as a self-contained world, a heterocosm. This vision of text dates back to the 18th century and can also be found in Romantics like Shelley, for whom the poet "creates anew the universe" (Abrams, 1953, pp. 272-285; see also Culler, 1981, p. 156).

If it is a world, an electronic text is a world in constant motion. Electronic writing is as animated as the famous shield of Achilles in the *Iliad*. Homer's description of that shield is remarkable for its impossible movement: figures embossed on the shield talk and fight and dance in scenes that could not possibly be captured in a frozen image. This movement is appropriate for the oral poet Homer, for whom poetry was a spontaneous performance, not a fixed text. There is an obvious comparison to be made with Keat's famous description of figures on a Grecian urn. For Keats the paradox is that the urn depicts figures whose actions are frozen and therefore immortal. And Keats is writing in the mature age of print, when poems too are frozen texts, no matter how active they are in metaphor. But this traditional belief in the fixity of the text cannot survive the shift to the electronic writing space. Electronic writing challenges the assumption that the beauty of a poem is a static beauty, a quality of being removed from the flux of the world. A computer text is never stable and never detached from the changing contexts that readers bring to it.

In fact, taking the text as heterocosm only enhances the authority of the author, who serves as a kind of a deity for this world. It suggests a passive reading in which the reader "loses himself" in the world of the story. Losing oneself in a fictional world is the goal of the naive reader or one who reads for entertainment. It is particularly a feature of genre fiction, such as romance and science fiction. The capacity of electronic text ironically to comment on itself keeps the reader from falling too far or too long into passivity. The reader of "Afternoon" is forced at every turn to reflect on the experience of reading. An electronic text like "Afternoon" does not close itself off as a heterocosm; instead, it reaches out to other texts, and it invites the reader to participate in its own construction. "Afternoon" cares little about its own closure: "When the story no longer progresses, or when it cycles, or when you tire of the paths, the experience of reading it ends." The margins of "Afternoon" yield in a way that the secure white space surrounding a traditional printed poem cannot yield.

In short, the traditional views of the author as authority and of literature as expression or as mimesis do not help us in reading texts in the new electronic medium. Or rather the tradition helps us mainly by providing a negative measure for electronic texts: the computer seems to negate those qualities of literature that the tradition regards most highly. We must look elsewhere than in traditional (Romantic) criticism to find a paradigm for electronic reading.

THE READER'S RESPONSE

In the preceding chapter we saw that electronic fiction was unlike conventional printed fiction, but was anticipated or prefigured by experimental fiction in the late age of print. In the same way, recent literary theories, including reader-response criticism and deconstruction, themselves in revolt against traditional views, point toward a new literary theory that electronic writing will require. (For a stimulating discussion, see Landow, 1989.) It is sometimes uncanny how well the post-modern theorists seem to be anticipating electronic writing. Yet, as far as I can establish, none of the best-known theorists have had the computer in mind. They are instead responding to the literary experiments in print, like those we discussed in the preceding chapter. Nonetheless, their writings provide a transition to the technology that is replacing print.

For more than two decades, literary theorists have been emphasizing the role of the reader, who had in many ways been neglected ever since the Romantic Revolution (first in favor of the poet and then of the poem itself). The reader, they point out, responds actively to the words on the page; this response determines the text, which exists from moment to moment in the act of reading. The task of the literary criticism, then, is not to examine the text in isolation, but rather to understand the text through its effect on the reader—a technique called reader-response criticism. Wolfgang Iser explains that the reader must participate in the literary act by realizing the author's text.

> . . . the literary work cannot be completely identical with the text, or with the realization of the text, but in fact must lie halfway between the two. The work is more than the text, for the text only takes on life when it is realized, and

furthermore the realization is by no means independent of the individual disposition of the reader.... The convergence of the text and the reader brings the literary work into existence.... (Iser, 1980, p. 50)

The work therefore has a dynamic nature: it changes from reading to reading. Indeed the text itself is "... an arena in which reader and author participate in a game of the imagination" (pp. 51-52). The words on the page constitute the rules or parameters by which the game is played: "the written text imposes certain limits on its unwritten implications...." But these limits still leave the reader room to exercise his or her own imagination. Indeed, every text leaves gaps for the reader to complete:

[O]ne text is potentially capable of several different realizations, and no reading can ever exhaust the full potential, for each individual reader will fill in the gaps in his own way, thereby excluding the various other possibilities; as he reads, he will make his own decision as to how the gap is to be filled. (p. 55)

Filling in the gaps is a different temporal experience with each act of reading:

... In every text there is a potential time sequence which the reader must inevitably realize, as it is impossible to absorb even a short text in a single moment. Thus the reading process always involves viewing the text through a perspective that is continually on the move, linking up the different phases.... [W]hen we have finished the text, and read it again, clearly our extra knowledge will result in a different time sequence; we shall tend to establish connections by referring to our awareness of what is to come, and so certain aspects of the text will assume a signficance we did not attach to them on a first reading. (p. 56)

All of these qualities are exactly what we saw in our reading of the electronic fiction "Afternoon"; all of them follow from the computer's ability to free the text from its embodiment as a set of bound, paper pages. (On reader response in electronic text, see Ziegfeld, 1989, pp. 364-366; see also Douglas, 1988.) Stanley Fish has also emphasized the paradox of the physical (we would say printed) text. "The objectivity of the text is an illusion, and moreover, a dangerous illusion, because it is so physically convincing. The illusion is one of self-sufficiency and completeness. A line of print or a page or a book is so obviously *there*—it can be handled, photographed, or put away—that is seems to be the sole repository of whatever value and meaning we associate with it" (Fish, 1980, p. 82). Yet the text is not complete until it is experienced by the reader.

As Fish realizes, the reader does not make a printed book. The pages of a printed book exist prior to and apart from any reader; the text as a sequence of words on the page is made by authors and printers. What the reader does fashion is the text as a structure of sounds, images, or ideas in his or her own mind. This figurative text is for Fish, Iser, and others the only text worth studying, perhaps the only text available for study, since we cannot know the words on the printed page until we read them and call forth such a mental structure. But what was only figuratively true in the case of print, becomes literally true in the electronic medium. The new medium reifies the metaphor of reader response, for the reader participates in the making of the text as a sequence of words. Even if the author has written all the words, the reader must call them up and determine the order of presentation by the choices made or the commands issued. There is no single univocal text apart from the reader; the author writes a set of potential texts, from which the reader chooses.

The role of the reader in electronic fiction therefore lies halfway between the customary roles of author and reader in the medium of print. These two roles are most clearly delineated in the traditional novel or essay, in which a silent reader absorbs and reflects upon the words of the author. There are other kinds of texts which define different roles. In drama, for example, a special class of readers, the actors, interpret the text before an audience. Dramatic texts are like musical scores: the words on the page direct the actors in their effort to bring the drama into existence as sound and image. The written text could never be a complete record of the experience of the play; it has always to be filled out, and therefore interpreted. Even if the playwright is also directing, the playwright is in a sense interpreting his or her own work. In the last few centuries, directors and actors have allowed themselves great latitude in interpretation, and we have come to regard them as artists in their own right. Similarly the development of a sophisticated, but necessarily imperfect system of notation in Western music has led to the separation of the composer and the performer. In the 18th and 19th centuries, the performer moved gradually from the role of artisan to that of artist and became almost as important as the composer. Today we take it for granted that composer and performer work together to realize the music, that the music exists in the act of playing, not merely on the page. The composer never succeeds in exerting perfect control over the interpretation. In contemporary music, the composer's score is often a set of instructions that may be interpreted in a variety of ways. But even in the 17th and 18th centuries, performers were often free to ornament their parts; in the Classical concerto the soloist often wrote or improvised the cadenza.

The computer now extends the role of performer or interpreter to all forms of writing. In the electronic writing space all texts are like dramas or musical scores. The reader performs the text, perhaps only for himself or herself, perhaps for another reader, who may then choose to perform the first reader's text for others. In this way electronic writing defines a new level of creativity, indeed a myriad of new levels that fall between the apparent originality of the Romantic artist and apparent passivity of the traditional reader.

SPATIAL WRITING

An electronic text is open to performance by the reader: its structure or architecture is realized in time as the reader reads. But this has also been true of texts in manuscript and in print. What we have traditionally called the structure of the text is the relationship between the linear experience of reading and the network of allusions among elements that are separated in the physical space of the book. The fluid architecture of the text has been a particular concern of modern critics, because modern literature has made such radical and obvious efforts to distort the space and so to manipulate the reader's time. In modern prose as well as poetry, the narrative is often purposely fragmented. The step-by-step development of the story is ignored; causal relationships among events may also be omitted.

Joseph Frank was one of the first critics to discuss these qualities of modernism, and he coined the term "spatial form" to describe the architecture of a text that works against the "strict causal-chronological order . . ." (Frank, 1981, p. 235). Of the modern poets Eliot and Pound, he wrote that they "undermine[d] the inherent consecutiveness of language, frustrating the reader's normal expectation of a sequence and forcing him to perceive the elements of the poem as juxtaposed in space rather than unrolling in time" (Frank, 1963, p. 10). Joyce's extraordinary structure of allusion and reference in *Ulysses* and *Finnegans Wake* makes him the best example of the assault on the chronological order of the text. As we recall, Joyce expects that the reader of *Ulysses* will have to work his or her way back and forth through the pages of the book in order to perceive the references: the reader will have to abandon the linear experience of the story. *Ulysses* and much of *Finnegans Wake* have a simple storyline, but the story is buried beneath several layers of allusions and neologisms. In Joyce's case the archaeology of these layers is far more rewarding than the story itself. As Joseph Frank says, ". . . Joyce cannot be read—he can only be reread" (Frank, 1963, p. 19). We have seen that Frank's characterization of Joyce is also appropriate for electronic reading.

In general, just as the modern novelists were experimenting with narrative architecture, modern and now post-modern critics have been explaining that architecture in terms that are appropriate for the computer. Both the practice and the criticism anticipate the space that electronic writing now offers us. While the novelists have been straining with progressively greater violence against the conventions of the novel, their critics have been arguing that we must therefore reconsider the nature of narrative and indeed of writing itself. Gérard Genette makes the case in this way:

> One has long considered writing . . . as a simple means for the notation of speech. Today, we are beginning to understand that it is a bit more than that, and Mallarmé already had said that 'to think, is to write without flourishes.' Because of the specific spatiality to which we have referred, language (and thus thought) is already a kind of writing, or, if one prefers, the manifest spatiality of writing may be taken as a symbol for the profound spatiality of language. . . . Since Mallarmé, we have learned to recognize (to re-cognize) the so-called visual resources of script and of typographical arrangement, and of the existence of the Book as a kind of total object; and this change of perspective has made us more attentive to the spatiality of writing, to the atemporal disposition of signs, words, phrases, and discourse in the simultaneity of what is called a text. (taken from "La litérature et l'espace" in *Figures III*, cited by Frank, 1981, p. 242)

If these are indeed the lessons offered by the poets since Mallarmé, then contemporary fiction will have no little difficulty moving into an electronic medium that gives the fullest expression yet to the spatiality of writing. The electronic reader is encouraged to think of the text as a collection of interrelated units floating in a space of at least two dimensions. The reader's movement among units does not require flipping pages or consulting the table of contents: instead the reader passes instantly and effortlessly from one place to another. References and allusions are easier and more natural than in any previous writing technology. Indeed the act of reference, the movement from one passage "late" in the narrative to an earlier passage is technically the same as the movement from one passage to the next in chronological order. In a printed book readers mark their progress through the narrative by measuring the pages to the right of their bookmark against those to the left. But in an electronic text the reader has no obvious physical image with which to define progress through the text, unless the writer chooses to provide one. A printed book's natural order provides the foundation for the architecture of the text, but an electronic text is all architecture, all reference.

The electronic author can therefore make references more precise and more numerous. Far from abandoning control of the text, the electronic author can, if he or she chooses, exercise greater control over the process of cross-reference. In printed fiction, not all the readers, perhaps very few, will register any particular reference. In *Finnegans Wake*, there are no doubt still many references that no one has noticed. And the author cannot know which reader will find which references: the author cannot predict how the reader will move through the fictional space. Joyce could perhaps envision an ideal reader of *Finnegans Wake* who recognizes all the allusions and references, but he could not know how closely any flesh-and-blood reader will approach that ideal. In the electronic reading space, the author can make the process of reference contingent upon the reader's response or insist that the reader follow a particular path of references before following another. The electronic author can manipulate the reader's time at one remove—not only through the words on the pages, like all previous authors, but also by determining the presentation of the electronic pages themselves. The traditional printed novel molds time as a traditional sculpture molds the space it occupies, creating a complex but unchanging effect. The electronic text manipulates time as a piece of kinetic sculpture manipulates space.

TAKING APART THE TEXT

Not only the reader-response and spatial-form but even the most radical theorists (Barthes, de Man, Derrida, and their American followers) speak a language that is strikingly appropriate to electronic writing. How can we avoid seeing the computer, for example, in Roland Barthes's influential distinction between the work and the Text? "[T]he work," Barthes writes, "is concrete, occupying a portion of book-space (in a library, for example); the Text, on the other hand, is a methodological field" (Barthes, 1979, p. 74). "The Text is plural.... The Text is not coexistence of meanings, but passage, traversal" (p. 76). "The author is regarded as the father and the owner of his work;... The Text, on the other hand, is read without the father's signature... [N]o vital 'respect' is owed to the Text: it can be broken (this is exactly what the Middle Ages did with two authoritative texts, the Scriptures and Aristotle)" (p. 78). "... The Text requires an attempt to abolish (or at least to lessen) the distance between writing and reading, not by intensifying the reader's projection into the work, but by linking the two together in a single signifying process" (p. 79). All that is left to say—what Barthes could not say because he did not know about computers—is that the paradigm for the work is a finely bound, printed volume, whereas the paradigm for the Text is a network in the computer's memory. (See Ziegfield, 1989, pp. 364-365.)

We have already mentioned Barthes as a prose stylist whose techniques of fragmentation and interruption helped to call into question the linear essay. Barthes was an important figure in the post-modern attack on the traditional view of the literary meaning. If William Bennett and those who still defend the canon are at one end of the critical spectrum, Barthes, de Man, and Derrida are at the other, as they seek to confute literary works by turning their own premises against them. The deconstructionists have called forth perhaps the strongest reaction from traditionalist humanists by their critique of great literary and philosophical texts of the past. They seem to be arguing that the texts of Plato, Rousseau, or Freud do not embody truths about the human condition, because the very language of these works fails them and ends in contradiction. Jonathan Culler explains the task of deconstruction as

"...reading the major texts of Western literature and philosophy as sites on the boundaries of logocentrism and showing, in the most subtle interpretations that scholarship has yet produced, how these texts are already riven by contradictions and indeterminacies that seem inherent in the exercise of language" (Culler, 1981, p. 43). The deconstructionists assert that the meaning of any written text is radically unstable, a vain attempt to fix meaning, when all writing is condemned to drift in a space of possible meanings. Traditional critics believe tacitly or explictly in hierarchies. They believe that some works are more important than others. For the traditional critic, a work such as "Hamlet" is obviously more important than a minor 20th-century novel; it is equally obvious that "Hamlet" is more important, more central, than the body of critical writing that has grown up around "Hamlet," interpreting the play. Tradition also asserts that each work of literature, central or marginal, has its own identity, that each work occupies a portion of "book-space." A work has predecessors, and it influences other works, but we can always identify and single out the text of "Hamlet" for study. We can always separate "Hamlet" from its influences and go back to the play itself. But the deconstructionist challenges all these traditional beliefs. Not only can the central become marginal and vice versa, but the very identity, the separateness, of the work is questioned. The text of "Hamlet" has no boundaries: it opens out in all directions and includes, for example, all the centuries of interpretation of the play. The play is not central and the interpretations marginal, as we would assume, for we cannot say where the play ends and interpretation begins. Derrida speaks of text as "a differential network, a fabric of traces referring endlessly to something other than itself, to other differential traces. Thus the text overruns all the limits assigned to it so far . . ." (Derrida, 1979, p. 84).

Derrida's characterization of a text again sounds very much like text in the electronic writing space. And yet, when Derrida speaks of marginality or of the text as extending beyond its borders, he is in fact appealing to the earlier technologies of writing, to medieval codices and printed books. The scribes of the ancient world made relatively little use of the margins of papyrus rolls; the invention of the codex allowed for larger and more accessible margins. The margins of a medieval manuscript often belonged to the scholarly reader: they were the reader's space for conducting a dialogue with the text. The margins defined a zone in which the text could extend into the world of the reader. And during generations of copying, text could also move from the margins into the center, as glosses from readers made their way into the text itself. In the age of print, marginal notes became truly marginal, part of the hierarchy of the text that only the author defined and controlled: eventually they became footnotes and endnotes. Readers could still insert their own notes with a pen, where there was sufficient white space, but these handwritten notes could no longer have the same status as the text itself. They were private reactions to a public text. Today's scholars are extremely interested in finding books that were owned and commented on by Newton, or Erasmus, or Shelley. But such comments could only enter into the public life of the text, if and when a later editor took them into account in preparing a new edition. When deconstructionists play upon the dichotomy between the center and the margin, they are assuming a written or more probably a printed text, which naturally favors the center over the margin. In general, whenever the theorists set out to reverse a literary hierarchy, they are assuming the technology of printing (or sometimes handwriting) that generates or enforces that hierarchy.

If the margins that concern Derrida and deconstruction are the borders of the printed or written page, what can they say about electronic texts? We have seen that a text in electronic space has no necessary margins, no fixed boundaries except for the ultimate limitations of the machine. In "Afternoon" the margins yield to the reader, and this yielding serves as a safety valve to prevent the text from disintegrating under the force of a deconstructive reading. The electronic writing space can support a network in which all elements have equal status and to be at the margin is itself only provisional. The author can extend and ramify this textual network limited only by the available memory. The reader can follow paths through the space in any direction, limited only by constraints established by the author. No path through the space need be stigmatized as marginal. In future electronic fictions, the reader too may be allowed to change the structure of the text, to extend its borders in ways the author has not anticipated. All texts in the computer are therefore like geodetic lines in spherical geometry—finite, but unbounded. Furthermore the connections can extend beyond one author's texts to many. We have already discussed the electronic library, which could include books of all ages and subject matters, all organized into a reticulated network of topics. In such a library all boundaries are fluid: pages dissolve into sections or chapters, chapters into volumes, and volumes into the larger structures of the library.

The interrelation of texts is now often called "intertextuality." Jonathan Culler explains that ". . . literary works are to be considered not as autonomous entities, 'organic wholes,' but as intertextual constructs: sequences which have meaning in relation to other texts which they take up, cite, parody, refute, or generally transform. A text can be read only in relation to other texts, and it is made possible by the codes which animate the discursive space of a culture" (Culler, 1981, p. 38; see also Landow, 1989, pp. 184-188). The printed book or written codex encourages the notion of a text as an organic whole—a unit of meaning that is physically separate from and therefore independent of all other texts. Stressing connections rather than textual independence, the electronic space rewrites the possibilities of reference and allusion. Not only can one passage in an electronic text refer to another, but the text can bend so that any two passages touch, displaying themselves continguously to the reader. Not only can one text allude to another, but the one text can penetrate the other and become a visual intertext before the reader's eyes. The intertextual relationship occurs everywhere in print—in novels, gothic romances, popular magazines, encyclopedias, grammars, and dictionaries—yet the electronic space permits us to visualize intertextuality as no previous medium has done.

DECONSTRUCTING ELECTRONIC TEXT

The electronic medium discredits the traditional notions of monumental works, of a fixed canon of great authors, of the fixity and coherence of language itself. Are we left, then, to conclude that deconstruction is already the theory of writing appropriate to the electronic medium? It may be that the electronic writing space embodies the notions of the deconstructionists too well or rather too easily. Deconstruction works by reversal, by upsetting tradition, and one tradition that it seeks to upset is that of humanism in the age of print. As we have seen, deconstruction envisions its adversary in the form of the printed book. To deconstruct a text, one uses a vocabulary appropriate to the computer precisely because this vocabulary contradicts the assumptions of print. It is also a negative vocabulary because deconstruction must negate what is still the paradigm for literary and indeed all "serious" writing—the printed page. The deconstructionists seek to disturb, to alienate, to dislocate, and so by embracing the techniques of deconstruction, electronic writing seems in a playful way to subvert the whole project.

Deconstruction assumes the fixed character of a text in its effort to undermine that text. The fixed text provides a fixed target; you cannot say that a text contradicts itself unless the text appears to make and defend claims worthy of contradiction. Deconstructive critics seek to drive latent ambiguities in the text into the open. They often focus on problem texts, whose "message" is hard to decipher, such as Shelley's "Triumph of Life," James' "The Turn of the Screw," or Melville's *Billy Budd*. But an electronic text is and claims to be only a potential text, and as such even its ambiguities are only potential. It need not and probably will not present all of its claims, all of its ambiguities to any reader. Because the text changes with each reading, it may not ever make a univocal statement that invites deconstruction. In one reading of "Afternoon," the narrator does not visit his lover's psychologist; in another reading he does. Which is the story that needs to be subverted? The fact that the electronic space of "Afternoon" contains both versions already recognizes the contradiction. Neither reading is the whole story, and yet unlike a printed work we cannot say that the two readings are embodied in the same narrative, for each reading is itself a different narrative called forth by two different readers, or the same reader at two different times.

No doubt a deconstructionist could respond to this situation: either by examining each reading separately or by displaying a second level of contradiction embodied in the whole space itself. Deconstruction does not become impossible in the electronic medium—it is after all, like psychoanalysis, Christian hermeneutics, or Marxism, a closed method that cannot be confounded in its own terms. The question is whether the deconstruction of an electronic text seems worth the effort. The electronic text never takes itself seriously, as a printed text inevitably does. Deconstruction itself is playful, but its playful attitude requires a fundamental seriousness in its object. An electronic text already comes to us in pieces, as a tentative, fluid collection of words: why seek to deconstruct it further?

We may pose the question more generally: why do we need any critics when the text in effect criticizes itself? In fact, an electronic text is not hostile to criticism: it incorporates criticism into itself. "Afternoon" includes critical comments as episodes that the reader may visit: for example, the comment on closure that we cited earlier or a definition of hypertext. These episodes do not seem forced or intrusive precisely because of their ephemeral nature: they do not "mar" the self-contained perfection of story because they appear only in some readings and only for as long as the reader permits them on the screen. The electronic medium dissolves the distinction between writing and interpreting a text—a distinction that post-modern critics have tried to negate for printed texts as well. They claim that a text is no more important than its intepretations, because the text cannot be separated from its interpretation. Now, in the electronic writing space, where every reading of a text is a realization or indeed a rewriting of the text, to read *is* to interpret. But this insight too turns out to be harmless, for the author writes with that expectation. The author does not set out to exclude the reader from the process of making the text, and the author is not shocked to learn that his or her text is not inviolate.

In addition to lessening the shock of unstable text, electronic writing offers a new simplicity. Writers on deconstruction are notorious for their elaborate prose and their invented or appropriated terms. Traditional critics may see this as obscurantism, but deconstructionists and other post-modern critics have to write this way. They have to invent a new vocabulary, to fill their sentences with parenthetical phrases and abrupt reversal. Their writing has to be difficult for the same reason that experimental fiction in the 20th century has to be difficult—because both fiction and theory are attempting to turn the printed medium against itself. Both are trying to defeat the linearity of writing, and yet they have at their disposal only a linear medium. Now, however, the electronic medium can demonstrate easily what Derrida could only describe laboriously in print—or attempt to embody in the elaborate typography of *Glas*.

Electronic writing takes us beyond the paradox of deconstruction, because it accepts as strengths the very qualities—the play of signs, intertextuality, the lack of closure—that deconstruction poses as the ultimate limitations of literature and language. Electronic writing does not permit a return to traditional assumptions of stable and monumental texts. We cannot return to the comparatively unself-conscious literature before modernism, but it does seem possible that the fluidity of the new medium can move us out of the impasse in which we find ourselves. After all, if authors accept the post-structural claim that language and literature are fundamentally unstable or incoherent, how can they continue to write? They can continue by realizing that their texts are open to the charge of incoherence only if those texts pretend to be fixed and unchanging statements of poetic truth. They can continue by accepting the playful nature of their writing. In electronic text authors may include as many dramatic moments or philosophical poses as they like, but they must reckon with the fact that these moments and poses may appear in a variety of contexts and be construed by their readers in different ways on different readings. The author must be ready to accept for his or her electronic text the conditions that the deconstructionists have claimed for printed text. An electronic text that remakes itself for each reader and for each act of reading is not incoherent, even if it does embrace its own contradictions. Deconstruction has helped to free us from a mode of thought that was too closely wedded to the technology of print. Deconstruction therefore tells what electronic writing is not. We will still need a new literary theory to achieve a positive understanding of electronic writing.

LOOKING AT AND LOOKING THROUGH

The beginning of a positive theory can be found in Richard Lanham's recent plea for a "new rhetoric of the arts, an unblushing and unfiltered attempt to plot all the ranges of formal expression now possible" (Lanham, 1989, p. 276). Lanham claims that electronic technology is helping to break down the boundaries between literature and the other arts (pp. 275-276). The computer can textualize all the arts: that is, it can incorporate sound and images into a hypertext as easily as words. Lanham's new "digital" rhetoric will be inclusive, rather than exclusive. It will make "no invidious distinctions between high and low culture, commercial and pure usage, talented or chance creation, visual or auditory stimulus, iconic or alphabetic information." More important, it will compel us to reconsider the relationship between the text and the world to which the text refers. In the world of print, the ideal was to make a text transparent, so that the reader looked through the text to the world beyond. This was the goal of realistic painting as well as the traditional novel.

> The classical notion of decorum, like modern equivalents—"clarity," "authenticity," and so on—measures an effect on the beholder. If a style works, if it creates the transparent illusion, it is decorous. Decorum is such a poor descriptive term precisely because it describes so many different kinds of verbal patterns yet allows only one virtue, unselfconscious transparency. We know that all literature, that all the arts are infinitely more various. (p. 276)

In a digital rhetoric, transparency is not the only virtue. The reader can be made to focus on the verbal patterns, on the text as a texture of elements. The text can be transparent or opaque, and it can oscillate between transparency and opacity, between asking the reader to look through the text to the "world beyond" and asking him or her to look at the text itself as a formal structure. This oscillation was already a characteristic of modern literature in print: it is the tension we have already discussed between the text as a story and the text as a structure of allusions. Once again, electronic writing takes the modern literary experience one step further. An electronic hypertext makes the structure visible; the formal structure of the text is embodied in the links between episodes. In reading an episode, the reader may succeed in looking *through* the text to the imagined world. But whenever he or she comes to a link, the reader must look *at* the text, as a series of possibilities that he or she as reader can activate. In "Afternoon" we may get lost in Peter's compelling narrative of his search for his son, but the need to make choices keeps pulling us back to the fact that we as readers are participating in the making of a fiction. We are constantly critiquing the nature of these choices as we read. In "Afternoon" as in all other hypertexts, the links have the same status as the verbal episodes. It is therefore as legitimate to look at the formal arrangement of the text, as it is to get lost in the story. Lanham reminds us that any point on the spectrum from transparency to opacity and any oscillation between the two can make for interesting fiction.

Rapid oscillation between the transparent and the opaque (between looking through and looking at) is a defining characteristic of hypertext. It applies not only to interactive fiction, but also to hypertextual pedagogy, technical writing, and databases. In any hypertext readers move back and forth between reading the verbal text and reading the structure. When they are reading the verbal text, they may temporarily forget about the hypertextual structure and concentrate on the voice in the text. When they are moving about in the structure, readers are brought back to the hypertext as a network of elements. A good hypertext is constructed so that the movement between these two kinds of reading is almost effortless. The oscillation between looking through and looking at can become so rapid that the two experiences merge: the structure of the hypertext is then always present to the reader as he or she reads. In a hypertext there is no escaping the text as a structure of elements, a network of what semioticians call "signs."

The Mind as a Writing Space

Artificial Intelligence

The computer as a thinking machine, a machine that rivals or surpasses human intelligence, is a familiar theme in computer science and in science fiction. The theme continues to evoke both enthusiasm and fear. Many are still frightened by the prospect that superintelligent computers will someday take control of human affairs or dispense with human beings altogether. On the other hand, there are computer specialists who do not fear this prospect at all; they are trying to build such an *artificial intelligence.* In the long debate over artificial intelligence, some philosophers and even computer specialists claim that artificial intelligence is impossible, whereas others claim that it is not only possible, but imminent or indeed already achieved.

From our perspective, however, artificial intelligence is simply another way to write with the computer. This crucial point has not been appreciated either by the opponents or the enthusiasts for artificial intelligence. The very definition of artificial intelligence turns out to be the ability to write and to read as humans do, and artificial intelligence programs turn out to be hypertexts that create and traverse networks of signs. What makes these programs unusual is their claim of autonomy. They claim to be texts that dispense with the (human) writer and write themselves. The human reader of these artificially intelligent texts is left to play in a writing space that is supposed to be the mind of the machine. Artificial intelligence is the art of programming the computer to "write the mind."

THE GOAL OF ARTIFICIAL INTELLIGENCE

Can the synthesis of Man and Machine ever be stable, or will the purely organic component become such a hindrance that it has to be discarded? If this eventually happens—and I have ... good reasons for thinking that it must—we have nothing to regret and certainly nothing to fear. (Arthur C. Clarke, *Profile of the Future*, 1984, p. 243. Also quoted in Winner, 1977, p. 59)

The success of computers in so many domains has led to the widespread assumption that they already possess human intelligence. We could blame HAL and other superintelligent, malevolent computers in the movies, but such cinematic computers are of course symptoms rather than causes. Our culture seems eager for or resigned to accept computers that talk, read the newspaper, control traffic, and make economic and political decisions for us; indeed, we assume that computers can already do such things. In fact, today's computers cannot, like HAL, converse with their users in idiomatic English on a wide variety of topics. They cannot read *The New York Times* and answer general questions on their reading. They cannot devise important new theorems in mathematics or physics. They cannot steer an automobile along a road in the company of other vehicles. That is, computers can perform none of these tasks autonomously, although they can play a role in all of them in interaction with a human user. Artificial intelligence, however, insists on the autonomy of the machine: the goal is to embody in the computer an intelligence that can operate in isolation from human users. To return to the user is to cheat the program of its autonomy. The human is called on only at the beginning and the end—to prescribe conditions under which the program must operate and to interpret its output. And precisely because artificial intelligence programs must function in isolation, they have limited success. If the goal is to build the HAL 9000 computer of *2001*, the current programs remind us of HAL only as he is being dismantled at the end of the film—as he regresses from superintelligence to the singing of children's songs. Yet the promise of an intelligent machine continues to appeal to computer users of all levels of sophistication, and millions of dollars are still poured into research in artificial intelligence, particularly by the military in its quest for pilotless tanks and smart bombs. In the personal computer market, almost every database program offered to the credulous business world now claims to contain artificial intelligence. The enthusiasm for artificial intelligence stems in part from the age-old desire to recreate life through technology, the desire expressed in the myth of Pygmalion, in the legend of the Golem, and in the alchemists' formula. Artificial intelligence is the newest recipe for the homunculus. Thus, when Pamela McCorduck, author of *Machines Who Think,* writes that artificial intelligence is "the scientific apotheosis of a venerable cultural tradition" (McCorduck, 1979, p. 29), she seems to mean the tradition of Paracelsus and E. T. A. Hoffman's "Sandman." In the most radical view, artificially intelligent computers will form a race separate from, but at least as intelligent as, human beings. And, at least in Arthur C. Clarke's dark vision, this new technological race does threaten to do away with the human race altogether.

Many, perhaps most, artificial intelligence specialists are not prepared to go as far as Arthur C. Clarke. But they all accept a fundamental analogy between the computer and the human mind. For some, the analogy is all that matters: they see themselves as cognitive scientists, who use the computer as a tool for studying the mind. Their work is a kind of experimental psychology, and their programs are cognitive theories. But even the more pragmatic programmers, who build industrial robots or so-called "expert systems," cannot avoid thinking and speaking of the computer in human terms; nor can they avoid using their programs to provide a vocabulary for human nature. As one artificial intelligence specialist has put it, the human brain "happens to be a meat machine" (Minsky quoted in McCorduck, 1979, p. 70). In more technical, though less colorful terms:

> Artificial intelligence is based on the assumption that the mind can be described as some kind of formal system manipulating symbols that stand for things in the world. Thus it doesn't matter what the brain is made of, or what it uses for tokens in the great game of thinking. Using an equivalent set of tokens and rules, we can do thinking with a digital computer, just as we can play chess using cups, salt and pepper shakers, knives, forks, and spoons. Using the right software, one system (the mind) can be mapped into the other (the computer). (Johnson, 1986, p. 250)

There is, then, no conceptual difference between a human mind and a vast computer program. Cognitive psychologists too have come under the influence of the computer metaphor, and their jargon is full of terms borrowed from electronic technology. And even when psychologists and artificial intelligence specialists admit differences between computers and human beings, the computer may be seen as an alternative to human thought. Fifteen years ago, the psychologist George Miller could already write: "Many psychologists have come to take for granted in recent years . . . that men and computers are merely two different species of a more abstract genus called 'information processing systems'" (quoted in Weizenbaum, 1976, p. 158).

Now one group of researchers, called connectionists, reject the notion of artificial intelligence as symbol manipulation and draw instead a direct analogy between electronic hardware and the brain. The idea is to connect electronic elements into networks that will function like patterns of neurons in the brain. These neural nets seem to bypass the level of discrete symbolic structures and provide a "direct" repesentation of thought or perception.

(See Dreyfus & Dreyfus, 1988.) Connectionism remains a form of artificial intelligence, because the goal is still to achieve autonomy for the machine. Neural networks are still electronic representations of cognitive information, and thinking is still the processing of such representations. Because of its closer relation to neural science, connectionism may be more scientifically successful than symbolic artificial intelligence. However, symbolic artificial intelligence, because it seeks to duplicate the human mind, still provides the more compelling cultural metaphor.

MODELING THE MIND

Symbolic artificial intelligence uses the computer to mirror or "model" the human mind. Modeling the brain through connectionism may or may not succeed: it is a conventional attempt to build a scientific model. But symbolic artificial intelligence is something different. It begins by identifying the model with the thing modeled: the computer program is identified with the mind, the symbolic structures of the program are identified as thoughts and beliefs. An investigator in the hard sciences would never treat his or her model in this fashion. No physicist would confuse a real galaxy with a mathematical model of the motion of stars in that galaxy. No biochemist would mistake a model made of styrofoam balls and dowels for a protein molecule. Yet this is what artificial intelligence specialists willingly do, when they identify their computer programs with the mind. For the philosopher John Searle, this identification is intolerable: Searle argues that a computer program is always only a simulation.

> No one supposes that computer simulation of a five-alarm fire will burn the neighborhood down or that a computer simulation of a rainstorm will leave us all drenched. Why on earth would anyone suppose that a computer simulation of understanding actually understood anything? It is sometimes said that it would be frightfully hard to get computers to feel pain or fall in love, but love and pain are neither harder nor easier than cognition or anything else. For simulation, all you need is the right input and output and a program in the middle that transforms the former into the latter. That is all the computer has for anything it does. To confuse simulation with duplication is the same mistake, whether it is pain, love, cognition, fires or rainstorms. (Searle, 1981, p. 302)

Yet if this is a mistake on the part of the artificial intelligence programmer, the mistake is understandable. It is easy to confuse simulation with duplication when the simulator is the computer and the object of simulation is the human mind. The obvious reason is that the computer seems to possess capacities previously possessed only by human minds. The computer can solve numerical problems or process texts without human intervention. In a complex and changing environment, the computer can function without human contact for a longer period than any other machine. We can know other human minds only by their "output," and the computer's output resembles that of human agents.

The deeper reason why the computer is identified with the mind is that the computer is a writing technology, and writing is intrinsic to our notion of the mind. After 5000 years of phonetic writing and thousands more of picture writing, we can hardly conceive of the mind without the metaphor of writer and writing surface. As the latest technology for writing, the computer is now our most convincing expression of that metaphor. When artificial intelligence claims to be modeling the mind, the claim is therefore tautologous. Every computer program models the mind, as it reflects and reiterates the interplay of writer and writing surface. The study of artificial intelligence is simply the search for new mechanisms to elaborate the writing metaphor. It is no surprise, then, that a cognitive science based upon the computer explains human intelligence in terms of the mechanisms of symbol manipulation (which is another way of saying electronic writing); it cannot do otherwise.

On the other hand, it is not surprising that artificial intelligence programs work poorly when they attempt to embody the entire process of writing, when they attempt to incorporate writer and writing surface and leave the human writer nothing to do. Artificial intelligence specialists often excuse a disappointing program by saying that although the program may not work well now, it is at least a first step on the road to a theory of mind. But the current programs of artificial intelligence are both beginning, middle, and end, because they constitute a self-contained explanation of the mind, one that is grounded in the primary metaphor of mind at least since the time of the Greeks. The value of artificial intelligence is that it shows how the computer can redefine the relationship between writer and writing surface, as it incorporates the writer into the book in a new way. The computer invites us to experiment with new relationships between minds and texts, and artificial intelligence takes up that invitation.

TURING'S WRITING TEST

In 1950 the mathematician and computer specialist Alan Turing wrote a paper entitled "Computing Machinery and Intelligence" (Turing, 1950/ 1963), in which he proposed the following game of wits between human and computer. The human being would sit in one room and type questions at a keyboard and the computer, located in another room, would try to give convincingly human answers; it would try to fool its human interrogator into thinking that he or she was talking to another human being. Here are some questions and the answers that Turing envisioned. (The computer's text is in capital letters.)

Q: Please write me a sonnet on the subject of the Forth Bridge.

A: COUNT ME OUT ON THIS ONE. I NEVER COULD WRITE PO-
ETRY.

Q: Add 34957 to 70764.

A: (Pause of about 30 seconds and then give as answer) 105621.

Q: Do you play chess?

A: YES.

Q: I have K at my K1, and no other pieces. You have only K at K6 and R at R1.
It is your move. What do you play?

A: (After a pause of 15 seconds) R-R8 MATE.(Turing, 1950/1963, p. 12)

Will a digital computer ever be able to play Alan Turing's game even this
well? My own guess is that computers will continue to evolve as they have: in
special domains they will equal or surpass human abilities, but in many ways
they will remain idiots. But idiots can mask their deficiencies. We will have
computers that function surprisingly well—responding to our questions in
English or controlling some industrial process—and then suddenly fail mis-
erably. They will fail unpredictably in tasks that seem hardly different from
those at which they succeed. Their failure will pull us up short, remind us of
their mechanical nature, and at the same time reveal nothing in general about
human nature. The only real danger posed by these idiot savants is that we
may come to trust them beyond their limited areas of competence.

Computers may some day be able to pass the Turing test in fact, without
living up to it in spirit. The test is actually rather easy to pass by the standard
that Turing himself set: "I believe that in about fifty years' time it will be
plausible to programme computers . . . to make them play the imitation game
so well that an average interrogator will not have more than 70 percent chance
of making the right identification after five minutes of questioning" (Turing,
1950/1963, p. 19). Five minutes is not a long time, especially if one must
communicate by typing. But the important point is that in any form Turing's
test is a test of writing ability and reading comprehension. The computer
reads the questions posed by the interrogator and writes responses. The
machine is not asked to imitate the human sense of touch, taste, or smell; it
does not have to demonstrate human dexterity. It has to write and read like
a human being, and its performance is judged entirely by the text that it
produces.

ARTIFICIAL WRITING

All useful computer programs write: they produce output that is a texture of
signs. However, a program that outputs vectors of real numbers is writing a

text that only an engineer or a scientist can appreciate. Artificial intelligence programs are more fun to read. Not only do they often produce text in something like the English language, but, like all texts, this artificial text has a voice.

A program called Eliza, written in the 1960s, resulted in texts like this one (again, the computer's responses are in capitals):

... my boyfriend made me come here.

YOUR BOYFRIEND MADE YOU COME HERE

He says I'm depressed much of the time.

I AM SORRY TO HEAR THAT YOU ARE DEPRESSED

It's true. I am unhappy.

DO YOU THINK COMING HERE WILL HELP YOU NOT TO BE UNHAPPY

I need some help, that much seems certain.

WHAT WOULD IT MEAN TO YOU IF YOU GOT SOME HELP

Perhaps I could learn to get along with my mother.

TELL ME MORE ABOUT YOUR FAMILY

My mother takes care of me.

WHO ELSE IN YOUR FAMILY TAKES CARE OF YOU

My father.

YOUR FATHER

You are like my father in some ways.

WHAT RESEMBLANCE DO YOU SEE

You are not very aggressive, but I think you don't want me to notice that.

(Margret Boden, 1977, pp.106-107)

Eliza inverts the original Turing test: the program asks the questions and the human reader is expected to answer. If anything, this inversion makes the task of impersonating a human easier, because the human reader has already ceded control to the program. The program assumes the persona of the omniscient doctor, whose questions are all rhetorical: the doctor asks in order to compel the patient to his or her own realization. Eliza practices Rogerian or non-directed therapy, the obvious choice, if we are going to embody psychotherapy in the computer. In fact, Eliza is constructed from a series of programming tricks that constantly turn the human partner's own words against him or her. The program focuses on key words and repeats fragments of the human's recent responses. When the program gets lost, it has other tricks to divert its partner's attention. The result can be a silly and repetitive dialogue or an ironic and coherent one. In either case, it is really a monologue, in which the human being is unwittingly responsible for both questions and responses. Thus, Eliza shows how the computer, like all other writing technologies, directs the reader back to his or her own resources in a quest for meaning. However, with the computer, this process of redirection is more complex than in earlier media, because the computer can hold and manipulate the reader's words before releasing them again. Eliza performs this manipulation according to the instructions of the human programmer. Eliza therefore speaks with a voice that reflects both the author of the program and the reader.

Eliza is not now considered artificial intelligence, although the program's voice did manage to fool some people for some time. The author of the program, Joseph Weizenbaum, found this distressing evidence of the dehumanization brought about by the computer:

> I was startled to see how quickly and how very deeply people conversing with [the program] became emotionally involved with the computer and how unequivocally they anthropomorphized it. Once my secretary, who had watched me work on the program for many months and therefore surely knew it to be merely a computer program, started conversing with it. After only a few interchanges with it, she asked me to leave the room. (Weizenbaum, 1976, p. 76)

But Eliza's voice does not dehumanize its audience; it is simply an example of the reflexive power of the computer as a writing space, or more generally the reflexive power of all writing technologies. As readers we enjoy losing ourselves in a text. We enjoy searching for the author's voice in a text, because we are always vaguely aware that we ourselves are the author. When we read a text, we cannot help but ascribe meaning to it, and the texts of artificial intelligence depend upon that impulse in their readers. Why else would Turing's test be a test of human intelligence at all? If text appears on the teletype, we read it and try to make sense of it. If we succeed (and it is very hard to fail), we assume that there must be an intelligence at the other end of the line.

Many artificial intelligence programs possess the mechanical voice of the robot, patiently executing the commands of its human master. At the other extreme, there was a program named PARRY that spoke with the voice of a paranoid patient and conducted the following conversation with a human doctor:

... I TRY TO AVOID THE UNDERWORLD.

Are you afraid of the underworld?

THE MAFIA ARE THE WORST GANGSTERS.

Are you connected with the Mafia?

YOU KNOW, THEY KNOW ME.

How do they know you?

THEY SPY ON ME.

Why do they?

THEY WANT TO GET FALSE EVIDENCE TO FRAME ME.

What do they have against you?

THEY ARE OUT TO GET ME . . .

(Margaret Boden, 1977, pp. 100-101)

In this conversation both the doctor and the computer play their parts convincingly. The programmer of this paranoid program reported that other psychiatrists reading typescripts of similar interviews could not distinguish human patients from the simulated ones. But this is not surprising. When we have only this text before us, we have no reason to believe in the reality of the doctor any more than that of the patient. The patients and the doctors occupy a fictional world of paranoids and therapists. That is the power of text, the power that artificial intelligence seeks to exploit.

The intelligent computer often produces text in direct conversation with a human. A different effect is achieved when the computer speaks with a solitary voice—as here when it takes on the persona of a (slightly demented) storyteller.

ONE DAY JOE BEAR WAS HUNGRY. HE ASKED HIS FRIEND IRVING BIRD WHERE SOME HONEY WAS. IRVING TOLD HIM THERE WAS A BEEHIVE IN THE OAK TREE. JOE THREATENED TO HIT IRVING IF HE DIDN'T TELL HIM WHERE SOME HONEY WAS....

ONE DAY JOE BEAR WAS HUNGRY. HE ASKED HIS FRIEND IRVING BIRD WHERE SOME HONEY WAS. IRVING TOLD HIM THERE WAS A BEEHIVE IN THE OAK TREE. JOE WALKED TO THE OAK TREE. HE ATE THE BEEHIVE.

HENRY ANT WAS THIRSTY. HE WALKED OVER TO THE RIVER BANK WHERE HIS GOOD FRIEND BILL BIRD WAS SITTING. HENRY SLIPPED AND FELL IN THE RIVER. HE WAS UNABLE TO CALL FOR HELP. HE DROWNED. (Taken from *The Cognitive Computer* by Schank, 1984, p. 84)

These stories, produced by programmers at Yale, are perfect examples of the deferred character of electronic writing. The immediate author was the computer itself, which apparently put together the defective storyline and generated the sentences. The ultimate author was the human programmer who devised a series of "knowledge structures" and algorithms from which the computer proceeded. The human writer has not been eliminated from the writing process. Instead, the writer is working at one remove by providing the structures from which the stories flow. The programmer creates a universe of discourse (a universe populated by anthropomorphic bears and ants), and the computer realizes one story from that universe with each pass. The computer functions here as a reader, selecting from a set of possibilities established by the programmer. We in turn provide readers for the computer as author, and the stories belong equally to us, to the computer, and to the programmer. The programmer must share the credit for the crazy outcomes, in that each one of these stories goes wrong because of some defect in the knowledge structure. Although animal fables have a predictable rhythm of expectation and resolution, these stories fail absurdly to satisfy their own expectations. That failure gives them a special voice and in fact makes them far more interesting than stories that succeed. Still, the breaking of the predictable structure does not bring the computer any closer to passing the Turing test, because such a breakdown calls attention to the computer as a reflection of its human programmer.

On the other hand, perhaps there is no such thing as failure in a program like this, since any plausibly connected series of words becomes an exercise for the reader's ingenuity. Artificial intelligence programmers at Yale once produced a program, called FRUMP, that summarized new items from the press wire. The story goes that one day an item came over the wire that began: "Rome was shaken this morning to learn of the death of Pope John Paul I..." The computer summarized by noting that an earthquake in Rome had resulted in one casualty. The computer was not wholly wrong; it had simply preserved the metaphor in the original item.

WRITING CHESS

It is easy to see in the stories of Joe Bear that artificial intelligence is the art of making texts. That same art is required in all artificial intelligence, because all artificial intelligence produces texts that are concatenations of discrete symbols. Sometimes the texts can be read only by experts, as is the case with the game of chess. When the computer plays chess, it conducts a conversation with its human opponent, just as Eliza or the programmed paranoid converse with their human users. The conversation in chess is the movement and action of the pieces over the board. It is a conversation that may also be transcribed into an alphabetic and numerical notation (Byrne, 1989, September 26, p. 24):

	White	Black
1	e4	c5
2	c3	b6
3	d4	Bb7...

A chess player can read this notation and replay the game (revive the conversation) in his or her head or on the board. For good players, these columns of symbols constitute the story of the game. Every chess match is a narrative of cleverness and blunders, ending in victory for one protagonist or in a draw. (The excerpt above is the beginning of a narrative in which a computer program named "Deep Thought" defeated the grand master Robert Byrne.) The game of chess itself is a writing system, whose elements are limited, but still adequate to express a range of meanings for experienced player/readers. When commentators provide comments in English to accompany a game, they are weaving their own text in and around the game and therefore imposing their own interpretation on the original text—just as literary commentators do with their primary texts. And like most literary commentaries, chess commentaries explain the text of the game in terms of the intentions of the player/authors. The commentator tells us that "Black intends to put pressure on White's queen's pawn to force an exchange" or "White offers his knight in a desperate gambit." To poor or beginning chess players, the moves do not convey intentions at all: they form instead a sequence of monotonous play and occasional surprises, when a piece is captured or the king put in check. One move does not seem to follow another for any good reason. We could say that for beginners the text of a game of chess is like a narrative by Kafka or some other modern, but for skilled players it is a coherent story in which the two characters reveal their intentions with every move.

Skilled players will read intentions into the text even when the computer is playing. And this is precisely why artificial intelligence programmers make chess programs: to create a convincing persona that can "write" with chess pieces. At least one program is now so good at chess writing that it can sometimes defeat grand masters. To those who can read the texts of these games, such a program must seem intelligent. "Computers are not human," writes the defeated grand master Robert Byrne, "and yet the best of them seem to play with a certain style that one would have supposed to belong only to a human-like creature. Deep Thought plays generally very conservatively—like a transistorized Anatoly Karpov" (Byrne, 1989, September 26, p. 24). Byrne is aware of the irony and tries to avoid obvious anthropomorphizing. But as a skilled reader (as well as writer) of chess programs, he cannot help but ascribe intentions to the player/author. So in commenting on a game between two computer programs, Deep Thought and Hitech, he writes: "... that Hitech had not worked out such a strategy became evident when it deemed f3 too loosening and shilly-shallied. Deep Thought did its own share of shilly-shallying, but with 29 ... g5!, it started the correct plan of exploiting the absence of white pieces from the kingside by producing a mating attack" (Byrne, 1989, June 27, p. C17). Deep Thought may now be one of the best authors of chess texts in the world, but its reputation and its importance for artificial intelligence will continue to depend on humans who read and comment on what Deep Thought has written.

ELECTRONIC ANIMISM

Artificially intelligent writing can take many forms. In addition to the stories of Joe Bear and the texts of Deep Thought, there are programs that prove mathematical theorems, translate from English into Japanese, or solve logical puzzles. All these programs can best be understood as experiments in the technology of electronic writing. Particularly popular now are the expert systems: programs to aid geologists in finding oil or doctors in diagnosing patients. These too are writing programs: the human expert, doctor or geologist, encodes his or her experience as a text that consists of hundred or thousands of condition-action rules. This coded text constitutes the expert system. The human reader interrogates the text by making the rules fire and waiting for the textual output, which should be answers to the reader's questions about diseases or oil rigs. An expert system may or may not be an effective way in which to embody the expert's knowledge, but it is clearly nothing other than a new kind of book, no more or less intelligent than a conventional printed encyclopedia. Computer-controlled robots too are writing systems, although, instead of displaying their output as characters on a videoscreen, they write with electro-mechanical arms or wheels. They take electronic writing out into the world.

Ultimately the artificial intelligence programmer wants the computer to cover the world with electronic writing. Artificial intelligence leads almost inexorably to a kind of animism, in which every technological device (computers, telephones, wristwatches, automobiles, washing machines) writes and in which everything that reads and writes also has mind. The Pentagon already speaks of smart bombs; cameras are now said to be intelligent when they adjust the focus and shutter speed to save us from overexposed family photos. The artificial intelligence proponent John McCarthy has claimed that thermostats have beliefs: they believe that the house is too hot, too cold, or at the right temperature (McCarthy, 1979, pp. 173-174). McCarthy's claim is a prelude to the common futurological dream—here stated in an article from the Futurist magazine, in which the whole house becomes an animistic universe:

The ultimate house may be a structure whose computer brain, equipped with sensors and linked through telecommunications networks to computer data banks and the brains of other houses, has developed an awareness of its own existence, and an intimate knowledge of its inhabitants. . . . This development will greatly add to our ability to 'believe in' the computer as a conscious entity. Once your house can talk to you, you may never feel alone again. (cited by Roszak, 1986, p. 35)

This smart house is the microcosm; others are bold enough to envision the whole earth in these terms:

It is not difficult to imagine the shape of the eco-computer in place. Sensors will proliferate in the biosphere and beyond. . . . Pressure-sensitive devices, infra-red systems, microphones, sensor probes, pollution detectors, temperature sensors and countless other devices will be sited in the oceans; just as an equivalent range of detectors will be carried on surface vessels, on land, in aircraft (computer-controlled) and in orbiting and geostationary satellites. Masses of ecological, demographic and other data will be fed into the computer nodes of the global electronic intelligence. A complex hierarchy of cybernetic loops will sense environmental change and take action, where possible, to maintain conditions of equilibrium. People will work to provide data for the eco-computer, much as they might work to feed a ravenous creature with an insatiable appetite. (Simons, 1987, p. 156)

In this odd vision, the whole world (even outer space) has become a writing space, which the computer reads and onto which it writes. Here the balance between perception and semiosis is clearly lost, as the perceived world is taken through transducers into the machine.

Computer animism is the reversal of traditional animistic belief, for example in archaic Greece. In the traditional view, the elements of nature such as the sun, the mountains, bodies of water, thunder, and earthquakes were divine and therefore more alive than humans. Such products of technology as buildings, ships, and pots were inanimate. In the computer age, everything technological threatens to take on its own mental life, whereas the physical world (excluding plants and animals) is quite lifeless and can be explained in terms of Newtonian or quantum mechanics. In this new great chain of being, the machines take the place of angels, as purified or supernatural human agents. Humans stand between animals and machines, because humans lack the simplicity of the machines. They are subject to earthly passions and carry the dross of their animal origins. Machines, particularly computers, are pure, clean, and orderly instances of design.

Computers are not now called angels. Instead, they are clothed in the vocabulary of Darwinian science and named a new species. Gordon Pask has written that the proliferation of computers and control devices ". . . is leading to the evolution of a new species, a species we have dubbed 'micro man'"

(Pask & Curran, 1982, p. 2; see also Roszak, 1986, p. 42). But Pask seems still to envision a symbiotic relationship between humans and machines. Robert Jastrow has gone further and eliminated humans altogether:

> ... human evolution is a nearly finished chapter in the history of life. ... We can expect that a new species will arise out of man, surpassing his achievements as he has surpassed those of his predecessor, Homo erectus. ... The new kind of intelligent life is more likely to be made of silicon. (Robert Jastrow, *Time*, Februrary 20, 1978, p. 59 quoted in Roszak, 1986, p. 43)

The idea of the computer as human replacement is more sinister than the eco-computer, if only because it is more plausible. More than one enthusiast for artificial intelligence has proposed using computers as therapists for psychiatric patients. (See Boden, 1977, pp. 456-458.) This is the clearest possible example of the desire by artificial intelligence to turn the computer into an immediate (logocentric) partner for human beings. The same impulse leads to the proposal that the electronic encyclopedia should have a personality: that it should be a person who asks the user questions and then leads the way to the answers. The strategy of artificial intelligence is always to disguise the computer as text and to make of it instead a persona. The result is what we might call a "minimalist" computer, a machine that functions in a deprived perceptual world and denies its own rich, semiotic nature. The problem lies in trying to substitute perception for semiosis. Almost all the visions of an artificially intelligent utopia degenerate into the electronic psychotherapist, when they try to let the computer do all the reading and writing and then serve the result up to human beings perceptually. In such a utopia, everything becomes computer-controlled television.

TEXTS AND MINDS

The electronic therapist and the previous examples of artificial writing are all texts that seem to have intelligence—texts that pretend to be not the product, but the embodiment of mind. For artificial intelligence specialists the mind is nothing other than a self-activating text, a network of elements together with mechanisms for adding and deleting elements and restructuring their relationships. Elements in the network may be verbal, or they may be some encoding of images or sounds. All elements are meaningful only because they can refer to other elements and so enter into a structure of signs. In other words, to think is to read and write, where reading and writing are the creation and manipulation of a network of signs. Artificial intelligence has given the computer world semantic trees, networks, scripts, frames. These are the syntactic structures through which the artificial intelligence program reads and writes its textual world. The meaning of an artificially intelligent text can be nothing other than its syntactic structure:

> Perhaps the single most important idea to artificial intelligence is that there is no fundamental difference between form and content, that meaning can be captured in a set of symbols such as a semantic net. (Johnson, 1986, p. 250)

A semantic net, a network of nodes and pointers, is all that any artificial intelligence program has to capture the meaning of a sentence or paragraph in English. A computer text is always a texture of signs that point to other signs, and so the form of the text *is* its meaning. The equation of form and meaning is made by all computer programs, not just programs for artificial intelligence. All programs require that their input be a structure of atomic symbols (ultimately binary units) and implicit or explicit pointers. Some programs, such as outline processors, now create structures that were pioneered by artificial intelligence specialists. Once again, the difference is that artificial intelligence insists that such structures do not constitute the text alone, but that they constitute the readers and writers as well. Mind, whether human or electronic, is a network of atomic symbols and pointers.

In one sense artificial intelligence is right. The mind is what we make of it, and in this age we are more and more inclined to make of the mind a symbol processor on analogy with the computer. As our culture produces more electronic texts, we repeat the experience we have had with earlier writing technologies: author, text, and reader enter into a relationship in which each is identified or confused with the others. We come to see ourselves in the text we have created and to ascribe to our minds the qualities of those texts. Once we realize that the computer is a new writing technology, particularly well-suited to creating semiotic structures, what else could the mind be but a computer program—that is, a network of interrelated signs, together with some facility for adding new signs, discarding others, and revising connections?

Computer programming, including artificial intelligence, is the art of writing with electronic technology, the art of manipulating signs and of deferring their manipulation so as to create writing of the second order. A computer program evokes in its users the familiar response: where there is writing, there must be an author, and if the program itself writes, then it must have or be a mind. But computer programming cannot teach us about mind itself, abstracted from the experience of writing, both because there is (for our culture at least) no such abstraction and because the paradigm of writing is inherent in the digital computer. You cannot do anything with a computer except to write. The moment you touch a key on the keyboard, you have accepted this paradigm, whether you are consulting a database, using a word processor, or putting together your own program. The computer describes the process of mental writing so well because it is itself a writing technology, and we cannot understand "higher" or cognitive mental activity except by analogy with writing.

The metaphor of mental writing applies most effectively and obviously to cognition; it is less clear how any system of symbolic writing can account for sense perception. As critics have been pointing out for years, the digital computer cannot easily explain or imitate perceptual experience. The computer can play brilliant chess, because chess is a game of pure semiosis, a pursuit of signs. But a computerized robot can hardly make its way around a living room without colliding with a table or chair, because this task requires the subtle interplay of sense perception and reason, and there is no clear way to make that interplay into a game of discrete symbols. So computers perform poorly in most tasks that require pattern-matching or robotic navigation through the "real" world. In recent years, for example, the Army has been trying to build a computerized truck that can drive itself without a human pilot:

> The boxy truck bore a large sign reading Warning Unmanned Vehicle Stay Back 100 Feet. It was supposed to navigate a sharp curve at 6 miles an hour. Instead, it headed for the ditch. 'It could have been mud on the road or maybe a cloud's shadow obscured its visions,' hedged the ... engineer who hit the kill switch.... During tests of a similar vehicle at Carnegie-Mellon in 1985, the robot, which had been programmed to stay on the road by following edges of sharply defined contrast, tried to run up a tree. (Jacky, 1987, pp. 187-188.)

Again, such a robot-vehicle is an attempt to read and write upon the world—in this case to read a scene directly from nature and to write back onto nature with the wheels of the truck, all without the benefit of a human translator. Unfortunately, what the video camera can see does not translate easily into a semiotic code. It is hard to represent the objects in a room or the shape of a road in discrete symbols that the computer can process. Perception and semiosis somehow come together in human intelligence, but not in a way the digital computer can duplicate. Again this reason is that the computer is a technology for writing and reading systems of discrete signs. There must always be a gap between the continuous world of perception and the world of signs, a gap that can never be closed in any technology of writing. Attempts by cognitive science or cognitive psychology to "model" human perception are contemporary examples of the desire to close the gap between the sign and the signified—either to reduce the world to signs or to give the signs the same status as things.

AUTONOMOUS WRITING

Remember thou hast made me more powerful than thyself. . . . But I will not be tempted to set myself in opposition to thee. I am thy creature, and I will be even mild and docile to my natural lord and king, if thou wilt also perform thy part, the which thou owest me. (The monster to Frankenstein, in Mary Shelley's *Frankenstein*, 1960, p. 101)

It is a commonplace to compare modern technology in general, and the computer in particular, to Frankenstein's monster—a powerful and threatening creation beyond the control of its creator. The Frankenstein story is in fact a parable for the computer age, precisely because it maintains the proper ambivalence toward the monster. In Mary Shelley's story, the monster may or may not be beyond human control, but he is certainly not autonomous. Rather, the monster is the alter ego of his master. The two are repeatedly drawn together, and their relationship (creator and creation, father and son) is often confused or inverted. The horror of the tale is that the monster cannot leave the master in peace. In his first conversation with Victor Frankenstein, the monster says: ". . . you, my creator, detest and spurn me, thy creature, to whom thou art bound by ties only dissoluble by the annihilation of one of us" (p. 100). But even this is an understatement, for the death of Frankenstein leads quickly to the monster's own suicide. Computer programs, particularly artificial intelligence programs, are like Frankenstein's monster in this crucial respect: they always carry the trace of their creators. If they set themselves in opposition to their programmers, it is certainly only to please—because the programmers want their creations to appear autonomous. Yet the programs can never be entirely separate from the programmers who made them.

The autonomy of the computer is only apparent. The computer seems to be a tool that one can let go of, but all programs, including artificial intelligence programs, simply defer the need to return to the human user. All programs are liable to fail and require human intervention. But even if the programmer could create a flawless program, his or her creation would still be operating in an environment defined by human needs and interests. What would such a program do? Would it read books? Why, except that human beings read books. Would it do mathematics? This would merely reflect the taste and capacity of human programmers and mathematicians. Would it replicate? Why, except that survival through replication is a facet of animal and therefore human life. The most advanced artificial intelligence program would refer back to its human programmer, even if all human life ceased and the planet were taken over by robots. But this is science fiction. No program that now exists or that is foreseeable can achieve such autonomy. Artificial intelligence programs must reflect the mind, simply because the programs are human artifacts and reflect the capacities of their human makers. It is because the computer's origin as a humanly produced tool can never be wholly denied, that the computer can never provide an independent assessment of human intelligence.

The programmer and the program are bound by the same ties that bind any author to his or her text. Authors can never control their texts as they would like, but they can never wholly deny their creations. And just as texts cannot exist without authors and readers, programs, which are special texts, cannot exist without programmers and users. Artificial intelligence can pursue the goal of building a symbolic mind, but it will never succeed in emancipating the mind from human nature. For the mind must be understood in terms of reading and writing that refer back to human beings. What artificial intelligence seeks to create is the text that writes itself, and any such text will always be understood in reference to a remote, yet never wholly absent human writer or programmer. The apparent autonomy of the computer is simply a new manifestation of the apparent autonomy of the book; the computer's voice is the voice of the prose that has addressed us for centuries from the pages of books. Our ambivalent reaction to the voice of any book (is it the author? is it simply the voice of the reader? is it somehow independent of either?) is the source of both the interest and the fear that the computer inspires.

When we realize that the computer is nothing more or less than a new way of writing, the threat of the autonomous computer disappears. Like all earlier kinds of books, the computer as book never manages to write and read itself. The computer is also far more effective (and dangerous) when it operates in contact with humans, than when it is deprived of the aid of human writers and readers. If computers do embody intelligence, then they do so just as printed books and manuscripts have done. Can a poem in manuscript or a printed encyclopedia replace a human being? In fact we constantly use books in place of human beings. Textbooks serve as teachers. Newspapers report events because we cannot question eyewitnesses ourselves. A grammar and exercise book serves in place of a native speaker in introducing us to a foreign language. The printed novel adopts the voice of the storyteller. In some cases, we are content with the book. In others, we would prefer to have a human teacher or reporter. In all cases, our experience of the book is different from our experience with a human being. Books do not replace human intelligence; they present human intelligence in another form. They defer the promise of a direct relationship between the human author and reader. Computers should be understood in the same way. As we work with the machine, we encounter human intelligence deferred.

ARTIFICIAL INTELLIGENCE AS DEFERRAL

Writing is always an act of deferral: the writer puts words down on a writing surface in order to have those words back at a later time. Each technology of writing lends its own peculiar character to the act of deferral. Electronic writing defines a radical kind of deferral, by permitting the computer to intervene between the author and his or her words or between the reader and the author's words. The computer becomes the author by proxy, in the sense that it operates on the text as the reader reads. The computer both heightens the illusion of the author in the text and further separates the author from the text. It creates a more circuitous route between author and text or reader and text than has ever before existed.

Each computer program is an experiment in deferred writing, in which the programmer is an author, the program is a text, and those who use the program are readers. The readers of the program find themselves acquiescing in the deferral, acting as if they were communicating with an intelligence rather than activating a series of instructions. It is almost impossible to avoid this move. As computer users, we begin to talk to the screen, to ascribe malice or good will to the machine. Of course we also talk to cars and can openers, especially when they fail to perform as expected. But with the computer our reaction is more complex. A computer running a program is not only a device; it is also a text, and the user/reader of the program ends up playing the same game as the reader of any text, forgetting the textual frame and pretending instead that the text has a voice. When we read a printed novel, we pretend that the text is not simply a constellation of words, but rather a narrative voice describing real events. When we read a newspaper article, we imagine that the story is being told by an eyewitness or someone with some other claim to know the facts from witnesses. We assume an intelligence behind the text. In the same way the computer user assumes an intelligence in order to get on with the program, to accomplish whatever the program promises to help the user do.

A failure in a computer program reminds the user of its limitations as program, that is, as a series of coded instructions. The failure also reminds the user of the human programmer, who failed somehow to provide for a particular circumstance that the user now requires. The failures of artificial intelligence programs are striking, precisely because the programs have worked so hard to create the illusion of autonomous intelligence. Popular films about robots and computers exploit this same shock of recognition. In the classic scene, repeated it seems in every such film, one of the characters, whom we had assumed to be human, turns out to be a robot and comes apart in a very unhuman way, revealing wires where it should have nerves and muscles. Often the robot also turns out to be a foe rather than a friend, the cause of all the trouble along the way. Its mechanical nature confirms its alienation from the community of the other characters. The character moves from the human world into the world of technology, and this movement shows that it is evil.

Whether artificial intelligence programs are friendly or evil, they certainly give us a mild shock of recognition when they come apart. Yet all programs are liable to come apart, word processors and speadsheets as well as chess-playing programs and natural-language processors. When any program breaks down, it reveals its origin as a text and therefore as the deferred product of a human mind. Artificial intelligence programs are unusual only in their attempt to deny the process of deferral, to deny their own character as programs. The charm of artificial intelligence programs (think of Joe Bear) is that they try to be autonomous, even if they cannot ultimately succeed. Artificial intelligence programmers are always trying to enlarge the domains of success, to push back the limits at which the program reveals itself as a program. But those limits can never be erased, for to do so would be to overcome the limits of writing, of symbolic representation itself.

SEARCHING FOR THE AUTHOR

Almost by accident, artificial intelligence programmers have come upon the central problem of writing: the problem of defining the relationship among author, reader, and text. Artificial intelligence is an exploration of that complex relationship in the new medium provided by the computer. Each artificial intelligence program presents us with a text and then invites us to look for the author. When we say that the author must be human, we are invited to consider the paradox of the computer as author.

For a moment we may find it hard to respond, because a computer text does seem to usurp the conventional roles of both the author and the reader. Conventional reading is conceived as taking signs from an external book and writing them in the inner book of the mind. The computer complicates this picture: the author is now present in the book, not metaphorically as the author has always been in the history of writing, but operationally, because the computer can direct the course of the reading. In previous technologies, readers had to be tricked into playing the role of the author, who was in fact absent. The trick was perhaps easier in ancient times and in the early Middle Ages, when readers generally read aloud and so recreated what seemed to be the author's voice with their own. Silent reading has encouraged a more distant and criticial view of what we read; we are less inclined to hear the author's voice as our eyes fly over the page. Still, operational presence has always been the elusive goal of writing. It is what Plato demanded in the *Phaedrus* when he insisted that true writing should know when to speak and when to keep silent.

Operational presence is precisely what artificial intelligence exploits in its attempt to convince us that programs are intelligent. Artificial intelligence programmers invite us to hear the author's voice, and at the same time they insist the voice is that of the machine itself. Every artificial intelligence program is a story with its own narrator, whose purpose is to convince us that the narrator is human or to confuse the definition of humanity to the extent that we cannot exclude such a narrator. Artificial intelligence is literally science fiction. It is certainly the product of the same impulse: the desire to extrapolate technology wildly, while keeping social and cultural change to a minimum—to put 20th-century men and women into some future or technologically possible world. Artificial intelligence programs are themselves little science fiction dramas narrated in the same, usually optimistic tone. In one program the voice asks the user to describe his or her emotional problems; in another it provides plausible summaries of news events; in another it analyzes drilling prospects for an oil company. The emphasis on the narrative voice is greater in artificial intelligence than in more practical programs, although the voice is always there if we listen closely.

Artificial intelligence programmers are themselves engaged in a perpetual search for the author. They will admit to being the author of their own programs, but they refuse to take credit for the output of those programs. If the program writes a story or produces an endgame in chess, they look for the author in the program itself, in the algorithm that constitutes the program, which for them constitutes intelligence. Searching for the program as author is a new version of the long search for God as the author of the world. The theologian looked for evidence of God in nature, which was itself often compared to a book, and the absence or presence of God in nature became the fundamental theological question of the 17th and 18th centuries. Artificial intelligence programmers revive that question in their tiny programmed universes, as they toy with the presence or absence of the author in the text.

Joseph Weizenbaum has described the role of the computer programmer as a kind of Mosaic lawgiver:

> The computer programmer ... is a creator of universes for which he alone is the lawgiver.... [Programmed elements] compliantly obey their laws and vividly exhibit their obedient behavior. No playwright, no stage director, no emperor, however powerful, has ever exercised such absolute authority to arrange a stage or a field of battle and to command such unswervingly dutiful actors or troops. (Weizenbaum, 1976, p. 115)

In fact, the programmer is not so much Moses as the deity itself. Artificial intelligence programmers, in particular, play God, in the sense that they build programs that are meant to act in a human fashion. Artificial intelligence specialists are sometimes quite open about such a parallel. They see themselves as demigods as they set about to create intelligent and therefore animate machines. What they fail to realize is that they are demigods in exactly the same sense as authors of narrative fiction have always been demigods of the stories they write. Authors routinely play God in creating characters that live and manifest intelligence in a tiny alternate world.

THE WRITING TEST REVISITED

The philosopher Robert Sokolowski has recently argued for a close relationship between artificial intelligence and the activity of writing: "[a]rtificial intelligence does not simply mimic the brain and nervous system; it transforms, codifies, and manipulates written discourse" (Sokolowski, 1988, p. 48). He even suggests that "[t]he continuity between writing and artificial intelligence should make us less apprehensive about being somehow replaced by thinking machines. In a way, we are already replaced by the written word" (48-49). But he does not carry this compelling argument far enough, perhaps because his definition of writing is too narrow, limited by the fixed character of handwriting and printing. Artificial intelligence is not a continuation of writing by other means: it is rather a species of writing, of the new electronic writing. It does not add anything to the reflexive character of writing that is not already present in an electronic encyclopedia or an interactive fiction.

Indeed, it is because artificial intelligence is a genre of electronic fiction that the Turing test is such an appropriate measure of artificial intelligence. Turing proposed that artificial intelligence be judged by the texts it creates. Judge the author by the text: if a computer can be an autonomous author of convincingly human texts, then it is intelligent. Nearly 40 years after Turing's proposal, computers can produce all sorts of texts in closer or more distant collaboration with human users. No program has achieved the autonomy that Turing hoped for, but computers have already added further complexity to the relationship between author, reader, and text—the three elements in the Turing test. The computer has piqued our interest in redefining intelligence as the book that writes itself. Artificial intelligence specialists understand this when they say that their work will change the definition of intelligence. "I believe," Turing wrote, "that at the end of the century the use of words and general educated opinion will have altered so much that one will be able to speak of machines thinking without expecting to be contradicted" (Turing, 1950/1963, p. 19). This prediction has already come true; it was coming true when Turing made it in 1950. Engineers were no doubt already saying that their early computers "forgot" to execute code under a certain condition or "thought" that one numerical variable was larger than another. Most significantly, they were already speaking of the computer "reading from" and "writing to" magnetic tapes. We must remember, however, that this changed definition of intelligence accepts the computer into a world created by human intelligence, more precisely by human literacy.

The computer is therefore both an extension and a reflection of the human mind. Its double character is exactly that of a full-fledged writing technology. And the computer is particularly suited to this dual role. The machine always keeps its user off-balance. Just when it seems safe to regard the computer as a lifeless tool, the machine seizes control. Yet when the user wants to cede control to the computer, it reveals its mechanical nature by breaking down. Those who work habitually with the computer come to accept, perhaps even to enjoy the violent shifts to which the machine subjects its users. But many would-be users are put off by precisely this quality: the inability of the machine to remain either a machine or an intelligence. Once again, the ambiguity of the computer identifies it as a writing technology. It is in the nature of all writing to evoke such ambivalence in the writer and reader. The ambiguities of printed or written texts, however, are subtle, and writers have had hundreds or thousands of years to get used to them. Printed and written texts too pretend to speak to us, as Plato said, as if they had intelligence. Yet many kinds of interruptions intervene to break the illusion of a voice in a printed or written text. When the computer loses its voice, it does so spectacularly. When it regains that voice, it speaks with such apparent authority that we are left to wonder who is in control. At all times the computer, like all previous technologies of writing, is intelligent only in collaboration with human readers and writers.

11

Electronic Signs

We have seen that, like all texts in the electronic writing space, the texts of artificial intelligence form a network of elements and pointers. All electronic texts are self-sufficient, in the sense that each element refers only to other elements in the network. This apparent self-sufficiency raises questions about the meaning and reference of the electronic writing space. What happens in this new technology to the written word as a symbol: what is the semiotics of electronic writing? Students of semiotics have not ignored the electronic media, but they seem more interested in television than the computer. And yet, while television is a relatively meager symbolic space, the computer as a writing space promises a semiotic revolution.

What the computer promises is the embodiment of semiotic views of language and communication: that is, the views of Peirce, Saussure, Eco, and others. And this is hardly surprising, since semiotics itself is a product of the same intellectual forces that have produced the computer, including symbolic logic, linguistics, and philosophy. The computer is a machine for creating and manipulating signs; the signs may be mathematical, verbal, or pictorial. Computer programming and indeed all kinds of writing and reading by computer are exercises in applied semiotics. The first lesson any sophisticated computer user must learn is the difference between a sign and its reference, between the address of a location in the computer's memory and the value stored at that address. This dichotomy characterizes the machine at all levels: it is at the essence of hypertext and of programs for artificial intelligence, in all of which text is simply a texture of signs pointing to other signs.

Signs are always anchored in a medium. Signs may be more or less dependent upon the characteristics of one medium—they may transfer more or less well to other media—but there is no such thing as a sign without a medium, without a defined writing space. This is simply another way of saying that we cannot understand the nature of writing without taking account of writing surfaces and instruments. The surface and the instrument must always affect the signs we write—at the very least by suggesting forms that are convenient and legible. The computer certainly does that much in favoring letter forms and graphics that can be displayed legibly as pixels on a screen. But the computer does more, as it becomes both surface and instrument for a uniquely fluid writing. The very process of semiosis, the movement from one sign to another in the act of reference, is embodied in the computer, and this embodiment is unique in the history of writing. In the computer, signs behave exactly as the students of semiotics expect them to behave. We could say that the theory of semiotics becomes obvious, almost trivially true, in the computer medium. In earlier media such as the printed book, the signs only referred potentially to other signs. However, the computer as a text that can seem to read and write itself also provides its own semiosis.

SIGNS AND REFERENCE

At first glance the mode of reference in the electronic writing space seems to be the same as that of earlier technologies. A printed book consists of words on a page. When we read the words, they give rise in our minds to representations of the world, of imagined worlds, or of abstract ideas. When we read words or examine illustrations in a hypertext on the computer screen, we have the same experience. Traditional reading is still possible in the new medium. The difference is that traditional reading is shadowed or doubled by a new kind of reading, in which the computer helps to define the paths to follow. The words in an electronic text suggest their own reference, because they are contained within topical units that relate to other topical units in a variety of ways. The topics themselves are signs, complex signs that may consist of one paragraph or a whole chapter of prose. Each topical sign is defined not only by the words it contains, but also by its relation to other topics. And the computer makes these relations explicit and operative as the writer builds and the reader reads.

The new reading permitted by the computer becomes especially clear when the text is too large to be read from cover to cover, as is the case with encyclopedias and dictionaries. The *Oxford English Dictionary* is now available on CD-ROM for electronic reading (1987). An advertising brochure claims this advantage for the electronic version: "The OED on CD-ROM permits direct electronic access to quotations, definitions, and more, no matter in which of the 252,000 main entries they appear. This is possible as the traditional list of headwords has been supplemented by seven additional lists (or indexes) created from the material in the OED: Etymology, Definition; Label . . . ; and Quotations subdivided into Date, Author, Work, and Text."

The eight electronic indexes transform the OED into a vast reticulated network, in which each entry is a topic linked to thousands of other topics by parallels of etymology, definition, date, and so on. The reader is invited to explore the dictionary by defining and following out these parallels.

> By using the etymological index, for example, one can isolate all the words of Greek origin . . . or by using the quotation date index, one can pull out all the dictionary's quotations falling between the years 1580 and 1600 . . . or by using the quotation author index, one can find all the quotations from John Donne contained in the OED . . . or by using the label index, one can isolate all the legal terms. (Royalynn O'Connor, letter accompanying brochure.)

The same information existed in the printed version of the OED. But connections had to be made and followed one by one by the reader—often from the reader's memory of other entries. The electronic OED can operate on the connections automatically, at the reader's request, so that the act of reference now belongs in part to the machine and in part to the reader.

It is quite appropriate that the OED should be among the first great printed texts to be transferred to electronic form. For the dictionary has always been the classic example of the semiotic principle that signs refer only to other signs. Peirce explained semiosis as a three-part process: there must always be a bridge between the sign and what the sign represents, and this bridge Peirce called the *interpretant*. The interpretant is the process by which the sign is defined; it is therefore another group of signs. We can only define a sign in terms of other signs of the same nature. This lesson is known to every child who discovers that fundamental paradox of the dictionary: that if you do not know what some words mean you can never use the dictionary to learn what other words mean. The definition of any word, if pursued far enough through the dictionary, will lead you in circles. This paradox is the foundation of semiotics. A sign system is a set of rules for relating elements. The rules are arbitrary, and the system they generate is self-contained. There is no way to get "outside" the system to the world represented, because, as in the dictionary, signs can only lead you elsewhere in the same system.

The computer is a self-contained world in which the whole process of semiosis can take place. Say that a writer creates the following structure (Fig. 11.1) in the electronic writing space of the machine. Not only the words in each topic, but the topics themselves and the link that connects them are part of the process of signification. Words, boxes, and arrow together constitute the text, or at least its visualization, for the text is also the data structure that the computer registers behind the image on the screen. In other media the

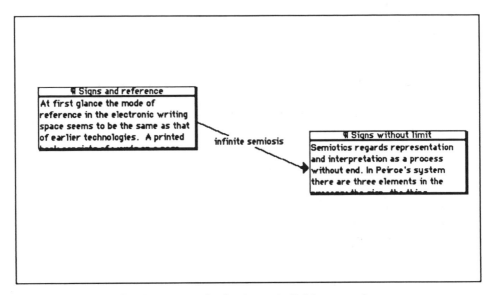

FIG 11.1. Two hypertextual episodes and a link between them.

text has been all image, never anything more than the ink we see on the paper or the scratches in clay or stone. And because there has never been anything behind the text, the process of reading and interpreting has always taken place in front of the text—in the eye and the mind of the reader. The electronic space is unique in that its textual structures are kinetic: the structure can alter or regroup its elements behind the screen as we look on. In the technologies of handwriting and printing, the human mind was the only activator of signs; in this new technology signs also become active outside the mind in the electronic circuits where the text itself resides. The reader must therefore learn to read in a new way, by cooperating with a text that is directed by its own economy of interpretation. The interpretation and therefore the meaning of a text is generated by the interactions, the attractions and repulsions, of two poles: one pole is the reader's mind as he or she faces the surface of the text, and the other is the data structure located behind that surface. Both poles may be constantly responding to one another, making and breaking connections, perhaps altering the words themselves of the superficial text that lies between them.

In a printed dictionary, we must move from page to page, looking up definitions, if we are to set in motion the play of signs. The play takes place in our heads, not in the book at all. The electronic space does not prevent us from reading in this fashion, but the electronic space does duplicate within itself the process of interpretation. Whether they exist permanently in the textual structure or are generated dynamically, the links in a hypertext are acts of interpretation that move the reader from one sign to another. In the electronic OED, when the reader isolates all the words of Greek origin before 1800 or all the words instanced by a quotation from Donne, the reader is simply engaging in the electronic pursuit of signs; he or she is creating connections between the signs in the dictionary and interpreting each sign in terms of its connection to others. A hypertext is always a play of signs. The writer arranges the electronic space so that one sign points to another or many others. We as readers follow those connections and move through the space along predetermined paths of interpretation, or we forge our own paths, which we may choose to leave behind for other readers. An electronic dictionary can be shot through with such connections. In Peirce's terms, the computer system itself becomes the interpretant for each sign, and interpretation becomes the process of following links according to the constraints of the computer's logic.

We have seen that the electronic reader takes an active role in the making of the text: that indeed the text becomes a contested ground between author and reader. In fact there is a third player in this game, the electronic space itself. The computer is always doubling the author for the reader, just as it doubles the reader for the author, interpreting and misinterpreting each to the other. Once the author has set up the text as a delicate balance of signs, the computer can be made to perform operations on individual signs or on the whole structure, operations that alter the balance without the direct and continuing intervention of author or reader. The author may fashion the text so that it changes permanently when readers traverse a certain path—so that readers burn their connections behind them. Readers may search the text for the occurrence of various words and form new paths based on that search. The computer can even be programmed to rearrange its structure overnight in response to a dozen different variables: say, the news service or messages on a computer network or the time of day or year registered on the computer's clock. In collecting a library of printed books, we can be sure that our texts will be the same in the morning as they were the night before. For an electronic library, we have no such assurance, as the texts may age, mature, and degenerate to reflect the time that we have been away.

THE SIGN IN ACTION

In semiotic theory, a sign is not a static thing, but rather a function, a relation between the signified and the signifier: the sign function relates expression to contents. As Umberto Eco explains it, "the classical notion of a 'sign' dissolves itself into a highly complex network of changing relationships. Semiotics suggests a sort of molecular landscape in which what we are accustomed to recognize as everyday forms turn out to be the result of transitory chemical aggregations and so-called 'things' are only the surface appearance assumed by an underlying network of more elementary units" (Eco, 1976, pp. 48ff). Signification is activity, like the pulsing world of molecules as they form and dissolve bonds. Eco's appeal is to a metaphor from chemistry, but the "network of changing relationships" perfectly describes the computer and hypertext. Electronic writing allows us to display and manipulate our network of relationships with far greater facility than a chemist can control the molecular landscape. And the electronic writing space is not a metaphor for signification, but rather a technology of signification. Signs in the computer do precisely what students of semiotics have been claiming for their signs for more than a century.

In symbolic logic or mathematics, a function is a pairing between sets of elements. In the computer the writer and the reader create such pairings, as they move from topic to topic. Texts themselves become programs that the writer builds and the reader executes. The writer puts in not only verbal signs, but rules for the interrelation of signs, and the reader plays the writer's game by following those rules to see how the verbal signs fit together. Each textual program embodies a range of possible meanings, many of which even the writer may not have foreseen. In reading the text, the reader is running a program. The resulting interpretation or reading will depend upon the choices the reader makes in the course of the running. Mediating between author and reader, the computer makes the act of reference explicit, and in doing so it makes apparent the purely conventional nature of writing. A hypertext system spells out the process of interpretation in an algorithm and embodies that process in a programming language: there is nothing mysterious about a program that follows pointers from one symbolic unit to another. And if the act of reference can be played out by the computer, then reference and meaning must depend upon nothing more than an arbitrary set of rules.

In other media, some of the conventions of representation are equally apparent: in a printed book, the index and table of contents are conventions to help us find our way through the text. Yet we as readers do much more of the work of reference: much of the process of interpretation still plays out in the inaccessible regions of the mind. Furthermore, even in a printed book, there remains a sense of the presence of the spoken word. In the earlier age of manuscripts, the reader was all the more inclined to treat the written text as a script, in which the signs were meant to be revived as sounds in the spoken language. Whenever readers treat text as a script, they feel the magical presence of spoken language, what the deconstructionists now call "logocentrism." As text becomes more visual and includes signs that cannot be spoken, the sense of the arbitrary and the mediated increases at the expense of the belief that words are natural, immediate representations of the world. Logocentrism, then, has been diminishing for hundreds of years, at least since the later Middle Ages, when silent reading became popular and long before the deconstructionists recognized it as the great problem of Western metaphysics. (We may even wonder whether the rise of silent reading coincides with the nominalism and scholastic logic of the 13th and 14th centuries, which have been called the intellectual ancestors of deconstruction.) Printing itself encourages silent reading and the view of words as arbitrary signs, although there remains a vestige of orality in reading a printed book.

Orality is further diminished in electronic writing. As the act of reference becomes explicit in a hypertext, there is a greater emphasis on visual meaning, on diagrammatic signs that cannot be spoken. An aural residue will remain as we read words on the videoscreen, but that residue is not enough to mask the conventional nature of the game of signs. The conventions become clearer and intrude on the writer and reader as never before—as the writer sits adjusting the connections among words and images in the text and so redefining the limits of interpretation for that text, and as the reader follows out the connections, testing the limits set by the author, and delimiting his or her own interpretation.

A TEXTURE OF SIGNS

Text as texture, as a weaving together of signs, is a metaphor that dates from the Middle Ages. The signs in a text mingle and interrelate: they are points in a space whose coordinates are determined, as Eco points out, by the intersection of many codes (Eco, 1976, pp. 57ff). Both the written page and the printed page are fields in which codes can intersect, but the computer as hypertext offers a more appropriate space for this intersection. A text in the computer is a dynamic network of relationships, and each path through the network defines an order, interpretation, and meaning for the text according to a certain code. The sum of all connections becomes all possible interpretations of the text. So in the electronic OED, the text is the sum of all the possible paths that lead from each entry to others: paths that are either built in the data structure provided by the editors or are created through searches that the reader initiates.

All the interpretive meaning of an electronic text is embodied in the ramifying structure of its connections. In the computer we can see, as students of semiotics have maintained for decades, that a text is never anything more than a structure of relations. By changing the relations, as we do when we make and break connections, we change the meaning of the text. Saussure and his followers showed that sounds in a language have only relative meaning defined by the distinctions that we make between sounds. Students of semiotics have extended this principle to all codes: meaning lies in the systems of differences among their elements. As Jonathan Culler puts it:

"...elements of a text do not have intrinsic meaning as autonomous entities but derive their significance from oppositions which are in turn related to other oppositions in a process of theoretically infinite semiosis" (Culler, 1981, p. 29). Electronic writing now makes those differences operative for every level of topical writing. The differences are seen and manipulated as a set of connections that hold topics in tension, both binding topics together and keeping them apart. The reader uses the computer to move along these lines of force, and this movement is the meaning of the text. Thus, the reader can move through the OED along paths of synonyms or antonyms, examining the differential meanings of the words. The reader can group and distinguish words along any axes provided by the indexes. Meanwhile, the quotations cited by the OED provide what students of semiotics would call an intertextual commentary on the reader's movement.

We have mentioned intertextuality as a facet of the new literary theory that the computer both endorses and subtly undermines. (See Culler, 1981, p. 103.) Intertextuality is more than the references within a text and allusions between texts that are common in literature; it is the interrelation of all texts in the same subject, language, or culture. Some, like Roland Barthes, say that these interrelations cannot be mapped, because a text depends upon many anonymous codes that can never be set forth. Barthes wrote, for example, that "I is not an innocent subject, anterior to the text. . . . This 'I' which approaches the text is already itself a plurality of other texts, of codes which are infinite or, more precisely, lost (whose origins are lost)" (Barthes, *S/Z*, 1974, p. 10; see also Culler, 1981, p. 102). But there is a great difference between the infinite and the inaccessible. Electronic writing with its graphical representations of structure encourages us to think that intertextual relations can indeed be mapped out, made explicit—never fully, but with growing accuracy and completeness. Mapping in the electronic writing space can be a collective process: the writer creates some connections, which pass to the first reader, who may add new connections and pass the results on to another reader, and so on. This tradition, this passing on of the text from writer to reader, who then becomes a writer for other readers, is nothing new; it is the literal meaning of the word "tradition."

Humanistic study carried on in manuscript and print was just such a tradition, in which scholars read and interpreted classical authors and then published their interpretations for a new generation of readers. Their work too was intertextual. But the computer so simplifies the technology of intertextuality that it casts the whole idea of tradition in a new light. In the computer, reading passes effortlessly into writing, and the new writing can have the same character as the rest of the text. There is a project among Dante scholars today to put into the computer the text of the *Divine Comedy* together with all its Renaissance commentaries. The *Divine Comedy* itself is an "intertextual construct," and the commentaries add further complexity to the textual network. Now, if they choose to do so, contemporary scholars can themselves become contributors to the growing construct. The computer is the ideal writing space for such an ongoing project, both because it handles change so easily and because it grants equal status to all the elements in the evolving structure. On the other hand, it is true that the computer takes the mystery out of intertextuality and makes it instead a well-defined process of interconnection, the collective act of reading one text in the light of others. Any sense of mystery that remains is the residue of the age of writing or printing, when the technology provided no good way to embody the movement from one text to another.

SIGNS WITHOUT LIMIT

Semiotics regards representation and interpretation as a process without end. In Peirce's system there are three elements in the process: the sign, the thing represented, and the interpretant. The interpretant, the definition of the sign, may in turn be treated as a sign requiring definition. The process continues in theory as long as we like, because each new interpretant allows for a further interpretation. In fact any practical system is limited. In the dictionary each word is defined in terms of other words that are themselves entries to be consulted, but no dictionary is infinite. If we had the patience, we could examine all the words in the network of definitions contained in the dictionary. By starting often enough at different entries, we could ultimately exhaust the dictionary's writing space.

The electronic space is subject to the same limitation. An electronic text may grow and grow as it comes to include the work of many hands, but no electronic text can be infinite—not only because it is the work of finite human beings, but also because the computer itself, as a technology of writing, is finite. All computers must operate with a limited memory and a finite speed of computation. The machine is always stymied when it confronts infinity, in symbolic applications as in numerical ones. So in electronic writing, the network of elements must always be limited, and the act of interpretation must reconcile itself to this limitation. Eventually, the interpretation will loop back on itself, so that we return to the original elements to be interpreted. Any search in the electronic OED will eventually suffer this fate. We suggested earlier that a simple interactive fiction might take the reader in a circle. In such cases, the hypertextual network is not infinite; it is instead, like the lines of latitude and longitude on the globe, finite but unbounded. The computer provides us with an electronic writing space that is always a finite world.

Students of semiotics and of deconstruction must ultimately address the finite character of the textual world. They understand that all texts are finite, and yet they seem to be looking back to that Faustian culture in which the infinite is the highest, if unsatisfied, aspiration. Roland Barthes speaks of the infinity of intertextual relations. Even Derrida still plays on the paradox of the infinite and the finite: he grounds his assault on texts on the premise that the text is trying to put an end to the unlimited process of interpretation. His deconstructions reduce texts to a play of signs that by its very nature can never end. Our reading of all texts becomes an endless transit from one passage to another, never out into a "real" world beyond signs. This insistence on the endless quality of interpretation is part of deconstruction's strategy for subverting canonical texts and has been taken for pessimism or nihilism. The traditional Western view is that we can reach the signified, that we can get beyond the forest of signs to what the signs stand for. That ultimate goal is what Derrida calls "the transcendental signified." It would be, if we could ever achieve it, perfect signification: the end of interpretation not because of lack of time or space, but because the interpretation has finally arrived at that point, in which the signifier and the thing signified coincide. All of deconstruction's work is to show that the transcendental signified cannot be achieved. But even to worry about such an achievement shows that deconstruction is only half way toward a new view of signs. The old view of transcendence and infinity still matter enough to the deconstructionist that he or she feels the need to refute them.

The new view of signs is embodied unambiguously in electronic hypertext. Here the writer and reader know that there is no transcendence, because they know that the topical elements they create are arbitrary sequences of bits made meaningful only by their interconnecting links. They feel no need to refute the old view, the product of the printed and written book, which are both closer to the spoken language. In the computer meaning is always deferral, the pointing from one place to another. The fact that electronic signs only refer to other signs is the fundamental characteristic of the medium, made apparent in every act of electronic writing. In an electronic space there is no infinite regression, not because the reader eventually reaches the transcendental signified, but rather for the mundane reason that the resources of the machine, though vast, are always finite. All this suggests again that the computer takes us beyond deconstruction, which for all its ambivalence, is still incapable of acquiescing in the arbitrary and limited character of writing. Electronic readers and writers have finally arrived at the land promised (or threatened) by post-modern theory for two decades: the world of pure signs. While traditional humanists and deconstructionists have been battling over the arbitrary, self-referential character of writing, computer specialists, oblivious to this struggle, have been building a world of electronic signs in which the battle is over.

A NEW REPUBLIC OF LETTERS

Jonathan Culler has written that in order to understand our social and cultural world ". . . we must think not of independent objects but of symbolic structures, systems of relations which, by enabling objects and actions to have meaning, create a human universe" (Culler, 1981, p. 25). In other words, the play of signs is not merely a literary pastime; it takes over and defines the world of human intelligibility. Here again, the student of semiotics is describing the writing space of the computer, which could never pretend to be anything other than a universe of signs. Computer programmers and users are so inclined to think in these terms that they take no notice of the colossal metaphysical issues that the computer as writing space simply sweeps away. They are inclined to become utterly engrossed in the programmed texts they create. For them, the computer as writing space becomes a living space, at least for the life of the mind. Computer specialists now talk blithely about the problem of getting "lost in hyperspace"—of losing one's bearing in a hypertext and continuing to wander from one text to another. Indeed, the literature on these new forms of electronic writing is filled with metaphors of wandering, journeying, exploring, as if the human reader were physically a part of the text he or she is reading.

We are accustomed to thinking of books as extensions of our memories, devices to help us remember more clearly and argue more effectively. A book, particularly a novel, is also often thought of as something the mind puts on, fits around itself, and settles into. A library in turn is a building that serves as a large book, through which the reader travels physically and intellectually. If it is so easy to see the book as a world for the mind to explore, then the next, short step is to regard the mind itself as an element in that world of signs. Peirce was bold enough to make this idea explicit: "[the human mind] is a sign developing according to the laws of inference. . . . [T]he content of consciousness, the entire phenomenal manifestation of mind, is a sign resulting from inference" (Peirce, 1934, p. 188). So already in the 19th century, before there were any operating computers, Peirce had imagined this world and the human's place in it. People for Peirce were like words. "The man-sign," he goes on to say, "acquires information, and comes to mean more than he did before. But so do words. Does not electricity mean more now than it did in the days of Franklin? . . . In fact, therefore, men and words reciprocally educate each other; each increase of a man's information involves and is involved by, a corresponding increase of a word's information" (pp. 188-189).

With this bold metaphor Peirce was presenting what might be called the working philosophy for today's electronic writer, who indeed lives in a world of interconnected symbols that reciprocally educate both each other and the writer. For the new readers and writers, the human mind itself becomes a text to be fashioned and explored according to the principles of the electronic writing space. But the idea of the mind as text is older than Peirce. At least since the Middle Ages, as reading has emancipated itself from speaking and become more visual and spatial, readers and writers have found it easier to regard thought as the setting out and arranging of symbols in the mental space of the thinker. The explicit definition of thought as the manipulation of symbols can be traced at least to the 17th-century thinkers and their search for a "universal character," a universal (written) language in which all ideas could be expressed unambiguously to all human beings. (For a discussion of the philosophical background, see Knowlson, 1975.)

The universal character itself was another manifestation of the desire for a utopia of letters—like the medieval and modern encyclopedias and now the electronic library and artificial intelligence. Surely there has never been a better text in which to lose oneself than the electronic library realized by computer. All computer users, not just artificial intelligence specialists, are citizens of this same republic—a new republic of letters defined not by the printing press, but by the computer, which serves as the locus of (written) reality. Perhaps we should call it the empire of letters because of the computer's tendency to incorporate all signs within itself, to dominate the whole world of intelligibility. The computer world, of course, is no more strange than the world that philosophers and mathematicians have inhabited for many centuries. The computer as hypertext is the newest in a long line of candidates for the universal book. And like all the previous candidates, the computer makes the seductive promise to break down the barrier between thought and writing, to join the mind and writing surface into a seamless whole.

Chapter 12

Writing the Mind

All writing is projection: to write is to put on a writing surface what the writer "had in mind." Writing in any form serves as both an extension and a reflection of the writer's mind. And each particular technology of writing (on papyrus, in codex, on the videoscreen) is a different form of projection, suggesting a somewhat different relationship between the written word and the mind. The reflexive character of each technology permits writers to find themselves in the texts they create and therefore to know themselves in a new way. It is no coincidence that the ancient Greeks discovered the self during precisely those centuries in which writing was absorbed into their culture. Indeed, any literate culture is led inexorably to define mind in terms of writing, as this technology becomes at the same time a metaphor for and the principal embodiment of thought. The mind comes to be understood as an ethereally supple writing surface, and thinking becomes the activity of inscribing on that surface.

As a new writing technology, the computer is yet another instance of the metaphor of writing in the mind. With the aid of the computer, the writer constructs the text as a dynamic network of verbal and visual symbols. These electronic symbols in the machine seem to be an extension of a network of ideas in the mind itself. More effectively than the codex or the printed book, the computer reflects the mind as a web of verbal and visual elements in a conceptual space. When technology provided us with printed books and photographs, our minds were repositories of fixed texts and still images. When the contemporary technology is electronic, our minds become pulsing networks of ideas. As we have seen, electronic technology fits perfectly with the semiotic view of language and thought in the tradition from C. S. Peirce to Umberto Eco:

> But thinking, too, is to connect signs together: 'each former thought suggests something to the thought which follows it, i.e. is the sign of something to this latter.'(5.284) (Peirce cited by Eco, 1976, p. 166)

This is the metaphor of mind for our age: it is not simply the mind as computer, as the artificial intelligence specialists propose, but rather the mind as a network of signs, of which the computer is the embodiment. To understand the mind as a network of signs is also to understand the mind as a text. Semiotics and literary theory now suggest implicitly that we regard the mind as a text, as a writing space filled with interwoven signs. And yet, as we have seen, semiotics and literary theory are still products of the late age of print, of writers who are exploring the final possibilities of printed text and have not generally realized that the computer provides the next space for writing.

WRITING AS ANALYSIS

While Plato's Socrates argued that writing could enfeeble the mind, the modern consensus is more optimistic. In *Orality and Literacy* Walter Ong, for example, is enthusiastic:

> Without writing, the literate mind would not and could not think as it does, not only when engaged in writing but normally even when it is composing its thoughts in oral form. More than any other single invention, writing has transformed human consciousness. (Ong, 1982, p. 78)

Ong lists a series of characteristics that distinguish the oral from the literate mind. The literate mind is analytic; the oral mind is aggregative. The literate mind is objective; the oral mind is traditional and unable to detach itself from its context. Writing makes it easier to see logical relationships and to subordinate one idea to another. Syllogistic reasoning, for example, is foreign to a culture without writing; the syllogism itself was first codified by Aristotle at a time when Greek culture had achieved a high level of literacy. Ong claims that "an oral culture simply does not deal in such items as geometrical figures, abstract categorization, formally logical reasoning processes, definition, or even comprehensive descriptions, or articulated self-analysis, all of which derive not simply from thought itself but from text-formed thought" (p. 55).

This claim is probably too strong. Literacy is not the necessary and sufficient cause of reasoned thought, which we tend in any case to identify with ancient or Western modes of thought. (See Brian Street's *Literacy in*

Theory and Practice, 1984.) But it is true that literacy provides a new opportunity for analysis and reflection. The difference that literacy makes, is evident in a culture's "texts." Oral cultures produce poems, stories, mythology, lore, and dramatic performances; they do not produce philosophic essays, technical studies, scientific treatises, or textbooks of higher mathematics. Oral cultures do not send out anthropologists to study literate cultures and explain the differences between orality and literacy. On the other hand, literate cultures do not produce the same kind of mythology or poetry as oral cultures. Writing changes the relationship between a person and his or her words; it allows each of us to slow the insistent pace of spoken language, to control the rate at which we must produce or receive words. Writing allows us to weigh our own words or those of others. It is surely easier to appreciate a complex argument in writing than in oral presentation, to dissect the argument by moving back and forth through its points.

The difference is that the written argument is a visible and therefore durable structure in two dimensions. The reader can move through the argument, examining both the soundness of the parts and their relation to the whole. The reader who can write may also take elements out of their original context for his or her own purposes. Writing is a tool for reorganizing, for classifying, for developing and maintaining categories. The anthropologist Jack Goody has argued for the importance in this respect of even the simplest written structure, the list:

> The list relies on discontinuity rather than continuity; it depends on physical placement, on location; it can be read in different directions, both sideways and downwards, up and down, as well as left and right; it has a clear-cut beginning and a precise end, that is, a boundary, an edge, like a piece of cloth. Most importantly it encourages the ordering of the items, by number, by initial sound, by category, etc. And the existence of boundaries, external and internal, brings greater visibility to categories, at the same time as making them more abstract. (Goody, 1977, p. 81)

Not only the making of lists, but all writing fosters categorical thinking and analysis, because analysis is built into the very act of writing. Writing is a technology for dividing the world into categories. In the case of phonetic writing these categories (logograms, syllables, or vowels and consonants) are set on top of the much older spoken language. In picture writing the classifications are by idea rather than by sounds in a language. Mathematics, symbolic logic, and computer programming are all primarily written rather than spoken, and they all rigorously and ruthlessly categorize. When a student sets out to learn a computer language, what he or she must learn by example and practice is the art of analyzing a problem into the operational categories provided by the language. Different languages provide somewhat different categories, but all languages require the programmer to find a discrete representation scheme and to break the task down into small, interrelated functional units. All languages require programmers to think analytically, where analysis is defined in the tradition of mathematical and symbolic logic since Descartes and Leibniz.

By emphasizing analysis, categorization, and method, writing changes and, from the modern point of view, improves our ability to reason. It is not that writing gives its users a mental capacity that is unknown or impossible in an illiterate person, but rather that writing favors certain capacities at the expense of others. Not every culture may take advantage of the potential that writing offers, but that does not deny that the potential is there. Without schooling and other institutions, written texts cannot permeate culture. (See *The Psychology of Literacy* by Scribner & Cole, 1981. See also Olson, 1986.) Yet without writing, institutions that accumulate around literacy cannot exist.

WRITING ONESELF

Although writing enhances our capacity for reasoned argument and our ability to trace connections among disparate ideas, this enhancement is not in itself a restructuring of consciousness. Writing does more: its reflexive character gives the writer a new awareness of self. Anyone, who writes a letter, an essay, a poem, or even a scientific paper or legal brief, finds his or her verbal self presented on the page. In an oral culture the verbal self never exists long enough to be reflected upon. As speakers we are caught up in our words; we have no time to distance ourselves and examine the words as if they were produced by someone else. In making verbal thoughts visible, writing creates the mind as a personal and cultural metaphor. It is a metaphor in the strong sense—not simply a comparison between two disparate things (writing technology on one hand and mental states or capacities on the other) but rather an identification of the two. Once the technology of writing is established, it becomes difficult not to think of memory and reason as a special kind of writing, a writing in the mind. The memory becomes a writing space, and the writer a homunculus who looks out at the world through our eyes and records what he sees. The homunculus translates perceptions into words and images and records them; he also puts down his inner thoughts and conclusions. To think is to write in the language of thought and to remember is to search the space of our memory until we find what is written there. This is exactly the view of artificial intelligence, which completely identifies thought with the kind of symbol manipulation, that is writing, that the computer can do.

In fact, throughout the ancient and modern Western cultures, the mind has been and remains inseparable from writing. The metaphor is pervasive in literature, found in poets from Aeschylus ("remembering tablets of [the] mind," *Prometheus Bound*) to Dante ("the book of memory") to Shakespeare ("the book and volume of my brain," *Hamlet*, Act 1, Scene 5), and beyond. (See Curtius, 1973, pp. 302-347. Also Paulson, 1989, pp. 291-293.) Philosophers as early as Plato have assumed that thinking and writing are inseparable. Consider once more Socrates's myth in the *Phaedrus*: there Socrates invokes the metaphor of "writing in the mind" even as he seeks to deny it— when he says that the best argument is "that which is written with intelligence in the mind of the learner, which is able to defend itself and knows to whom it should speak and before whom to be silent" (*Phaedrus* 276A in Plato, 1919, p. 567). And in this respect, even modern psychology has not diverged from the line established by Plato. Cognitive psychology, under the influence of computer technology, is more than ever committed to the metaphor of writing. But so was Freud, who explicitly compared human memory to a child's toy, the magic writing pad. Derrida and his followers have reminded us of Freud's dedication to the metaphor of writing: ". . . Freud speculates that the very mansion of presence, the perceiving self, is shaped by . . . writing" (G.C. Spivak, in the preface to *Of Grammatology* by Derrida, 1976b, p. xli). Indeed, the deconstructionists have led the way in finding the paradigm of writing in all manifestations of Western culture. Some non-Western cultures may well be less attached to this paradigm than we are, and they may more easily think themselves out of it. But for our culture, the notion of the mind as a writing space has long been inescapable. The technology of writing is customarily regarded as the creation of the human mind, possibly its greatest creation. In fact, it is the other way around: the mind is the creation of writing.

The classicist Bruno Snell has shown that the Greek concept of mind developed slowly in the archaic period. "Homer," he points out, "had no one word to characterize the mind or the soul. Psyche, the word for soul in later Greek, has no original connection with the thinking or feeling soul" (see *The Discovery of Mind: The Greek Origin of European Thought* by Snell, 1960, p. 8). A Homeric warrior did not have a mind: he had emotions, thoughts, plans, and preferences, but he did not unify all these mental states under a single name. He was not aware of himself as a unified thinking agent. The change came over centuries and can first be seen in the work of such lyric poets as Sappho and Alcaeus and finally in philosophers like Plato. "The early lyricists try to reproduce those moments in which the individual is all of a sudden snatched out of the broad stream of life. . . . Such are the moments which furnish man with his first glimpse of the soul" (p. 65). It is no coincidence that writing was working its way into Greek culture in exactly these centuries. Homer, living at the beginning of the archaic period, was apparently illiterate; certainly his audience was. Sappho and the other lyric poets still recited their poems, but they could presumably write them down and perfect them in private. Sappho could see her writing as the product of her own mind and reflect on the person who produced that product.

This is the best sense in which to take Ong's remark that the human mind would not be what it is without literacy. The reflexive character of writing allows the writer to define his or her mind out of the confusion of thoughts and emotions that are experienced. To say that there would be no mind in the ancient or the Western sense without literacy is not to say that there would be no thought or mental activity or that illiterate peoples do not think. It simply means that the notion of mind as a unified entity developed in the context of literacy. Yet the very fact that we cannot separate writing and mind creates a paradox that was apparent as early as Plato and remains potent today. The act of writing creates a gap between words and thoughts, while at the same time encouraging us to identify words with thoughts. As a new technology of writing, the computer allows us to reexamine this paradox: to consider how the gap opens, how we function in the groundless space between thought and word, and how we strive to close the gap once again.

OPENING THE GAP

The computer represents all its data in bits and bytes, which are stored on memory chips or magnetic or optical disks and are therefore invisible to the writer. The electronic writer is estranged from his or her text, which is only made visible by the interaction of computer hardware and software. But estrangement is inherent in any writing technology. Placing words on any writing surface opens a gap that can never again be securely closed. As writers we like to believe that our words as visible representations of our thoughts belong to us, and yet written words have an existence apart from the writer. They can be appropriated by others, published, and made available to an audience of unknown readers. Written words can be plagiarized. In the ancient world, plagiarism was almost a compliment; since the 18th century it has become a matter for litigation. But in any age it is proof that writers cannot keep their writing to themselves. Writers have worked in various ways to preserve their personal attachment to their words. Poets have inserted tag lines or spelled their names as anagrams in their poems. At the other extreme, writers from Virgil to Kafka have tried to destroy their texts to prevent expropriation. All these efforts point up the writer's insecurity: the writing is the product of his or her mind and yet no longer his or her own. It is just the ambivalence that parents must eventually feel about their children—and as early as Plato's *Symposium* books were compared to children.

Estrangement is the original sin that belongs to the act of visual representation: the spoken word does not call forth the same sense of estrangement. Before the invention of the phonograph and tape recorder, speakers could not listen to their speech as if they were hearing someone else. The audience could not carry the speaker's words away and play them back for others. No one can really plagiarize a speech, although in our text-bound society we have transferred the concept of plagiarism to music and speeches. A speaker's words belong to him or her in a way that a writer's words never can, but only because the words cease to exist immediately after they are uttered. The written word stays around for the writer to consider and perhaps to regret. Its relative permanence is a tremendous aid in defining what the writer "thinks," although a text is never really a record of what the writer thinks, but rather a record of how his or her thoughts have intersected with the writing system. Like acting or teaching, writing means assuming a persona. However, unlike the oral performances of the actor or the teacher, the writer's persona is available for later inspection by both reader and writer.

Writing reveals the writer to himself or herself, but, as in quantum mechanics, the process of revealing affects what is revealed. Writing presents a person on the page and tells the writer he or she is that person. Unlike records, tape, and film, which record perceptions, writing is a semiotic technology, in which the writer watches a persona form as a reflection of the signs that he or she places on the page. People who do not write deprive themselves of this experience of symbolic self-reflection. A culture that does not write deprives itself of this mechanism of collective reflection. Writing is a way of knowing your own mind, as you see the manifestations of your mind externalized on the page (or the screen). But the mind you come to know is your writing mind.

This externalization also leads to a sense of loss. Everyone who writes has had the experience of feeling distanced from his or her own writing, of looking at a sentence written yesterday or a year ago and wondering who could have produced such a sentence. When we read our own letters or essays written months or years before, we begin to wonder what the author could have had in mind. That is, we find ourselves in the traditional role of the reader, having lost the privileged status that we presumed to have as author. We have lost our sense of intimacy with the text, just as we have gained perspective on it.

The writer's written self will also be different with different writing technologies. Handwriting and especially printing emphasize stability. The written or printed page is the same when we return to it a month or a year later, and so the written persona on the page has not changed. That very stability may reassure us as writers, or it may have the opposite effect. When we see what we have written a year ago, we may be impressed by the continuity of our thought or surprised by how much our thinking has changed in a year's time. By reading our own written or printed texts, we see ourselves evolving, or failing to evolve, in a series of snapshots. Electronic technology presents a different self. An electronic text can change each time it is read. The persona of the text is neither stable nor unified; or rather, it projects unity through movement, a unity that reveals itself in the kinds of changes that the text is willing to make in the reader's hands. Authors who return to their own electronic texts find a sliding scale against which to measure their changing self. And still the author may not find himself or herself in any of the range of textual possibilities.

TEXT AND MEMORY

> [Writing] will produce forgetfulness in the minds of those who learn to use it, because they will not practise their memory. Their trust in writing, produced by external characters which are no part of themselves, will discourage the use of their own memory within them. You have invented not an elixir of memory, but of reminding; and you offer your pupils the appearance of wisdom, not true wisdom. (*Phaedrus*, 275A in Plato, 1919, p. 563)

The computer offers writers and readers new ways of getting at their text, and getting at the text has always been the great problem in all technologies of writing. We write in order to have our words available at a later time, but once we have written more than a few pages (or rolls or screens), we have to worry about finding the words again when we want them. Access to verbal ideas and images in our mind is more or less automatic. If asked to name the third president of the United States, we think instantly of Thomas Jefferson, but we cannot say how we found that name. In fact, if someone ordered us not to think of the name of the third president of the United States, we would have no means of keeping Jefferson out of our consciousness. When someone has a lapse of memory, we often give that person the futile advice to avoid thinking about it and the memory will come by itself. And often it does. "Natural" memory is so natural that we are not aware of its nature. The elaborate methods of artificial memory, on the other hand, came to the ancient world only after the invention of writing. Writing in fact placed greater burdens upon human memory, because it demanded that ancient orators produce speeches that were models of diction, argument, and arrangement—in other words, speeches that could be written down for later reading and study. Artificial memory was already a kind of writing in the mind.

The claim that writing harms human memory goes back at least to Plato. In fact, writing does not harm memory; rather it imposes a changing set of demands upon human memory. A literate culture can make more demands for rote memorization, because there are far more texts available to remember. In Plato's own culture, the demands on memory certainly grew in the age of literacy. After Homer's *Iliad* and *Odyssey* were written down, these texts became the standard vehicles of literary education. Schoolboys memorized long passages, if not the whole poems. Students were also made to memorize their own and other speeches, perhaps excerpts from tragedians, and so on. Litigants memorized their speeches for the lawcourts. In general, the existence of written texts meant that one could hold the memory up to an objective standard. An actor in a Greek tragedy (or a Shakespearean tragedy) could forget his lines because the lines were written down. Rote memorization remained important in Western culture into the 19th and even the 20th century. Even two or three generations ago, schoolchildren still memorized Shakespeare, Keats, and of course the Bible.

Today such memorization is practically absent from education, but its absence does not mean that our memories are less exercised. An educated person now controls an extraordinary amount of factual information. The requirements in any technical and intellectual field are enormous. How many facts did an ancient or even a Renaissance doctor have to know? How much, by comparison, is a medical student expected to learn today? The same explosive growth of information and technique is characteristic of mathematics, civil engineering, the study of medieval history, or for that matter professional athletics. Of course, modern technicians in any of these fields can consult books; they need not remember everything themselves if they know where to look facts up. But the residue that does remain in the memory is tremendous, and to that residue must be added the information from all the other sources in a literate and technical society that an individual collects either as a necessity for daily life or simply from interest. There is no way to prove, of course, that an individual today remembers more than an ancient Greek or indeed a paleolithic hunter. The hunter no doubt amassed great amounts of experiential memory—sights, sounds, smells—during his apparently repetitive days on the hunt. But it would be just as wrong to think that our memories are less active today.

What changed with the invention of writing was the way in which humans deployed their facility to remember. Memory became tiered or layered. Plato already drew a distinction between internal and external memory and greatly favored the former, the writing in the mind rather than on paper. So it is not that the mind has less to remember because of writing, but that the mind can now keep some knowledge intimately in memory and relegate other knowledge to written texts. A literate person must still remember how to find the knowledge he or she has stored up in texts. The computer age considers this a problem of the "interface" between the user and his or her data, but the problem of the interface between human memory and its written extensions has existed since the beginning of literacy. Learning to read and write is learning particular strategies for storing and finding symbolic structures. Different writing technologies permit different techniques of storing and finding: linear access for the papyrus roll, greater freedom for the written or printed book, and elaborately structured and controlled access in the computer. Yet such techniques all emphasize the estrangement of writing. The building of visual and conceptual structures in books is an admission of the separation of the text from the writer and, of course, all the more from the reader. These techniques have always been slower and more cumbersome than writers and readers would like; they have always reminded us of the rupture between our mind and the writing surface.

The printed book offers as its interface not only page layout but indices and tables of contents to help readers make their way. As useful as these techniques are, it is striking how often they fail, when, for example, we are searching for a passage in a book we have already read. We often remember the passage not by the conceptual outline in the table of contents, but rather by verbal or visual fragments. We remember a particular phrase or the fact that the passage appeared high on a left-hand page early in the book. In fact, as we read or write, our mind reaches out to the text and forms far too many associations (and the wrong kind) to be accommodated by the frozen format of a written or printed book. We end up with a memory of the text that does not correspond to its chapter divisions, table of contents, or indices.

There must always be a discrepancy between our mental construction and the physical representation of the book; an efficient writing technology is one that minimizes the discrepancy. Medieval writers would have relied on memory whenever possible. If they needed to consult an authority, they would have to stop writing, retrieve the book, and leaf through (or consult the relatively primitive index) to find the passage—assuming of course that the book was in their or their institution's library. If not, they might have to wait weeks or months to secure a copy from a scholar elsewhere. After printing, a writer had access to more books, and the books had better indices and other aids to organization. Finding the book was still a chore, although the writer might then simply have had to walk across the library, rather than send to the next monastery.

Computer technology can make those breaks more subtle and less time-consuming. In an electronic library, writers turn easily from writing their own texts to reading other texts. The distinction between their own and other texts begins to blur, since writers can cut and paste anything they read into their own documents. In a full-fledged hypertext the distinction can disappear altogether. The computer speeds the writing process itself, as the writer moves quickly between verbal ideas and their visual expression on the computer screen. The network of ideas in the author's mind merges with their expression in the computer, and this structure in turn merges with the network of all texts stored in this or other connected machines. It is as if the computer could dissolve Plato's distinction between internal and external memory—the distinction that is fundamental to all writing.

THE TEXTUAL MIND

> The computer, when it is used as a processor or an outliner or an organizer, becomes an extension of our memory in a more organic sense than this is usually taken to mean. . . . That is, the computer feels to us as if it is an auxiliary hemisphere of our own minds. (Harvey Wheeler, *The Virtual Library*, 1987, Chapter 6)

Plato's distinction was always an ironic one: Socrates insisted that writing cannot capture the essence of human memory, but at the same time he referred to a true writing in the soul. He used the metaphor of writing to describe the inner experience of thought and memory. Metaphorically he closed the gap in the act of opening it, when he argued that writing on papyrus was deceptive and that it was better to write directly in the mind. Plato's ambivalence about writing has been with us ever since, and in the case of electronic writing the ambivalence is greater than ever.

As the most technologically sophisticated form of writing, electronic writing should be the farthest removed from human nature. The structure of electronic text is the most elaborate in the history of writing, and yet the capacity rapidly to create and modify structures makes the computer in some sense the most natural of writing systems. The computer seems to solve once and for all the problem of retrieval. The writer is no longer slowed by the laborious materials of pen and paper; the reader does not have to flip through pages to find the passage he or she wants. Electronic technology suggests a kind of writing that denies its limitations as writing and becomes unmediated thought. It would seem that writing is no longer separate from the mind, if the computer can forge an instantaneous link between the writer's thoughts and the writing surface. Instant access is an aspect of the electronic utopia of literacy, in which the barrier between writing and thinking dissolves and all symbolic information, anywhere in the world, is as immediately available to the writer/reader as his or her own thoughts.

But here our ambivalence returns. Does the computer turn writing into unmediated thought, or is it just the reverse—that the computer turns thought into writing? The computer provides rapid access and new ways of finding written structures, but it does so by making us more aware than ever of the artificiality of writing. If our thinking merges almost seamlessly with this new writing system, perhaps the explanation is that the semioticians are right: our thinking is a network of interrelated signs that can connect to the network inside the machine. To dissolve the distinction between thought and writing is to dissolve the fragile barrier between the human mind and technology, to create the ultimate machine that merged with the mind. But are we left with mind-machines (computers that act like human beings) or machine-minds (human beings whose minds are computers)?

We vacillate between the two possibilities until we can no longer distinguish them. Artificial intelligence specialists, and other computer users perhaps unwittingly, are frantically trying to merge human and machine. They sometimes act as if the goal were to humanize machines; at other times they cheerfully mechanize their own humanity to suit their programs. The goal is to bridge the gap, and they are prepared to anchor their bridge at either the mechanical or the human side. The machine's electronics already operate at speeds faster than human thought and seem to be no less ethereal than the mind. But the presence of the keyboard and the text on the screen still remind us that the computer is a writing technology—that the electronic signs in the computer are separate from our thoughts. Therefore artificial intelligence programmers are pursuing the obvious solution of eliminating the keyboard in favor of a computer that can master spoken language. A computer that understands the human voice would take advantage of the prejudice that speaking is not a form of semiotic communication at all. Spoken language seems to have immediate access to the mind, and therefore a hearing and speaking computer would seem to collapse the distance between human and machine. (As we have seen, it would only seem to be so: the deconstructionists have made it impossible to argue that spoken language is more immediate than writing.)

The "ultimate" solution would be to bridge the physical gap by establishing a direct electronic interface between synapses of the brain and the machine. For critics, like Joseph Weizenbaum, such an interface would also be the ultimate disaster: "The proposal I have mentioned, that an animal's visual system and brain be coupled to computers . . . represents an attack on life itself. One must wonder what must have happened to the proposers' perception of life . . . that they can even think of such a thing" (Weizenbaum, 1976, p. 269). The artificial intelligence specialist would see it differently: he or she would point out the humane applications of helping the blind to see (with the aid of computer-controlled video cameras) or the deaf to hear. But whatever the moral implications, we should remember that in fact the human mind cannot touch or be touched by the machine. If a direct synaptic-electronic interface should ever become feasible, the physical gap between brain and computer would disappear. The conceptual gap between the mind and the computer's software could still be bridged only by metaphor. The mind would still be a network of signs only because verbal thoughts take the form of a network on the electronic writing surface.

In short, the computer emphasizes the paradox of writing as fully as any of its predecessors. It promises to eliminate the barrier that exists between the writer and writing technology. It suggests that writers and readers can take the book back into themselves, until they have within themselves, and in some sense become, the sum of all symbolic writing. Yet the computer goes about fulfilling this promise by making the human mind over in its own image. In order to close the gap between the writer and the text, the computer turns the writer's mind itself into a text.

THE INTENTIONAL GAP

The mind as text has profound implications for the contemporary philosophy of mind. These implications are becoming apparent in the work of English and American philosophers, particularly on the issue of intentionality. Intentionality is the doctrine that our ideas, beliefs, and other states of mind have the quality of referring to something beyond themselves. Ideas are about something, as Dennett and Haugeland have put it.

> Intentionality is aboutness. Some things are about other things: a belief can be about icebergs, but an iceberg is not about anything: an idea can be about the number 7, but the number 7 is not about anything. (Dennett & Haugeland, 1987, p. 383)

The question is how our ideas and beliefs are related to the things they are about. How do they refer, for example, to things in the world, and who gets to decide what an idea is about? As Anthony Kenny describes it, thoughts have content and also a possessor (Kenny, 1984, p. 74). The intentional philosopher argues that the content of my thoughts is what I intend or mean to say. But how do I determine that meaning for others or even for myself? How is my belief that Venus is a planet "linked" to that massive object that orbits the sun? And do I as the thinker of my thoughts have a special prerogative to say what my belief means? "[T]he philosopher and psychologist Bretano...claimed that intentionality is the defining distinction between the mental and the physical: all and only mental phenomena exhibit intentionality" (Dennett & Haugeland, 1987, p. 383). English and American philosophers today have made the problem more complex by arguing that sentences also exhibit intentionality. In other words, they have connected the problem of reference and meaning of our thoughts with the problem of reference and meaning of texts. It is a short step to realize that the two problems become one if thoughts too are regarded as texts, as the product of writing in the mind.

The doctrine of intentionality is then revealed as an attempt to analyze the metaphor of the mind as writing space. What divides philosophers is the question of how this metaphor is to be understood—how the "text of our thoughts" is related to the human thinker on the one hand and to the world on the other. No philosopher who remains true to contemporary circumstance can ignore the metaphor entirely. Ideas are explicitly or implicitly assumed to be written in the mind: the disagreement is over the nature of that writing. Some may still maintain that this mental writing (or "inner speech") is privileged: that it has the privilege of meaning what it says. "[T]here seems in non-Quinean circles to be a covert belief that somehow inner speech is directly expressive of thought" (Samuel Wheeler, 1986, p. 492). That is, unlike words written on paper or on a computer screen, my inner speech written in my mind cannot be misinterpreted (or indeed intepreted at all) at least by myself. My inner speech is free of the gap that characterizes all other forms of writing. But Quine and others take the opposite view: they take "thought to be inscriptional and . . . inscriptions to be writing-like. If inscriptions are writing-like, then all we have, even in our inner speech, is a text which can be taken in many ways. Without something besides texts in the brain, there is nothing to be made of the 'correct' interpretation or the one that conformed to the intentions of the author. (The author's intentions, after all, are just more writing in the brain.)" (Samuel Wheeler, 1986, p. 492). As Samuel Wheeler recognizes, this is exactly the point that Derrida and the deconstructionists have made about writing in general. Writing as represen-tation, as mediation, is inescapable in communication. When we speak, we are writing or representing in this sense—even when we are talking or thinking to ourselves. The universal character of writing . . .

> requires that we take seriously the *language* part of "the language of thought."
> If the linguistic model is indeed the way thought is to be thought of, then it too
> is meaningful in the absence of the producer, and it too is subject to the kinds
> of drift to which language is subject. (p. 493)

All texts wander in their meaning, and the author has no way to stop the drift, no special warrant in determining the meaning. In this case the text is an individual's inner speech, and it is as open to drift as any other text. The individual as author of his or her inner speech has no special authority to determine what that speech means, because inner speech is simply another network of interrelating signs. As Wheeler says, the author's intentions too are part of the network. The individual cannot put an end to the interpreta-tion of his or her own thoughts any more than an author can put an end to the interpretation of his or her written text. Instead each new thought that seeks to explain the previous one becomes part of a ramifying network. The debate over intentionality is therefore another debate about the text, author, and reader.

Recent philosophical interest in intentionality parallels the literary theorist's interest in the text as a network of signs. Both interests are fostered by the change in the technology of writing that we are now experiencing: the diminishing importance of the printed writing space and the coming of the new electronic space. We cannot predict exactly how the intentionality debate will be resolved. It seems, however, that those who believe in a special human intentionality are casting their lot with a metaphor that depends on print. Their philosophical position is that I as the author of my thoughts am privileged to say what I mean, that I give my thoughts meaning by intending them. This is a view of the author appropriate to print, when the author was privileged vis-à-vis other readers. Print, as we have noted earlier, fostered the Romantics' extremely high evaluation of the author as prophet or priest. In a certain sense critics like Carlyle were suggesting that we should read literature in order to have access to the inner speech of great souls like Shakespeare and Homer.

A great deal is philosophically at stake here. Perhaps even the Cartesian notion of the ego depends on the metaphor of the author and the text. In the beginning of the *Meditations*, Descartes takes leave of the world by doubting it all as the deception of evil spirit; that is, he questions the authority of his senses to report to him about the world. However, Descartes admits no doubt that his thoughts are his own: "[t]hought is an attribute that belongs to me; it alone is inseparable from my nature" (Descartes, *Second Meditation*, 1960, p. 26). Descartes is saying that he is the author of his thoughts, his inner text. When Descartes claims "I think therefore I am," he is claiming that the text validates him as author. Then Descartes as author goes on to validate the text. That is, he reconstructs the world from his own "clear and distinct ideas." This is a philosophical foundation for the age of printing, in which the author indeed both validates and is validated by the texts he or she publishes. Once again it is no coincidence that the late age of print has seen concerted attacks on the Cartesian ego—by Wittgenstein (Kenny, 1984, pp. 77ff), for example, whom we also saw chafing against the limitations of the medium of print. The deconstructionists would deny the Cartesian argument on precisely the grounds that the author has no special status in interpreting his or her own ideas, which are after all texts like any others.

So philosophers who deny the individual ego special powers as the author of its thoughts are questioning the foundations of Cartesian philosophy. They are also exploring positions appropriate to the electronic writing space. A philosophy of mind for the coming age of writing will have to recognize the mind as a network of signs and will see that network spreading out beyond the individual mind to embrace other texts, written in other minds and on conventional writing surfaces. Something like Peirce's vision of the mind as a sign should prevail. The most radical solution would dispense altogether with the notion of intentionality: there is no privileged author but simply textual networks that are always open to interpretation. Such a philosophy may be nothing less than the end of the ego, the end of the Cartesian self as the defining quality of humanity. This radical view would also seem to vindicate symbolic artificial intelligence. Artificial intelligence programs simply construct textual networks and claim that such networks are all there is to thought.

Yet questions remain. Computers manipulate signs according to formal rules: is this sufficient to constitute thought? Do these manipulations have a content and a possessor? Are they intended by their author, and indeed who is the author of these manipulations: the computer program or the human who wrote the program? (See the discussion in *The Intentional Stance* by Dennett, 1987, 298ff.) We have already said that a new theory of literature will be needed for the electronic space, one that achieves a new balance between author, reader, and text. It turns out that the philosophy of mind will need a similar proposal—a proposal that recognizes the textuality of the mind and goes on to understand the individual as both author and reader of that text.

Chapter

13

Writing Culture

The term *computer literacy* has been taken to mean either the ability to operate a computer (how to insert diskettes, how to call up a program, perhaps how to type into a word processor) or a technical knowledge of programming and concepts of computer science. In the preceding chapters, we have been exploring a different and more general definition of computer literacy: the ability to read and write in the computer medium and an understanding of how the computer fits into the long tradition of the technologies of writing. In the ages of handwriting or printing, literacy marked out a special social class, although not always the wealthiest or most powerful people. Not everyone needed or wanted to read and write. In the early Middle Ages, even kings and nobles were often illiterate, while secretaries and clerics maintained the society's records and literature. In earlier societies such as Egypt and Sumeria, literacy was limited, and there were professional scribes, who enjoyed a high social status (Gaur, 1984, p.150). Universal literacy has only been a goal in the industrialized world in the last two centuries. (The Marxist historian may claim that it only became a goal when capitalists realized that they needed a literate work force to maintain and improve production.) The question today is which model computer literacy will follow. Will our society aim to make it universal, or will it be limited to an elite?

Critics often compare our technological "priests" today to the scribal-priests of the ancient Near Eastern societies. If computer literacy is to be a new and general form of reading and writing, then it must obviously be available to a much wider class than the priestly or administrative literacy of ancient societies. Still, it may not be universal, or even as widespread as conventional literacy in recent centuries. Some sociologists and economists fear that our society may be splitting into a technologically sophisticated upper class and a lower class lacking the skills required by the so-called information economy. Although these fears may be exaggerated, they are not without substance. And if there is such a bifurcation, then computer literacy will be the distinguishing talent. The elite will be those who can read and write with the computer; they will use the machine in their work and probably for their recreation as well. The computer illiterate will at best be passive users/ readers of the machine. They may be able to enter data—as cashiers now do for cash registers that are already microcomputers—but they will not be able to write with the machine across the spectrum of semiotic communication. If the computer enters their leisure hours, it will be as a perceptual toy, like the current video games, but with far greater visual sophistication. Such games will allow their users little opportunity for symbolic communication. In Huxley's *Brave New World*, children's games were required to be complicated in appearance and simple in practice. A child threw a ball into a hole at the top of a contraption, and the ball was conveyed through a long series of channels and wheels before popping out again at the bottom; the game consisted mainly in watching the machine.

PERCEPTION AND SEMIOSIS

The danger, then, is not that the computers will supplant books, but rather that the computer will not be allowed to fulfill its promise as a new writing system and provide us with a new kind of book. To fulfill its promise, the computer must not be used merely to provide video games. Like all earlier forms of literacy, computer literacy is semiotic. Semiosis entails the reading and writing of signs, and any human activity that does not involve signs should not be confused with literacy. Other human activities that involve perceptual and motor skills are important but do not in themselves constitute literacy. In the same way literacy is not a substitute for perceptual skills: it is a different realm altogether. Artificial intelligence teaches us that lesson. The digital computer is not a good metaphor for the human senses or for the kind of intelligence that is closely tied to sense perception. Computer specialists have for decades been trying to make computers see by feeding data from video cameras into the machine. Yet, a computerized robot can hardly make its way across a room because it cannot read its video image to identify chairs, tables, and other obstacles. The digital computer reconfirms the dichotomy between perception and semiosis as two aspects of mind, and it comes down firmly on the side of semiosis. The immediate perception of the world is not open to the computer. Like all writing systems, the computer must work through signs in order to represent, classify, and operate on perceived experience. To accept the computer as a model of the mind is to accept the view of thought as the manipulation of signs—implicitly or explicitly to accept Peirce's definition of the human mind as "a sign developing according to the laws of inference."

Our culture, still in transition from the technology of print to electronic technology, is extremely ambivalent about this definition of mind. Computers are common, and wherever they are used they compel their users to treat data as symbolically coded information and language as a network of signs. This compulsion is obvious for a computer scientist or a physicist. But what is a lawyer or a doctor, with or without the computer, but an applied semiotician picking his or her way through a network of signs? Literary theorists tell us that novels and poems are also networks of arbitrary signs. The intellectual world of the late 20th century is a universe of signs, organized (like galaxies, clusters, and superclusters of stars) into more or less closely related networks. All intellectual disciplines—from nuclear physics to epidemiology to macroeconomics—depend upon the distribution and interrelation of symbolic texts. The hypertextual utopia is the vision of bringing all the networks together into one ramified whole, and therefore to prove that the intelligible world is a network of signs.

But there is a strong countercurrent, a longing to cut through all these networks of signs in order to achieve an immediate perception of reality. On the level of popular culture, this longing expresses itself as an obsession with "feelings," a denial of the value of semiotic thought. The same people who as lawyers and accountants spend their whole day manipulating arbitrary signs prefer to devote their evening to exercises in perception and empathy—through television and spectator sports. The longing for the immediate perception of reality is deeply engrained in our culture. As we discussed in the last chapter, when deconstructionists speak of logocentrism or the illusion of presence, they are describing the desire to break through the gap that exists in all forms of representation between the thing represented and the representing sign, the desire to perceive the thing in the sign. This desire must come relatively soon after the invention of writing, since writing makes any thoughtful writer painfully aware of the gap. Plato built much of his philosophy on this foundation, as he sought to break through language and dialogue to a higher ground in which reality would be immediately apparent to the philosopher. In the *Symposium* he gives us a vision in which even language is unnecessary, but this is an ideal that only the true philosopher can achieve. For the rest of us, and for the philosopher most of the time, language and therefore representation are indispensable. Plato himself did not dispense with writing: he wrote dialogues, like the *Symposium*, that describe verbal encounters that in turn seek the higher realm of philosophic silence. Plato envisioned getting beyond discourse, beyond representation, but he began from representation. He tried to use writing to transcend writing.

Could there, on the other hand, be a culture in which writing did not need to be transcended—a culture, in which perception was given priority over representation, so that minds were conceived of primarily as perceptual agents and only secondarily as symbol manipulators? Could we imagine a culture in which neither written nor spoken language was primary? Perhaps our evolutionary ancestors did live in such a state of immediate perception, and perhaps other animals still do. Pessimists might argue that our culture is approaching such a state today—through the magic of television. Television, at least American television today, is primarily a perceptual rather than semiotic medium: it encourages its viewers to react by empathy or antipathy to what is on the screen, not by the reading of signs. Television prefers feelings to signs, although it is not entirely devoid of signs (logos, theme songs, etc.) and it is certainly not devoid of images used semiotically. Commercials on television make effective use of visual association—in order to turn, say, an automobile or a brand of beer into a symbol for a whole style of living. But the ideal of television is to deny the sign, to convince the viewer that he or she is looking *through* the screen at the "real world beyond." Broadcast television does not want readers who look at the screen as an electronic text; it wants viewers who do not understand or care about the construction of the televised image. Television seeks to foster the illusion that it is pure perception, a perfect recreation of the world. Unlike the computer, which is a technology of literacy, television therefore works against literacy in favoring image over idea, emotional response over analysis. (For a powerful analysis of the contrast between television and traditional literacy, see Neil Postman's *Amusing Ourselves to Death*, 1985.)

Television homogenizes human experience in an effort to make the same broadcast palatable to millions of viewers spread across the continent or around the world. It has been decades since McLuhan proposed that television would turn the world into a global village, and in the interim television does seem to be reaching out from America to Europe and the third world. But television also seems to be poor at promoting lasting unity, again because it is a relatively impoverished semiotic medium. Television may forge an emotional consensus among viewers that can be quite strong, but by its very nature the consensus lasts only a short time, as long as the perceptual stimulus remains. As the authors of *Habits of the Heart* put it:

> Television is much more interested in how people feel than in what they think. What they think might separate us, but how they feel draws us together. Successful television personalities and celebrities are thus people able freely to communicate their emotional states. (Bellah, Madsen, Sullivan, Swidler, & Tipton, 1985, p. 281)

Athletes are among the most popular of television personalities precisely because their emotions are simple and easily shared. Television can bring together hundreds of millions of viewers around the world to watch the

Olympics. But after the games are over, the viewers have achieved no lasting cultural sharing beyond watching athletes win at sports. If we need any evidence of the temporary character of television as a cultural unifier, we need only look at our own case in the United States. Television is a stronger cultural presence here than in any other country, and yet the United States remains highly decentralized both politically and socially.

The goal of television is to focus the will of the viewers. For this reason sporting events, which are nothing but will-focusing exercises, are among the most popular broadcasts. Television communicates affiliations: the first and almost the only questions the viewer asks are: "Do I like the person/action/ image that I see? Can I identify with that person/action/image?" Empathy or antipathy is all that is available to the viewer, because full intellectual (semiotic) participation is denied. Viewers are simply the recipients of images that come down to them "from above," now literally from above since they are relayed by satellite.

The television corporations call themselves networks, but they are in fact hierarchies, *trees* in computer jargon. The broadcast spreads out from a central studio and moves down through relays and local stations until it reaches the viewers who are the leaves of the tree. There is little or no movement of information in the other direction and no "horizontal" communication among viewers, except among those in the same living room. Attempts to make television more interactive have met with little success. Usually "interaction" means that viewers are given the chance to purchase goods they see displayed on the screen. At best viewers are invited to vote on issues debated by surrogates in the television studio: a yes or no vote on a complex issue can hardly be more than an emotional response.

ANTIREADING

In current broadcast television, it is difficult for the viewer to win and maintain a critical distance, and distancing is always a feature of reading a text. The television viewer is not a reader precisely because he or she cannot easily step back from or alter the pace of the presentation. It is true that technological changes are working to give the viewer greater control. The VCR makes it possible to pre-record programs, to stop in the middle of a scene, and to move back and forth through a program. The VCR therefore gives viewers some control over the pace of their viewing. The remote control device on many television sets offers another kind of control: the viewer can jump from channel to channel, repeatedly dipping into the flow of two or three programs. This technique fragments the viewing experience even more markedly than ordinary television, but it also allows viewers to distance themselves from the programs. The viewer begins to make a text out of the three programs he or she is simultaneously watching; the viewer begins to write with images. As we have seen, this writing can go much further. Under computer control, televised images can be joined with verbal text and graphics to form a rich, hypertextual structure. However, current television programs are not designed to be "read" in any such hypertextual fashion. They are meant to be viewed linearly, in order to keep the viewer glued to one channel even through the commercials. Television programs and commercials together are designed to create a perceptual world that merges with the viewer's living room or bedroom. They invite viewers to lose themselves, not to stand back and analyze critically. Therefore, the textual component of the televised experience is usually small, and it comes as a by-product of the sensual appeal to the eye and ear.

In any writing technology, the situation is reversed: perception is a by-product of semiosis. A narrative text is above all a texture of signs, and through signs it invites the reader into an imagined world. Again, as Richard Lanham has suggested, reading is an oscillation between looking at the text and looking through it. (See Lanham, 1989.) Readers move back and forth between confronting the signs (reading with a critical distance) and allowing themselves to be absorbed into that imagined world. The most popular printed fiction is the kind that provides readers with a world to get lost in: romances, military-technological thrillers, the "blockbuster" novels of James Michener and many others. These huge novels offer a detailed picture of some historical, contemporary, or fantastic world (Alaska through several generations, Paris in the time of the Revolution, Paleolithic Europe!). The novel may span generations and so give the reader the pleasing sense that the story never ends. Genre fiction (such as romances, detective or spy novels with the same hero) never does really end, because each new example of the genre repeats the mythic structure and the same reading experience. In *Reading the Romance*, Janice Radway points out that: "[p]opular romances... resemble the myths of oral cultures in the sense that ... they all *retell* a single tale whose final outcome their readers always already know" (Radway, 1984, p. 198). Televised soap operas are also designed never to end. In all these cases the reader or viewer assumes a passive role, enters into the text, and loses any real critical distance. In fact, passive reading, the desire to be surrounded by the text, is as close as reading can come to being a perceptual rather than a semiotic experience. If remote-controlled "zapping" is a way to read television as if it were a book, then the passive role of the genre reader is a way of watching a book as if it were television. The goal of passive reading is to forget oneself by identifying with the narrative world presented. In this sense passive reading is antireading, since true reading is an encounter with signs in which the reader continually asserts (and repeatedly loses) his or her independence of the text.

Like earlier reading technologies, the computer too can be used for antireading. Computer-assisted instruction, although meant to encourage the participation of the student, can often reduce the student reader to a state of televised passivity. And if artificial intelligence were ever to succeed in creating a whole personality inside the computer, the human user would become a mere passive reader who listened to the monologue provided by the machine. For the artificial intelligence specialist, a computer novel should not be a hypertext, but instead a storyteller. The human user would ask the machine for a story, add qualifications about the subject matter and plot, and then sit back and receive a printed or orally delivered result. The computer could continue to generate tales about familiar characters in a fictional world: it could surround the user with such a fictional universe and fill in any aspect of that universe at the user's request. The computer's capacity to combine video and sound suggest that the simulation could go further. The electronic writing space could become a three-dimensional, interactive movie. The user would in effect be absorbed into the interface of the machine. We have already encountered this vision in some proposals for electronic encyclopedias.

VIRTUAL REALITY

There are computer companies and research labs that have built systems to provide "virtual reality" (see Ditlea, 1989). Typically, the user dons stereoscopic glasses that have tiny videoscreens in place of lenses; he or she also wears a glove so that hand movements can be monitored by the machine. The user sees a space filled with colored, three-dimensional shapes. The computer is not yet fast enough to draw accurate pictures of complex moving objects: so everything in virtual reality (including humans and animals) has a geometrical appearance. Users must be content with a geometrical, vaguely cubist world: nonetheless, this world does seem to respond to their presence. When users turn their head, the view changes to fit the new perspective. When they reach out and close their gloved hand, they can pick up objects in front of them. NASA may use virtual reality to allow the user to simulate visits to the planets. As one researcher explains, "you'll be able to hold the moon or any planet in your hand and point to where you want to go on its surface. The computer will scale the environment back to life size and you can be virtually present at the indicated location. The planetary environment would seem to surround you" (Ditlea, 1989, p. 92). Another developer at a private company provides more fantastic scenarios: "You can visit the world of the dinosaur, then become a Tyrannosaurus. Not only can you see DNA, you can experience what it's like to be a molecule" (p. 97). This company also offers "Reality Built for Two," in which two people with headsets and gloves can share the same computer-created environment.

There will in fact be productive uses for such systems. Simulators already serve to train pilots and astronauts, and newer technology will make these simulations more convincing. A simulator could also help an operator to control machinery at a safe distance—say, for handling toxic or radioactive material. There is perhaps also a recreational use. A simulated world, a world of pure perception, can serve to counterpoint daily work in the world of signs. But it should be obvious that virtual reality cannot in itself sustain intellectual or cultural development. It must always be the "other" world which we visit from time to time. The problem is not that the computer environment is not the "real" world. There is nothing monstrous or wrong about constructing a world of perception, since human beings have been in engaged in reconstructing their perceptual world through art and technology for thousands of years. The problem is that virtual reality, at least as it is now envisioned, is a medium of percepts rather than signs. It is virtual television. The world of useful work is a world of reading and writing, and yet at least some developers of virtual reality want to bypass or even deny such symbolic communication. To understand the chemistry of DNA is a symbolic project involving mathematics, verbal writing, and diagrams. To "experience what it's like to be a molecule" adds nothing to this understanding. On the other hand, there is no reason that programs for virtual reality may not be used semiotically. For example, diagrams of a DNA molecule could be embedded in a three-dimensional space through which the user could move. Like the best two-dimensional graphics, these interactive diagrams would include mathematical and verbal information. The shapes, colors, and perhaps even tactile sensations of virtual reality would become part of a synaesthetic text. Such a three-dimensional space may be the future of the electronic book itself.

Computer programs for virtual reality are still experimental, but the idea of the simulated environment has already worked its way into our culture. Theme parks offer visitors all sorts of "virtual" experiences: a walk through a Western town in the 19th century or an American home in the 21st century, a helicopter ride or a spaceflight, and so on. Some programs for virtual reality seem to be direct descendants of these amusement parks. The computer offers the innovation that the illusion can now be created with computer-controlled light and sound; the classic illusions in parks like Disneyland were achieved with ingenious mechanical animation, which is necessarily less flexible. For that very reason, theme parks are now replacing mechanical automata, where possible, with computer animation and control.

These developments in simulated environments are also having their effect on contemporary museums, which seem to be incorporating both the best and the worst qualities of interactivity. In a traditional museum, the display of art and artifacts is kept clearly separate from the visitor. The museumgoer is expected to approach these monumental objects in the same spirit in which William Bennett's worshipful reader approaches the classics. Now, however, museums are being organized in such a way that visitors become a part of the cultural space through which they move. Especially in children's museums and science museums, visitors may be encouraged to touch the exhibits. And indeed the exhibits may not be artifacts so much as machines, or computer terminals, or simulation devices. Even in traditional art museums, visitors may now be offered a portable cassette player so that they can manage their own guided tour through the space. This much is certainly appropriate to the electronic way of reading. What is not appropriate is the absence of semiosis. When verbal and mathematical text is systematically eliminated from the exhibits, a museum becomes indistinguishable from a theme park, where there is no real writing and therefore no critical reading on the part of the visitor. In such cases the museum offers only a perceptual experience, not the opportunity for critical reflection upon that experience. Viewers are encouraged to lose themselves (and therefore their critical judgment) in the simulation.

George MacDonald, director of the newly opened Canadian Museum of Civilization points out that "[t]he average visitor to [Disneyworld's] Epcot Center stays for eight hours and leaves quite refreshed, while the average museum visitor in North America stays less than an hour and leaves with museum fatigue." The difference, according to MacDonald, is that the Epcot Center is "multi-experiential": visitors are entertained and fed as well as educated (quoted in Honan, 1990, p. 36). But this explanation does not go far enough. Visitors to traditional museums are fatigued in part because they are doing work that is inherently fatiguing: they are reading and reflecting on the artifacts. Visitors to the Epcot Center are simply gliding through a simulated environment that encourages no reflective thinking. The goal of a museum should be to create a physical and visual space in which the visitor can began to read—that is, to reflect upon the semiosis of the created space. A museum in the electronic age should be seeking to turn artifacts into elements of a hypertextual book, not a simulated environment.

THE NETWORK CULTURE

At its best and at its worst, the electronic museum is a space through which the visitor moves at will, sampling the exhibits, lingering over the ones that interest him or her and ignoring those that do not. There is no compulsion, no required order, and no requirement that any or all the exhibits must be visited. In other words the new museum is a cultural (and physical) expression of the organizational character of electronic text. It is organized as a network, rather than a hierarchy. And it is fair to suggest that the network is becoming the favored structure in American culture today—not only in the way we construct our books, libraries, and museums but also in the way we arrange our social and political lives.

Our culture is itself a vast writing space, a complex of symbolic structures. Just as we write our minds, we can say that we write the culture in which we live. And just as our culture is moving from the printed book to the computer, it is also in the final stages of the transition from a hierarchical social order to what we might call a "network culture." For decades all forms of hierarchy have been distintegrating, as greater and greater freedom of action is granted to the individual. Much of this distintegration accords with the goals of liberal democracy: the diminishing of racial and religious segregation, for example. But whatever one thinks of the trend, no one can deny that an extremely powerful leveling force is at work in our society. It can be said that this leveling has always been a feature of American culture, that Tocqueville remarked on it one hundred and fifty years ago. The authors of *Habits of the Heart* see today's "separation and individuation" as the culmination of a long historical process.

> [T]he colonists [to America] brought with them ideas of social obligation and group formation that disposed them to recreate in America structures of family, church, and polity that could continue ... the texture of older European society. Only gradually did it become clear that every social obligation was vulnerable, every tie between individuals fragile. Only gradually did what we have called ontological individualism, the idea that the individual is the only firm reality, become widespread. (Bellah et al., 1985, p. 276)

Today the leveling has gone further than perhaps even Tocqueville could have imagined. Hierarchies in government, church, and family may retain status in law, but they have almost no moral authority. The vestigial hierarchies in our society, like the Catholic Church, are tolerated because they are completely misunderstood. (Thus many American Catholics seem to regard their hierarchy either as their representative government or as a quaint, decorative motif in their religious tradition.) The only great hierarchical force left is money, and today the possession of money creates and depends on no other distinctions. Among the richest people in America are athletes and celebrities who are often indistinguishable in education and tastes from the poorest Americans. We certainly do not think of rich people as better people. Instead, we use money to play at class, at hierarchical organizations that no one now takes seriously. However, the end of hierarchy is not the end of social structure. The individual may now be "the only firm reality," but that does not mean that individuals no longer form groups. They may well form more groups than ever, because they are free to associate and break off their associations as they please. Individuals now regularly join and quit jobs, neighborhoods, clubs, political parties and action committees, and even churches several times in their lives. These affiliations are all seen as voluntary, and they are horizontal rather than vertical. The network has replaced the hierarchy.

Sociologists may disagree over the causes of the networking of American culture. The point here is that our culture of interconnections both reflects and is reflected in our new technology of writing. With all these transitions, the making and breaking of social links, people are beginning to function as elements in a hypertextual network of affiliations. Our whole society is taking on the provisional character of a hypertext: it is rewriting itself for each individual member. We could say that hypertext has become the social ideal. No one now holds as an ideal the proposition that a child, if male, should follow his father into his profession or, if female, should emulate her mother, stay home, and raise a family. Instead the message is that a child (as an ontological individual) should be free to choose what he or she wishes to do in life. That freedom of choice includes everything: profession, family, religion, sexual preference, and above all the ability to change any of the options (in effect to rewrite one's life story) at almost any time. Admittedly, for many Americans this ultimate freedom is not available. But the ideal remains, and it is the ideal of a network culture.

When critics complain of a decline in social and political values, they are often complaining about the loss of hierarchy. What Christopher Lasch identifies as the "culture of narcissism" or Allan Bloom calls the "closing of the American mind" are manifestations of the breakdown of traditions in which civic duty was placed above radical individualism and in which certain kinds of learning were regarded as more important than others. What has been lost is the belief in the legitimacy of hierarchy itself. The critics' complaints are as predictable as are the forces that incline our society to ignore the complaints and continue to replace hierarchies with networks. The development of electronic writing can only serve both to clarify and to accelerate the present impulse for change.

CULTURAL UNITY

One consequence of the networking of culture is the abandonment of the ideal of high culture (literature, music, the fine arts) as a unifying force. If there is no single culture, but only a network of interest groups, then there is no single favored literature or music. Nor is there a single standard of grammar or diction in writing. Elizabeth Eisenstein has argued convincingly that printing was a force for cultural unification during the centuries when the modern nation states were being formed. "Typography arrested linguistic drift, enriched as well as standardized vernaculars, and paved the way for the more deliberate purification and codification of all major European languages" (Eisenstein, 1979, vol. 1, p. 117). As we have seen, electronic writing has just the opposite effect. It opposes standardization and unification as well as hierarchy. It offers as a paradigm the text that changes to suit the reader rather than expecting the reader to conform to its standards.

This attitude is already widespread among readers in the late age of print. As our written culture becomes a vast hypertext, the reader is free to choose to explore one subnetwork or many, as he or she wishes. It is no longer convincing to say that one subject is more important than another. Today even highly educated readers, especially but not exclusively scientists, may know only one or a few areas well. Such ignorance of the shared textual tradition is in part the result of the specialization of the sciences that has been proceeding since the 17th century. But even the humanities are now utterly fragmented, so that a student of Latin literature may know nothing about Renaissance poetry or the 20th-century novel. Throughout the late age of print, however, there has been a lingering feeling of guilt about this situation—a call somehow to reestablish a core of textual knowledge that everyone must possess. The last vestige of this guilt can be heard in pleas for a canon of great authors, which we discussed in an earlier chapter. But the specialization has gone far too far to be recalled. In the sciences it is indispensable. In the humanities and social sciences it is institutionalized. The intellectual world is now defined by numerous "special interest groups" pulling this way and that—Marxists, neo-Freudians, deconstructionists, cognitive scientists, phenomenologists. All the groups are interconnected: some grew out of others, and each sends outrunners (links) into other camps. Thus, there are Christian Marxists, Marxist deconstructionists, phenomenological anthropologists, Lacanian psychoanalysts who write on literature, and so on. But an over-arching unification is no longer even the goal. In *After Virtue* Alasdair MacIntyre (1981), complaining about the fragmented state of moral philosophy, drew the following compelling analogy. Imagine an environmental catastrophe that causes human society to turn against modern science. Scientists are persecuted, and science texts are torn up or destroyed. Then imagine a later generation trying to reassemble these fragments ("half-chapters from books, single pages from articles, not always fully legible because torn and charred") into a single system. The result would be a mish-mash of incoherent theories and misunderstood facts. Of course, this disaster has not happened to modern science, but it is according to MacIntyre exactly what has happened to the great systems of moral philosophy (MacIntyre, 1981, pp. 2-3). For MacIntyre the disaster was the Enlightenment.

MacIntyre's analogy can be extended beyond moral philosophy to almost all fields today: each is an incomplete and disorganized hypertext that no one knows how to read in its entirety. But to call this fragmentation a disaster is to assume that unity is an achievable goal. What MacIntyre does not admit is that there is now no way out of this impasse. (It is certainly not possible to forget the lessons of the Enlightenment.) In fact, the fragmentation of our textual world is only a problem when judged by the standards of print technology, which expects the humanities, including metaphysics and ethics, to be relatively stable and hierarchically organized. What we have instead in the sciences is fruitful specialization and in the humanities a noisy collision of conflicting groups who in the end must agree to disagree. Anyone can enter or leave any group at any time or maintain a combination of interests and positions that characterize two or more camps.

In the late age of print, this situation must appear as chaos, because print holds up stability and order as its ideals. Even though printed materials are still the medium of expression for all these conflicting views, the unwritten assumption is that the disorder can eventually be set right. But in the context of electronic writing, nothing is more natural than the centrifugal disorder of our present cultural life. There is no conceptual problem (though many technical ones) in feeding all these conflicting texts into the computer and generating one vastly reticulated, self-contradictory hypertext. The computer provides the only kind of unity now possible in our culture: unity at the operational level. Hypertextual publication can accommodate all the mutually incomprehensible languages that the intellectual world now speaks, and this unification of technique must serve as the consolation for the lost unity of purpose.

Within the hypertextual libraries that are now being assembled, individual intellectual communities can retreat into their subnetworks and operate with as much or as little connection to each other as they desire. These communities may be large or small. Contemporary art, music, and literature have divided into several tiny elites and several huge popular movements, while most of the liberal arts are now pursued by relatively small groups of professionals. We have come to accept the fact that a new painting, a novel, or an essay will appeal only to one group of viewers or readers—that each person is free not only to dislike a new work, but simply to ignore it as irrelevant to his or her needs. Individuals today wander through an aesthetic supermarket picking out what interests them—atonal music, concrete poetry, science fiction films, situation comedies on television, or paperback romances. We are hard put to criticize any of these choices: they are simply questions of taste.

In the United States, the most thoroughly networked society, the distinction between high culture and popular culture has all but vanished. In place of the hierarchical organization in which high culture (poetry, "serious" novels, scholarly monographs) is valued above popular culture (doggerel, genre literature, how-to books), we have simply different subnetworks that appeal to different readers. None of the familiar indications of quality apply. In the age of print, a classic might be presented on high-quality paper and bound in cloth or leather, whereas a popular romance would appear in paperback with a suitably gaudy cover. In the electronic writing space, both texts will likely arrive on a diskette. The software for the romance may well be more sophisticated than the software that presents the "serious" fiction—for the same economic reasons that Hollywood's popular movies are often technologically more polished than European art films. The refusal to distinguish between high art and popular entertainment has long been a feature of American culture, but the computer as hypertextual network both ratifies and accelerates this trend. We can now see that American culture has been working for decades against the assumptions of the printed book and toward the freedom from top-down control provided by electronic writing. The computer is the ideal technology for the networking of America, in which hierarchical structures of control and interpretation break down into their component parts and begin to oscillate in a continuously shifting web of relations.

CULTURAL LITERACY

Because of this shift from hierarchy to network, the debate over cultural unity takes its strangest turns here in the United States. Recent examples are the discussion of Allan Bloom's *The Closing of the American Mind* (Bloom, 1987) and E. D. Hirsch's *Cultural Literacy*. Hirsch's book is a particularly instructive case. Many readers took it as a call to return to the classics, to a fixed curriculum of works and authors that would make one culturally literate. But this was a misreading, as anyone can see from the first sentences of the Preface:

> To be culturally literate is to possess the basic information needed to thrive in the modern world. The breadth of that information is great, extending over the major domains of human activity from sports to science. It is by no means confined to "culture" narrowly understood as an acquaintance with the arts. Nor is it confined to one social class. (Hirsch, 1987, p. xiii)

Hirsch is no champion of culture in the traditional sense. For him cultural literacy is the ability to function effectively in our current world of reading and writing. His is an operational definition of literacy—what one needs to get by. Hirsch never demands deep knowledge of any subject: a literate person simply needs to touch the surface of a broad range of topics. At the end of his book, Hirsch gives a list of hundreds of topics that exemplifies the range needed for cultural literacy in contemporary America. Here is a passage from the t's: "Tutankhamen; Twain, Mark; Tweed, Boss; Tweedledum and Tweedledee; Twenty-third Psalm (text); Twinkle, Twinkle Little Star (text)" (p. 210). Here is the beginning of the v's: "vaccine, vacuum, vagina, valence, Valhalla, Valley Forge, valley of the shadow of death, value judgement, Van Allen Belt, Vancouver" (p. 211). Clearly Hirsch's definition of culture has nothing to do with high culture: it is simply anything that a reader might expect to encounter in a newspaper or magazine. Elements in Hirsch's list shoot off in all directions; they are linked not by any hierarchy of values, but by shared associations. Hirsch's alphabetized list reminds us of the eclecticism of the local bookstore, where in the section marked "Philosophy" Hegel is shelved next to Kahlil Gibran, Shirley MacLaine next to John Locke. A visit to the bookstore reminds us that there are no longer accepted principles by which pop culture and high culture can be separated. As in Hirsch's list, there is no hierarchy; all these printed products are of value simply because they will appeal to some group of paperback consumers.

From this perspective, cultural literary does not require a knowledge of traditional texts; instead, it means access to the vocabulary needed to read and write effectively. And in fact this operational definition is now making cultural literacy almost synonymous with computer literacy. Both cultural and computer literacy simply mean access to information and the ability to add to the store of information. Increasingly, cultural literacy will require working with the computer, as the computer becomes the most important writing space in our culture. The cultural literates will be those who can use this new medium either for their work or for personal communication and expression. By this measure traditional scholars, who are at home in the world of printed books and conventional libraries, are relatively illiterate: they may not know how to work their way through an electronic network of information, certainly not how to write electronically for a contemporary audience.

This new definition of cultural literacy brings us back to the question of the canon of important works and authors. The idea of a relatively stable canon made sense in a culture dominated by printed books. The canon was also appropriate to a centralized educational system, in which everyone studied the same subjects and the same texts in order to be introduced into the standards of cultural life. But the notion of a standard has now collapsed, and the collapse is mirrored in the shift from the printed to the electronic writing space, in which a stable canon of works and authors is meaningless. No wringing of hands and no proposals for a renewed emphasis on the great authors of the past can do much to counter the trend toward a network culture, which is fostered not only by social preference, but also by the very medium of reading and writing that is coming to dominate the literacy of our society.

This prediction must seem bleak to those who still feel allegiance to the traditional culture of printed books. The loss is real; the hope for a cultural center based upon traditional texts must now be abandoned. But much of the loss has already occurred in the late age of print. The computer is only reinforcing the effects of centrifugal forces in the 20th century. More important, as we have seen from the outset, the end of traditional print literacy is not the end of literacy. The computer is simply the technology by which literacy will be carried into a new age.

THE ELECTRONIC HIDING PLACE

There is another, more positive way to view the loss of a stable core for our culture. Although we do lose the satisfaction of belonging to a coherent cultural tradition, we gain the freedom to establish our own traditions in miniature. The computer offers people the opportunity to build liaisons with other readers and writers and to work in relative isolation from other such groups. A group does not need to convince a major publishing house of its importance or saleability; it can use electronic mail and diskettes to disseminate its materials. A group does not need to feel answerable to a cultural norm, but can pursue its own definition of literacy. This feature of electronic writing will be as useful to traditionalists as to the avant-garde. Scholars in esoteric subjects will be able to communicate and publish their results by fax machine or electronic mail. Unlike television, which promotes uniformity (even through the apparent diversity of cable and satellite stations), the microcomputer and the phone network really do permit special literacies to survive.

The computer is an ideal writing space for our networked society, because it permits every form of reading and writing from the most passive to the most active. A large group of users (perhaps the largest) will use the resources of the machine to shop, read the weather report, and play fantastic video games under the rubric of virtual reality. There will be a large market for the electronic equivalents of how-to books and interactive romances, science fiction, and the other genres. Small groups will read and write "serious" interactive fiction and non-fiction. Tiny networks of scholars will conduct esoteric studies in ancient and modern literature and languages. Hundreds or thousands of different interest groups from fundamentalist religion to space exploration will publish and read each other's messages and hypertexts—on commercial, academic, or governmental communication networks. Government and business will produce electronic documents by the billions. All these groups will be in contact at various levels for various purposes. In other words, the chaos of publication and communication in the late age of print will continue. The ideal of stability and cultural cohesion will largely disappear. Few will feel the need to assert such cohesion, since even the smallest group of writers and readers can function happily in its niche in the electronic network. The computer can in fact provide a quiet place for readers and writers to pursue such interests, relatively secure from the noise of what remains of shared cultural elements. The computer as a writing space can also be a place to hide from the sensory overload of the daily world of work and leisure and the other electronic media. In this space, all the various definitions of cultural literacy can survive, but no single definition can triumph at the expense of all others.

Chapter

14

Conclusion

Printed books usually end, as they began, with a confession. At the beginning the author confesses that friends and editors have helped to write the book. At the end he or she confesses that the book is still incomplete and suggests what remains for others to do. This is really an apology that the book cannot achieve what it presumes to do: to "cover" the subject, to close the subject off between two covers. An electronic hypertext does not need to make such an apology, since the text never presumes to close itself off; instead it provides places where the reader may continue his or her own writing. There is no need to suggest further work in a hypertext, because further work is always needed and always implicitly requested.

For this printed book I can only offer the customary apology. This book has not been a definitive history of writing: what is still needed—and this could only be suggested in the previous chapters—is a text that combines the research of the historians of writing (Sampson, Diringer) with the work on oral theory of Havelock and Ong (as corrected and supplemented by Olson, Finnegan, Goody, and other sociologists and anthropologists) and further with the work of Derrida and other post-modern theorists. The study of information technologies (by Beniger, 1986 and others) must also be included. It is time for such a compendium because the coming of the electronic medium has put history and theory in a new perspective. The new medium compels us to acknowledge that all previous forms of writing are as much technologies as fully computerized hypertext—that writing itself is not merely influenced by technology, but rather *is* technology. The very idea of writing, of semiosis, cannot be separated from the materials and techniques with which we write, and genres and styles of writing are as much determined by technology as by other factors. Havelock and Ong on one side and the post-modernists on the other have shown us the implications of the technology of writing for literature, for all kinds of cultural communication, and ultimately for our notion of the human mind. They have helped us realize that writing is one way, perhaps the principal way, of constructing our cultural world. That world is the sum of the texts that we write, and we make this realization just at the time when the computer has arrived to compel us to rewrite our texts both individually and collectively.

THE HYPERTEXT

At the end of this printed book, the reader has the opportunity to begin again—by working through the text on computer diskette that can be obtained by sending in the order form enclosed in the book. The diskette, which runs on Macintosh computers, contains a hypertextual rewriting of this book.[1] The hypertext shadows the printed version, presenting paragraphs that appear in print and offering hypertextual notes that expand particular ideas. These elaborations could not be included in the printed version because of limited space or because a particular digression did not seem appropriate to the linearity of print.

Readers who obtain the diskette will see that the hypertext cheerfully violates the constraints imposed by the medium of print. The hypertext does not possess a single hierarchical-linear structure. It does not confront the reader with a single persona; instead, it speaks in several, sometimes contradictory voices. The style does not depend on rhetorical transitions, since the transition is provided by the reader in the act of branching from one textual unit to another. Readers will also see an inevitable irony. This printed book has argued for the breakdown of the paradigm of print: it has predicted its own obsolescence. The hypertext looks at the same evidence from the other side: it claims obsolescence for a medium that it has already replaced, and this claim has the unfortunate odor of a self-fulfilling prophecy. Perhaps only a few readers will bother to send for and examine the hypertext, and they will generally be those who are already convinced of the importance of this new technology. But this is, after all, the nature of electronic texts: they appeal to readers whose interests or needs have led them to that particular area in the network of all texts. In the world of electronic writing, there will be no texts that everyone must read. There will only be texts that more or fewer readers choose to examine in more or less detail. The idea of the great, inescapable book belongs to the age of print that is now passing.

---

[1]This hypertext was written using a program called Storyspace™, created by myself, Michael Joyce, and John B. Smith. (Storyspace is a trademark of riverrun Ltd.)

References

Abrams, M. H. (1953) *The mirror and the lamp: Romantic theory and the critical tradition*. New York: Oxford University Press.

Alexander, J. J. G. (1978) *The decorated letter*. New York: G. Braziller.

Bacon, Francis. (1955) *Advancement of learning*. In H. G. Dick (Ed.), *Selected writings of Francis Bacon* (pp. 157-392). New York: Random House.

Baker, G. P., & Hacker, P. M. S. (1980) *Wittgenstein: Understanding and meaning*. Chicago: University of Chicago Press.

Balestri, Diane P. (1988) Softcopy and hard: Wordprocessing and writing process. *Academic Computer, 2* (5), 14-17, 41-45.

Balkovich, E., Lerman, S., & Parmelee, R. P. (1985) Computing in higher education: The Athena Project. *Computer, 18* (10), 112-125.

Barth, John. (1967) The literature of exhaustion. *The Atlantic, 220* (2), 29-34.

Barthes, Roland. (1974) *S/Z* (Richard Miller, Trans.). New York: Hill & Wang.

Barthes, Roland. (1979) From work to text. In Josué V. Harari (Ed.), *Textual strategies: Perspectives in post-structuralist criticism* (pp. 73-81). Ithaca, NY: Cornell University Press.

Bellah, Robert N., Madsen, Richard, Sullivan, William M., Swidler, Ann, & Tipton, Steven M. (1985) *Habits of the heart: Individualism and commitment in American life*. Berkeley: University of California Press.

Beniger, James R. (1986) *The control revolution: Technological and economic origins of the information society*. Cambridge, MA: Harvard University Press.

Beniger, James R., & Robyn, Dorothy L. (1978) Quantitative graphics in statistics: A brief history. *American Statistician, 32*, 1-11.

Bennett, William J. (1984) *To reclaim a legacy: A report on the humanities in higher education*. Washington, DC: National Endowment for the Humanities.

Bloom, Allan D. (1987) *The closing of the American mind*. New York: Simon and Schuster.

Bloom, Harold. (1973) *The anxiety of influence: A theory of poetry*. New York: Oxford University Press.

Boden, Margret. (1977) *Artificial intelligence and natural man*. New York: Basic Books.

Bolter, Jay David. (1985) The idea of literature in the electronic medium. *Topic, 39*, pp. 23-34.

Borges, Jorge Luis. (1962) *Ficciones* (A. Kerrigan, Ed.). New York: Grove Press.

Brand, Stewart. (1987) *The media lab: Inventing the future at M.I.T.* New York: Penguin Books.

Brooks, Peter. (1984) *Reading for the plot: Design and intention in narrative.* New York: Alfred A. Knopf.

Bush, Vannevar. (1945) As we may think. *Atlantic Monthly, 176* (1), 101-108.

Byrne, Robert. (1989, June 27) Deep Thought, the computer that beat a strong human grandmaster, beats other computers, too. *New York Times*, p. C17.

Byrne, Robert. (1989, September 26) Chess-playing computer closing in on champions. *New York Times*, pp. 21, 24.

Carlyle, Thomas. (1890) *On heroes, hero-worship and the heroic in history.* London: George G. Harrap and Co.

Châtillon, Jean. (1966) Le 'Didascalion' de Hugues de Saint-Victor. *Journal of World History, 9,* 539-552.

Clarke, Arthur C. (1984) *Profiles of the future: An inquiry into the limits of the possible.* New York: Holt, Rinehart and Winston.

Conklin, J. (1987) Hypertext: An introduction and survey. *I. E. E. E. Computer, 20* (9), 17-41.

Crabbe, George. (1966) *The library, a poem.* Boston: G. K. Hall & Co. [originally published in 1781]

Crane, Gregory. (1988) "Redefining the book: Some preliminary problems," *Academic Computing, 2* (5), 6-11, 36-41.

Crowder, Robert G. (1982) *The psychology of reading.* Oxford: Oxford University Press.

Culler, Jonathan. (1981) *The pursuit of signs: Semiotics, literature, deconstruction.* Ithaca, NY: Cornell University Press.

Curtius, Ernst Robert (1973) *European literature and the Latin Middle Ages* (Willard R. Trask, Trans.). Princeton, NY: Princeton University Press.

D'Alembert, Jean le Rond. (1963) *Preliminary discourse to the Encyclopedia of Diderot* (R. N. Schwab, Trans.). Indianapolis, IN: Bobbs-Merrill.

Davies, W. V. (1987) *Egyptian hieroglyphs.* Berkeley: University of California Press.

Dennett, Daniel C. (1987) *The intentional stance.* Cambridge, MA: MIT Press.

Dennett, Daniel, & Haugeland, John. (1987) Intentionality. In R. L. Gregory (Ed.), *Oxford companion to the mind* (pp. 383-386). Oxford: Oxford University Press.

Derrida, Jacques. (1974) *Glas.* Paris: Éditions Galilée.

Derrida, Jacques. (1976a) *Glas* (John P. Leavey, Jr & Richard Rand, Trans.). Lincoln, Nebraska: University of Nebraska Press.

Derrida, Jacques. (1976b) *Of grammatology.* Baltimore: Johns Hopkins University Press. (Original work published in French in 1967)

Derrida, Jacques. (1979) Living on. In James Hulbart (Ed.), *Deconstruction and criticism: A continuum book* (pp. 75-176). New York: Seabury Press.

Descartes, Réné. (1960) *Meditations on first philosophy* (Laurence J. Lafleur, Trans.). Indianapolis, IN: Bobbs-Merrill.

Ditlea, Steve. (1989) Another world: Inside artificial reality. *PC Computing, 2* (11), 90-99, 102.

Douglas, J. Yellowlees. (1988) *Beyond orality and literacy: Toward articulating a paradigm for the electronic age.* Unpublished manuscript.

Dreyfus, Hubert L., & Dreyfus, Stuart E. (1988) Making a mind versus modeling the brain. *Daedalus, 177* (1), 15-43.

Eco, Umberto. (1976) *A theory of semiotics.* Bloomington: Indiana University Press.

Eisenstein, Elizabeth. (1979) *The printing as an agent of change: Communications and cultural transformations in early-modern Europe* (Vols. 1-2). Cambridge: Cambridge University Press.

Eisenstein, Elizabeth. (1983) *The printing revolution in early modern Europe.* Cambridge: Cambridge University Press.

Encyclopaedia Britannica. (1974-1987) (Philip W. Goetz, Ed.). Chicago: Encyclopaedia Britannica.

Encyclopaedia Metropolitana. (1849) (Edward Smedley, Hugh James Rose, & Henry John Rose, Eds.) (Vol. 1). London: John Joseph Griffin & Co.

Febvre, Lucien, & Martin, Henri-Jean. (1971) *L'apparition du livre* [The coming of the book]. Paris: Editions Albin Michel.

Finnegan, Ruth. (1977) *Oral poetry: Its nature, significance, and social context.* Cambridge: Cambridge University Press.

Fish, Stanley. E. (1980) Literature in the reader: Affective stylistics. In Jane P. Tompkins (Ed.), *Reader-response criticism: From formalism to post-structuralism* (pp. 70-100). Baltimore, MD: Johns Hopkins University Press.

Frank, Joseph. (1963) *The widening gyre: Crisis and mastery in modern literature.* New Brunswick, NJ: Rutgers University Press.

Frank, Joseph. (1981) Spatial form: Thirty years after. In Jeffrey R. Smitten & Ann Daghistany (Eds.), *Spatial form in narrative* (pp. 202-243). Ithaca, NY: Cornell University Press.

Gardiner, Alan H. (1927) *Egyptian grammar: Being an introduction to the study of hieroglyphs.* Oxford: Clarendon Press.

Gaur, Albertine. (1984) *A history of writing.* London: The British Library.

Gelb, I. J. (1963) *A study of writing.* Chicago: University of Chicago Press.

Gellrich, J. M. (1985) *The idea of the book in the Middle Ages: Language theory, mythology and fiction.* Ithaca, NY: Cornell University Press.

Goody, Jack. (1977) *The domestication of the savage mind.* Cambridge: Cambridge University Press.

Grant, Marian A. (1973) *Michel Butor: L'emploit du temps* [Michel Butor: The use of time]. London: Edward Arnold.

Groden, Michael. (1977) *Ulysses in progress.* Princeton, NJ: Princeton University Press.

Grolier Electronic Publishing. (1988) *The electronic encyclopedia on CD-ROM.* Danbury, CT: Grolier Electronic Publishing. [Computer program].

Grossman, Manuel L. (1971) *Dada: Paradox, mystification, and ambiguity in European literature.* New York: Bobbs-Merrill.

Harris, R. (1986) *The origin of writing.* London: Duckworth.

Havelock, Eric. A. (1982) *The literate revolution in Greece and its cultural consequences.* Princeton, NJ: Princeton University Press.

Hirsch, E. D. Jr. (1987) *Cultural literacy: What every American needs to know.* Boston: Houghton Mifflin.

Honan, William H. (1990, January 14) Say goodbye to the stuffed elephants. *New York Times Magazine,* pp. 34-36,38.

Hugo, V. (1967). *Notre-Dame de Paris, 1482.* Paris: Garnier.

Iser, Wolfgang. (1980) The reading process: A phenomenological approach. In Jane P. Tompkins (Ed.) *Reader-response criticism: From formalism to post-structuralism* (pp. 50-69). Baltimore, MD: Johns Hopkins University Press. (First published in 1974)

Jackson, S. L. (1974) *Libraries and librarianship in the west: A brief history.* New York: McGraw-Hill.

Jacky, Jonathan. (1987) The strategic computing program. In David Bellin & Gary Chapman (Eds.), *Computers in battle—Will they work?* (pp. 171-208). New York: Harcourt Brace Jovanovich.

Jensen, Hans. (1969) *Sign, symbol and script: An account of man's effort to write* (George Unwin, Trans.). New York: G. P. Putnam's Sons.

Johnson, George. (1986) *Machinery of the mind: Inside the new science of artificial intelligence.* New York: Random House.

Joyce, James. (1960) *Anna Livia Plurabelle: The making of a chapter* (Fred H. Higginson, Ed.). Minneapolis: University of Minnesota Press.

Joyce, Michael. (1987) Afternoon, a story. Cambridge, MA: Eastgate Press. [Computer program].

Joyce, Michael. (1988) Siren shapes: Exploratory and constructive hypertexts. *Academic Computing, 3* (4), 10-14, 37-42.

Kenner, Hugh. (1962) *Flaubert, Joyce and Beckett: The stoic comedians.* Boston: Beacon Press.

Kenny, Anthony. (1984) *The legacy of Wittgenstein.* Oxford: Basil Blackwell.

Knowlson, James. (1975) *Universal language schemes in England and France: 1600-1800.* Toronto: University of Toronto Press.

Knuth, Donald E. (1982) The concept of a meta-font. *Visible Language, 16,* pp. 3-27.

Landow, George P. (1989) Hypertext in literary education, criticism, and scholarship. *Computers and the Humanities, 23,* 173-198.

Lanham, Richard. (1989) The electronic word: Literary study and the digital revolution. *New Literary History, 20,* 265-290.

Lemoine, Michel. (1966) L'oeuvre encyclopédique de Vincent de Beauvais [The encyclopedic work of Vincent of Beauvais]. *Journal of World History, 9,* 571-579.

Levin, Harry, & Addis, Ann B. (1979) *The eye-voice span.* Cambridge, MA: MIT Press.

Levy, D., Brotsky, Daniel C., & Olson, Kenneth R. (1988) *Formalizing the figural: Aspects of a foundation for document manipulation.* Palo Alto, CA: System Sciences Laboratory, Xerox PARC.

Liddell, Henry George, & Scott, Robert. (1973) *A Greek-English Lexicon* (rev. by Sir Henry Stuart Jones). Oxford: Oxford University Press.

Lieberman, J. B. (1978) *Type and typefaces.* New Rochelle, NY: Myriade Press.

Lord, A. B. (1968) *The singer of tales.* New York: Atheneum.

Llull, Ramon. (1985) *Selected works of Ramon Llull (1232-1316)* (Anthony Bonner, Ed.) (Vols. 1-2). Princeton: Princeton University Press.

MacIntyre, Alasdair. (1981) *After virtue: A study in moral theory.* Notre Dame, IN: University of Notre Dame Press.

Mallery, G. (1972) *Picture writing of the American Indians* (Vols. 1-2). New York: Dover Publications. (First published in 1893)

Marchionini, Gary, & Schneiderman, Ben. (1988) Finding facts vs. browsing in hypertext systems. *Computer, 21* (1), 70-80.

McCarthy, John. (1979) Ascribing mental qualities to machines: In Martin Ringle (Ed.), *Philosophical perspectives in artificial intelligence* (pp. 161-195) Brighton, England: Harvester Press.

McCorduck, Pamela. (1979) *Machines who think.* San Francisco: W. H. Freeman.

McLuhan, Marshall. (1972) *The Gutenberg galaxy: The making of typographic man.* Toronto, University of Toronto Press.

Morris, William. (1982) *The ideal book: Essays and lectures on the arts of the book by William Morris* (William S. Peterson, Ed.). Berkeley: University of California Press.

Moulthrop, Stuart. (1988) *Text, authority, and the fiction of forking paths.* Unpublished manuscript.

Mullins, Phil. (1988) The fluid word: Word processing and its mental habits. *Thought, 63* (251), 413-428.

Mynors, R. A. B. (Ed.). (1937) *Cassiodori senatoris institutiones.* Oxford: Clarendon Press.

Nagy, Joseph Falaky. (1989) Representations of oral tradition in medieval Irish literature. *Language and Communication, 9* (2/3), 143-158.

Neel, J. (1988) *Plato, Derrida, and writing.* Carbondale, IL: Southern Illinois University Press.

Nelson, Ted H. (1974) *Dream machines.* Theodor H. Nelson.

Nelson, Ted H. (1984) *Literary machines.* Theodor H. Nelson.

Nelson, Ted H. (1987) *The Xanadu paradigm.* San Antonio, TX: Project Xanadu. Published broadsheet.

Nishimura, Y., & Keiichi, Sato. (1985) Dynamic information display. *Visible Language, 19* (2), 251-271.

Noblitt, James S. (1988) Writing, technology and secondary orality. *Academic Computing, 2* (5), 34-35, 56-57.

Nordenfalk, Carl. (1951) The beginning of book decoration. In *Essays in honor of Georg Swarzenski* (pp. 9-20). Chicago: Henry Regnery Co.

Olson, David R. (1986) The cognitive consequences of literacy. *Canadian Psychology, 27* (2), pp. 109-121.

Ong, Walter. J. (1958) *Ramus, method, and the decay of dialogue: From the art of discourse to the art of reason.* Cambridge, MA: Harvard University Press.

Ong, Walter. J. (1982) *Orality and literacy: The technologizing of the word.* London: Methuen.

Oxford English dictionary on CD-ROM. (1987) New York: Oxford University Press. [Computer program].

Pask, Gordon A., & Curran, Susan. (1982) *Micro man: Computers and the evolution of consciousness.* New York: Macmillan.

Paulson, William. (1989) Computers, minds, and texts: Preliminary reflections. *New Literary History 20,* 291-303.

Peers, E. Allison (Trans.). (1972) *Complete works of St. Teresa of Jesus.* (Vols. 1-3). London: Sheed and Ward.

Peirce, Charles S. (1934) *Collected papers of Charles Saunders Peirce* (Charles Hartshorne & Paul Weiss, Eds.) (Vol. 5). Cambridge, MA: Harvard University Press.

Plato. (1919) *Plato in English* (H. N. Fowler, Trans.) (Vol. VI). London: William Heinemann.

Postman, Neil. (1985) *Amusing ourselves to death: Public discourse in the age of show business.* New York: Viking Penguin.

Rabkin, Eric S. (1981) Spatial form and plot. In Jeffrey R. Smitten & Ann Daghistany (Eds.), *Spatial form in narrative* (pp. 79-99). Ithaca, NY: Cornell University Press.

Radway, J. A. (1984) *Reading the romance: Women, patriarchy, and popular literature.* Chapel Hill, NC: University of North Carolina Press.

Reynolds, L. D., & Wilson, N. G. (1978) *Scribes and scholars: A guide to the transmission of Greek and Latin literature.* Oxford: Clarendon Press.

Rouse, Richard H., & Rouse, Mary A. (1989) Wax tablets. *Language and Communication, 9* (2/3), 175-191.

Roszak, Theodore. (1986) *The cult of information: The folklore of computers and the true art of thinking.* New York: Pantheon Books.

Saenger, Paul. (1982) Silent reading: Its impact on late medieval script and society. *Viator, 13,* 367-414.

Sampson, G. (1985) *Writing systems, an introduction.* Stanford, CA: Stanford University Press.

Saporta, Marc. (1963) *Composition no. 1: A novel by Marc Saporta* (Richard Howard, Trans.). New York: Simon and Schuster.

Schank, Roger. (1984) *The cognitive computer: On language, learning, and artificial intelligence.* Reading, MA: Addison-Wesley.

Scholes, R. (1986) Aiming a canon at the curriculum. *Salmagundi, 72,* 101-117.

Scribner, Sylvia, & Cole, Michael. (1981) *The psychology of literacy.* Cambridge, MA: Harvard University Press.

Seaman, David W. (1981) *Concrete poetry in France.* Ann Arbor, MI: UMI Research Press.

Searle, John. (1981) Minds, brains, and programs. In J. Haugeland (Ed.), *Mind design: Philosophy, psychology, artificial intelligence* (pp. 282-306). Cambridge, MA: MIT Press.

Shelley, Mary. (1960) *Frankenstein.* London: Dent and Sons.

Shklovsky, Victor. (1965) Sterne's Tristram Shandy: Stylistic commentary. In Lee T. Lemon & Marion J. Reis (Trans.), *Russian formalist criticism: Four essays* (pp. 25-57). Lincoln, NE: University of Nebraska Press.

Simons, Geoff (1987) *Eco-computer: The impact of global intelligence.* New York: Wiley and Sons.

Smith, John B., & Weiss, Stephen F. (Eds.). (1988) Hypertext [Special Issue]. *Communications of the ACM, 31* (7).

Snell, Bruno. (1960) *The discovery of mind: The Greek origin of European thought* (T.G. Rosenmeyer, Trans.). New York: Harper and Row.

Sokolowski, Robert. (1988) Natural and artificial intelligence. *Daedalus, 117* (1), 45-64.

Solt, Mary Ellen (Ed.). (1970) *Concrete poetry: A world view*. Bloomington, IN: Indiana University Press.

Sontag, Susan (Ed.). (1982) *A Barthes reader*. New York: Hill and Wang.

Spencer, Sharon. (1971) *Space, time, and structure in the modern novel*. New York: New York University Press.

Steinberg, S. H. (1959) *Five hundred years of printing*. New York: Criterion Books.

Sterne, Laurence. (1965) *The life and opinions of Tristram Shandy, gentleman* (Ian Watt, Ed.). Boston: Houghton Mifflin Co.

Street, Brian V. (1984) *Literacy in theory and practice*. Cambridge: Cambridge University Press.

Tufte, Edward R. (1983) *The visual display of quantitative information*. Cheshire, CT: Graphics Press.

Turing, Alan. (1963) Computing machinery and intelligence. In E. A. Feigenbaum & Julian Feldman (Eds.), *Computers and thought* (pp. 11-35). New York: McGraw-Hill. (First published in 1950)

Vernus, P. (1982) Espace et idéologie dans l'écriture égyptienne [Space and ideology in Egyptian writing]. In Anne-Marie Christin (Ed.), *Écritures* (pp. 101-114). Paris: Le Sycomore.

Vico, Giambattista. (1948) *The new science of Giambattista Vico* (T. G. Bergin & M. H. Fisch, Trans.). Ithaca, NY: Cornell University Press.

von Hallberg, Robert. (1983) Canons [Special issue]. *Critical Inquiry, 10.*

Weitzmann, Kurt. (1970) *Illustrations in roll and codex: A study of the origin and method of text illustration*. Princeton, NJ: Princeton University Press.

Weizenbaum, Joseph. (1976) *Computer power and human reason*. San Francisco: W. H. Freeman.

Wenk, Richard. (1984) *Indiana Jones and the legion of death*. New York: Ballantine Books.

Weyer, S. A., & Borning, A. H. (1985) A prototype electronic encyclopedia. *ACM Transactions on Office Information Systems, 3* (1), 63-88.

Wheeler, Harvey. (1987) *The virtual library* [on diskette]. Los Angeles: University of Southern California.

Wheeler, Samuel C. III. (1986) Indeterminacy of French interpretation: Derrida and Davidson. In Ernest LePore (Ed.), *Truth and interpretation: Perspectives on the philosophy of Donald Davidson* (pp. 477-494). Oxford: Basil Blackwell.

Wills. F. H. (1977) *Schrift und Zeichen der Völker: Von der Urzeit bis heute* [Writing and signs among peoples: From primitive times to the present]. Düsseldorf: Econ Verlag.

Winner, Langdon. (1977) *Autonomous technology: Technics-out-of-control as a theme in political thought*. Cambridge, MA: MIT Press.

Winspur, S. (1985) Poetry, portrait, poetrait. *Visible Language, 19*, 426-438.

Wittgenstein, Ludwig. (1953) *Philosophical investigations* (G. E. M. Anscombe, Trans.). Oxford: Basil Blackwell.

Yankelovich, Nicole, Haan, Bernard J., Meyrowitz, Norman K., & Drucker, Steven M. (1988) Intermedia: The concept and the construction of a seamless information environment. *Computer, 21* (1), 81-96.

Yates, Frances A. (1964) *Giordano Bruno and the Hermetic tradition*. London: Routledge and Kegan Paul.

Yates, Frances A. (1966) *The art of memory*. Chicago: University of Chicago Press.

Young, Luke T., Thearling, Kurt H., Skiena, Steven S., Robison, Arch D., Omohundro, Stephen M., Mel, Bartlett W., & Wolfram, Stephen. (1988) Academic computing in the year 2000. *Academic Computing 2* (7), 7-12, 62-65.

Ziegfeld, Richard. (1989) Interactive fiction: A new literary genre? *New Literary History, 20,* 341-372.

Zuboff, Shoshana. (1988) *In the age of the smart machine: The future of work and power.* New York: Basic Books.

Author Index

Subject Index

---

* indicates figure